PENGUIN BOOKS

A GUIDE TO PROUST

Terence Kilmartin has been Literary Editor of the *Observer* since 1952. His publications include translations of Henri de Montherlant: *The Bachelors* (1960), *The Dream* (1962), *Chaos and Night* (1964), *The Girls* (1968), *The Boys* (1974); *André Malraux: Anti-Memoirs* (1968), *Lazarus* (1977) and *Charles de Gaulle: Memoirs of Hope* (1971). His translation of Proust's *A la recherche du temps perdu* was published by Penguin in 1983 under the title *Remembrance of Things Past*. For this three-volume edition, based on the Pléiade text (1954), Terence Kilmartin revised C. K. Scott Moncrieff's original English translation and incorporated new material. Volume one contains *Swann's Way (Du côté de chez Swann,* 1913) and *Within a Budding Grove (A l'ombre des jeunes filles en fleurs,* 1919). Volume two contains *The Guermantes Way (Le côté de Guermantes,* I and II, 1920 and 1921) and *Cities of the Plain (Sodome et Gomorrhe,* I and II, 1921 and 1922). Volume three contains *The Captive (La prisonnière,* 1923), *The Fugitive (Albertine disparue,* 1925) and *Time Regained (Le temps retrouvé,* 1927).

A GUIDE TO PROUST

Compiled by
Terence Kilmartin

PENGUIN BOOKS

Penguin Books Ltd, Harmondsworth, Middlesex, England
Viking Penguin Inc., 40 West 23rd Street, New York, New York 10010, U.S.A.
Penguin Books Australia Ltd, Ringwood, Victoria, Australia
Penguin Books Canada Ltd, 2801 John Street, Markham, Ontario, Canada L3R 1B4
Penguin Books (N.Z.) Ltd, 182–190 Wairau Road, Auckland 10, New Zealand

First published by Chatto & Windus · The Hogarth Press 1983
Published in Penguin Books 1985

Printed and bound in Great Britain by
Cox & Wyman Ltd, Reading

CONTENTS

FOREWORD

This book is intended as a guide through the 3,300-page labyrinth of *Remembrance of Things Past* not only for readers who are embarking on Proust's masterpiece for the first time but for those who, already under way, find themselves daunted or bewildered by the profusion of characters, themes and allusions. It also aims to provide those who have completed the journey with the means of refreshing their memories, tracking down a character or an incident, tracing a recurrent theme or favourite passage, or identifying a literary or historical reference. Perhaps, too, the book may serve as a sort of Proustian anthology or bedside companion.

The task of compiling the book would have been infinitely more laborious without the pioneering work of the late P. A. Spalding, whose *Reader's Handbook to Proust* was published by Chatto & Windus in 1952 and reissued, in a revised edition edited by R. H. Cortie, by George Prior in 1975. My debt to Spalding will be obvious to anyone who is familiar with that book. I have also, like him, been greatly helped by the work of his French predecessors, Charles Daudet (*Répertoire des Personnages de "A la recherche du temps perdu"*) and Raoul Celly (*Répertoire des Thèmes de Marcel Proust*); and to a lesser extent I have drawn on Jacques Nathan's *Citations, références et allusions de Proust*. But, more than to any of these, I have to acknowledge a debt to the editors of the Pléiade edition of *A la recherche*, whose very detailed index (150 pages in double column of small type) was an indispensable aid, especially in identifying historical personages and literary allusions.

Spalding divided his *Handbook* into two main sections, an Index of Characters and a General Index covering themes, objects, incidents, places and real people. The Pléiade Index is also in two parts, an *Index des Noms de Personnes* and an *Index des Noms de Lieux*, in each of which the real and the fictional are juxtaposed, RACINE cheek by jowl with RACHEL, for example, and TANGIER jostling TANSONVILLE. It seemed to me that it would be simpler and clearer to sub-divide the General Index and to separate the fictional characters from the hundreds of names of writers, painters, composers and historical figures of every kind that occur in the novel. So this book consists of four separate indexes — of Proust's characters; of real or historical persons; of places; and of themes. Since the places index is comparatively short, it includes both the real and the fictional, the latter being identified by the symbol (f). The revised edition of the translation contains a synopsis at the end of each volume, and so I have not included one here.

I have referred to the narrator throughout by the initial M, for Marcel. How do we know he was called Marcel? Proust is careful, almost from the beginning to the end of the novel, to avoid giving the narrator a name. Only twice does he allow his guard to slip — first, teasingly, early in *The Captive*, when Albertine on awakening murmurs "My darling — " and the blank is then filled in with the name Marcel, "if we give the narrator the same name as the author of this book" (Vol. III, p. 69), and the second time, later in the same volume, when Albertine addresses him unequivocally as "My darling dear Marcel" in her note from the Trocadéro (pp. 153–4).

Page references are to the three volumes (indicated by Roman Bold numerals) of the new and revised edition of *Remembrance of Things Past*, translated by C. K. Scott Moncrieff and Terence Kilmartin, published by Chatto & Windus and Penguin Books in Britain, and by Random House and Vintage Books in the United States.

INDEX OF
CHARACTERS

Princesse de Parme's tip: 816; his appreciation of moneyed clients: 856. His role in Nissim Bernard's relations with a young waiter: 873–4, 884. Conversations with M; relations with clients ("business first"); his letter from Charlus: 1021–6. His familiarity with the chauffeur: 1028, and interest in the chauffeur's tip: 1058. His pleasure in M's special dinners: 1119. His remembered remarks about Albertine exacerbate M's jealousy; M sends him a photograph of Esther Lévy for identification: 111 79–81, 371. Sent by M to Balbec to make inquiries about Albertine's behaviour in a bathing establishment: 502; his letter: 523–31. Sent by M to Touraine; second letter with revelations concerning Albertine's relations with the laundry-girls: 533–6, 540. His revelations concerning Saint-Loup: 697–9.

A.J. *See* Moreau, A. J.

ALBARET, Céleste. Lady's maid in the Grand Hotel, with whom M strikes up a friendship during his second visit to Balbec: 11 875–9. Brichot gives the etymology of her name: 962. Her grief at M's departure: 1163. Her strange linguistic genius: 111 10, 127.

ALBERT. *See* Guastalla, Albert, Duc de.

ALBERTINE Simonet. Niece of M. and Mme Bontemps; at school with Gilberte; "the famous Albertine": 1 552. Her insolence, according to her aunt: 643–4. M misses the opportunity of meeting her: 674. Her first appearance among the "little band" at Balbec — "a girl with brilliant, laughing eyes and plump, matt cheeks, a black polo-cap . . . pushing a bicycle": 846–53. The name "Simonet": 858–9, 865, 874–5, 904. Is she the girl M sees with an English governess?: 887–8. M sees her from a window of Elstir's studio; her beauty spot; Elstir identifies her; her social position: 902–6. The different Albertines: 916–17. M introduced to her at Elstir's: 929–36. Location of the beauty spot: 933, 936, 938. Conversation with her on the esplanade; her jaunty slang: 936–42. Encounters with Andrée, Octave, the d'Ambresacs; her taste and intelligence: 943–6. Plays "diabolo": 947 (cf. 992). Her attitude to Gisèle: 948–50. Her hair: 951. Cycling in the rain: 954 (cf. 111 498). Her craze for amusement: 955. Discusses dress with Elstir: 960–61. Her attitude to Bloch's sisters: 964. Her voice and vocabulary: 970–1. Her note to M: "I like you very much": 972. Her reaction to Gisèle's essay: 972–6. The game of "ferret": 980–83. Her hands: 980–81. Her ringing laughter, "somehow indecent" like the cooing of doves or certain animal cries: 981 (cf. 11 808, 823–4, 887, 1154, 111 115, 125, 171). Her kindness: 985. "I knew now that I was in love with Albertine": 987–91. In her room at the hotel; the rejected kiss: 993–6. Her charm and attraction and social success: 997–9. "The multiple utilisation of a single action": 1000–01. Explains her refusal to allow M to kiss her; the little gold pencil: 1003–4. The moral esteem she inspires in M, and the consequences thereof: 1005. Her changing face: 1009–11. Her abrupt departure from Balbec: 1013. Visits M in Paris; changes in her appearance and vocabulary; allows him to make love to her; her frankness and simplicity: 11 363–84. Second visit; accompanies M to the island in the Bois and to Saint-Cloud: 401–4. M gives her a box for *Phèdre* and arranges to meet her after the Prince de Guermantes's party: 669, 728, 735, 750–52. He anxiously awaits her return: 755–7; her telephone call: 757–60; her visit: 761–5. Denies knowing Gilberte Swann: 764 (cf. 111 15–16, 383). At Balbec again; sends word to M asking to see him: 790; M refuses: 795. The manager's annoyance with her: 803. Françoise's dislike of her: 804, 815–16. M at last decides to see her: 807–8. Recrudescence of M's desire for her: 810–12. He sends Françoise and the lift-boy to fetch her: 815–22. Dances with Andrée in the Casino at Incarville; Cottard's remarks: 822–5. Her secret life, unknown to M: 826. The visit to Infreville; her lies: 827–30 (cf. 111 104). Observes Bloch's sister and cousin in a mirror: 830–1. M's changed attitude towards her: 831–3. Introduced to the Cambremers: 835. Her admiration for Elstir: 838. Reveals a knowledge of Amsterdam: 843 (cf. 111 392, 400, 438). M "has things out" with her; his spurious confession of love for Andrée; accusations, denials, reconciliation: 853–63. Picnics with M near Balbec: 866; and further afield: 869. His suspicions and her reassurances: 870–1. Her attitude towards young women: 880–3. Flirts with Saint-Loup at Doncières station: 887–8. Reproaches and reconciliation: 889, 893–4. M's mother raises the question of his marriage to Albertine: 958. Invited (as M's cousin) to la Raspelière: 1002, 1005. Expeditions with M; paints the church of Saint-Jean-de-la-Haise: 1026–7. The toque and veil: 1028. Motor-car drives; visit to the Verdurins: 1029–38. The church of Marcouville-l'Orgueilleuse: 1046–7. Amorousness after drinks at a farm: 1047–8. Lunch at

Rivebelle; her interest in the waiter: 1048–9. Further outings; nights on the beach; M's growing jealousy and anxiety: 1050–53. Reputed intimacy with Morel: 1065 (cf. III 612–13). Visits to the Verdurins; the little train; her make-up: 1068–70, 1132. Her clothes admired by Charlus: 1089–90 (cf. III 220–23). How she gives herself away when lying: 1133–4. Avoids Saint-Loup: 1144–5. M's decision to break with her: 1149–50. Sudden reversal on hearing of her friendship with Mlle Vinteuil and her friend; M persuades her to spend the night in the Grand Hotel and return to Paris with him next day: 1151–62. "I absolutely must marry Albertine": 1169. Living with M in Paris: III 1–2. Sings in her bath: 3. Mamma's disapproval: 5–7. Changes in her vocabulary and appearance: 10–11. Outings with Andrée; the Buttes-Chaumont: 11–13 (cf. 396, 560, 622). M's feelings for her — jealousy without love: 13–23. Admits having known Gilberte: 15–16. Her fastidious taste in clothes: 24–5. The syringa incident: 48–9. Her dissimulation: 50–56. Her elegant clothes; her gold ring; her intelligence: 57–8. Memories of her at Balbec: 61–3. Her sleep: 63–8, and awakening: 68–9 (cf. 394). Visits M in his bedroom; her love play; her good-night kiss; makes him promise to work: 69–75. Aimé's ambiguous remarks about her; a new access of jealousy; 79–82. Her plan to visit Mme Verdurin; renewed suspicions; "a fugitive being"; lying a part of her nature: 83–93. Visits to aerodromes: 100–01. Her lie about Infreville exposed: 104 (cf. II 827–30). Denies knowing Bloch's cousin: 106 (cf. 348). M kisses her while she sleeps the sleep of a child: 108–11. Her morning visit; plans to go to the Trocadéro instead of the Verdurins after a ride with Andrée; M warns her of the danger of riding accidents: 115–16. Her fondness for the street-criers and their wares: 122–4. Rhapsody on ice-creams: 125–6. Visit to Versailles with the chauffeur: 127–30. Journey to Balbec with the chauffeur: 132 (cf. 339–40). Her contradictory lies: 141–2. Léa at the Trocadéro; M's frenzy of jealous suspicion; sends Françoise round with a note requesting Albertine to return home: 142–51; she complies, and sends an affectionate note ("What a Marcel!"): 153–4. Her new ring: 162–3. Her knowledge of painting and architecture: 164–5. Expedition to the Bois de Boulogne: 166–73. Feels herself a prisoner; her desire to escape: 173–5. Her technique in lying:

176–8, 187–91. M visits the Verdurins without her: 191; Charlus regrets her absence: 220, 222–3. Vinteuil's music revives M's love for her: 254–5, 260, 267, 308, 334. Her lighted window: 336. Her attitude to M's jealousy: 337. Her annoyance on learning of his visit to the Verdurins: 338. Admits that her trip to Balbec with the chauffeur was an invention: 339–40. Denies having been intimate with Mlle Vinteuil and her friend: 341–2. Her interrupted phrase ("get myself b. . .") of which M finally discovers the meaning: 343–6. Crushed by M's feigned decision to break with her there and then: 346–7. Her intimacy with Bloch's cousin Esther: 348. Her visit to Léa's dressing-room: 351 and her three-week trip with Léa: 357–9. Reconciliation: 365. M visits her in her room and finds her already asleep: 366–7. Does she want to leave him?: 367–70. Attempts to dispel his suspicions: 371. Fears of her departure: 373–4. Her interest in old silver and Fortuny gowns: 375–8. Plays the pianola: 378–80, 388–90. Revelation about Gilberte: 383. Conversation about literature: 382–7. Watching her sleep once more: 394. Why she had returned to Paris with M; her relations with Andrée; her lie about the Buttes-Chaumont: 395–400. The Fortuny gown: 401. Quarrel with M about Andrée; refusal to kiss him: 402–8. Noise of her window being opened during the night: 409. Visit to Versailles: 412–14. Makes eyes at a woman in a pastry-cook's: 416–17. Her sudden departure: 422. "Mademoiselle Albertine has gone!": 425. Her farewell letter: 427. Her behaviour just before her departure: 433–5. M learns that she has gone to Touraine: 438. How to get her back; plan to send Saint-Loup in search of her; Saint-Loup's reaction to her photograph: 441–50. Her letter from Touraine and M's reply: 461–70. Her forgotten rings: 471–4. Her third letter: 476–8. Saint-Loup's report: 480–4. Her death in a riding accident: 485. Her two posthumous letters: 486–7. She continues to live in M after her death; his memories and regrets: 488–525. Aimé's revelations about the bathing establishment at Balbec: 525–31. His inquiries in Touraine and revelations about the laundry-girl: 533–40. Fragmentation into many different Albertines: 540–5. She appears in M's dreams: 549–51. Andrée denies having had illicit relations with her: 557–60. M's love for her survives in his pursuit of women of her type and background: 562–8. Stages on the road to indifference:

570, 605–9. Andrée's revelations — her own relations with Albertine; Albertine and Morel; the syringa incident: 612–14. Albertine's reason for leaving M; the Buttes-Chaumont; her relations with Octave: 621–37. M nearing total indifference, in Venice: 637, 641–2. Brief and fortuitous reawakenings of her memory: 654–6. A telegram which M believes to be from her accelerates his return to indifference: 656–60. The Austrian girl who resembles her: 663–4. M's "reflex" memory of her at Tansonville: 716–17. He discusses her with Gilberte: 726–7. He no longer thinks of her: 751. Retrospectively, her exclamation on being caught by Françoise *in flagrante delicto*: 851. Linked with Saint-Loup in M's memory: 878–9. Had been of use to him by causing him unhappiness: 947. The inspiration of his book: 954.

ALBON, Old M. d'. Smiles at a remark by Mme de Guermantes: III 1041.

ALIX, the "Marie-Antoinette of the Quai Malaquais", one of the "three Parcae"; at Mme de Villeparisis's reception: II 200–07.

AMBASSADRESS, Turkish. At the Guermantes': II 555–60; why she irritates M: 684–5; her social utility: 685.

AMBRESAC, M., Mme and Mesdemoiselles d'. At Balbec; related to Mme de Villeparisis, despised by Albertine; Saint-Loup engaged to one of the girls?: I 944–5 (cf. II 30). Mme d'Ambresac at the Opéra: II 35. Saint-Loup denies the engagement rumour: 103–4. Competition for the hand of Daisy d'Ambresac: 419–20. Saint-Loup talks to her at the Princesse de Guermantes's reception: 724.

AMONCOURT, Mme Timoléon d'. Offers the Duchesse de Guermantes some Ibsen manuscripts; her wit, beauty and obligingness: II 690–92.

ANDRÉE. The eldest of the "little band" of girls at Balbec, the "tall one". Jumps over the old banker: I 849 (cf. 943). Plays golf: 939. Introduced to M by Albertine: 943–4. Complexity of her character; lies to M; quarrels with Gisèle: 946–9. In the Casino; her sympathetic disposition; her friendship with Albertine: 954–6. Her comments on Gisèle's essay: 972–6. Her hands; the game of "ferret": 980–83. M's doubts as to her kindness: 984–6. M pretends to prefer her to Albertine; her jealousy: 989–93. Her mother and Albertine: 997–9. M finds her a neurotic, sickly intellectual like himself: 1005–6. "A camellia in the night": 1008. Dances with Albertine in the Casino at Incarville: II 823–5. Expresses abhorrence of Sapphic behaviour: 830. Her tender ways with Albertine: 831–2. M pretends to be in love with her: 857, 859–62. She and Albertine avoid each other: 870–1. M prefers her to Albertine: 1150–51. Albertine's chaperone in Paris: III 9, 11–12, 15–16. The syringa incident: 48–9. Intensification of her defects; denounces Octave ("I'm a wash-out"); M's suspicions of her: 53–6 (cf. 97–8, 1113–14). Her voice on the telephone: 94–7. Albertine murmurs her name while asleep: 109. Her lies dovetail with Albertine's: 177, 225, 339. Her secret life with Albertine: 395–9. M quarrels with Albertine over her: 404–5. M invites her to come and live with him after Albertine's departure: 478, 486. M jealous of her: 543. Visits M after Albertine's death; admits to her own Sapphic tastes but denies having had illicit relations with Albertine: 556–60. Her second visit; has forgotten Albertine: 609–10; confesses her relations with Albertine; new version of the syringa incident: 612–16; her defamatory remarks about Octave, whom she later marries: 616–18; her explanation of Albertine's departure: 621–6. Third visit to M; further revelations about Albertine and a new explanation for the latter's departure (a plan to marry Octave): 627–9, 633–4. During the war, now married to Octave, remains M's friend: 752. Her friendship with Gilberte: 1032–3.

ANDRÉE'S mother. Mentioned by Albertine at Balbec: I 944, 886. Her social position and attitude to Albertine: 997–9. Her hair: 1008. Her "horses, carriages, pictures": III 9.

ANTOINE, the Guermantes's butler. Françoise's opinion of him and his "Antoinesse": II 18; his arrogant air: 23; his anti-Dreyfusism: 306–7.

ARCHIVIST, encountered *chez* Mme de Villeparisis: *See* Vallenères.

ARGENCOURT, Comte d', later Marquis d'. Belgian Chargé d'Affaires in Paris. At Mme de Villeparisis's reception: II 217–20, 229–30; speaks of Maeterlinck's *Seven Princesses*: 235–7, 257; his anti-semitism: 241–2; his rudeness to Bloch: 251–4. Meets M and Charlus in the street; Charlus's opinion of him: 302. "A terrible snob": 464. At Mme Verdurin's musical *soirée*;

his changed attitude to Charlus: III 274. During the war, arrested and released: 884. After the war, at the Guermantes *matinée*, has become an amiable old dotard: 961–6.

ARGENCOURT, Dowager Comtesse d' (*née* Seineport), mother of the above. Bluestocking hostess: II 464.

ARPAJON, Vicomtesse or Comtesse d'. At the Guermantes dinner-party (one of the "flower maidens"): II 444–5. Mistress of the Duke: 497, 500. Conversation with M about the archives in her château: 506–7. Her opinion of Flaubert: 508, and of Victor Hugo: 510–12. Quotes Musset for Hugo: 514. Ridiculed by Mme de Guermantes: 515, 518. Addressed by the latter as "Phili": 523. At the Princesse de Guermantes's, declines to introduce M to the Prince: 674–6. Jealous of Mme Surgis-le-Duc, who has succeeded her in the Duke's affections: 676. Drenched by the Hubert Robert fountain: 681–2. Cultivates Odette: 774–5. Her brilliant tea-parties: 1032. Doubts the existence of M. Verdurin: III 275. In her old age, seems at once unknown and familiar: 979–80. Her death discussed at the Guermantes *matinée*: 1024–7.

AUBERJON, Duchesse Gisèle d'. Summoned by Mme de Villeparisis to help with her theatricals: II 221.

AYEN, Duchesse Jane d'. Charlus deplores the conversation at her house: III 312.

BABAL. *See* Bréauté-Consalvi.

BALLEROY, Mme de. Great-aunt of a niece of Mme de Guermantes: III 189.

BASIN. *See* Guermantes, Basin, Duc de.

BARRISTER from Cherbourg. Staying at the Grand Hotel, Balbec: I 726–8. Entertains the Cambremers to lunch: 738–40. Orders trout from Aimé: 742. Irritated by Mme Blandais: 754. Visits Féterne: 758. M learns of his death: II 778.

BAVENO, Marquise de. Comments on Oriane's "Teaser Augustus" pun: II 483.

BEAUSERFEUIL, General de. Overhears Swann's Jewish witticism at the Guermantes' reception: II 723. The Prince de Guermantes consults him about Dreyfus: 731, 734.

(*See* Monserfeuil: it is clear that the two names apply interchangeably to the same general.)

BEAUSERGENT, Marquis de (Mme d'Argencourt's brother). In

Mme de Cambremer's box at the Opéra: 11 52. At the final Guermantes party, now an aged colonel: 111 981.

BEAUTREILLIS, General de. At the Guermantes dinner party: 11 511. His anti-Dreyfusism: 516.

BELLOEUVRE, Gilbert de. Young golfer at Balbec, remembered by M: 111 620.

BERGOTTE. Distinguished writer recommended to M by Bloch, who lends him one of his books: 1 97. His style, and its effect on M: 101–4. Swann speaks of him; an admirer of Berma: 105–6. A great friend of Gilberte: 107–8, 149. His booklet on Racine presented to M by Gilberte: 437, 444. Quotations from this concerning *Phèdre*: 478. Norpois's unfavourable opinion of him — "a deliquescent mandarin": 510–13 (cf. 11 228). Luncheon party at the Swanns'; the man with the goatee beard and snail-shell nose and the gentle bard with the snowy locks: 587–601. His voice and his style; "Bergottisms"; his family: 592–9. Vices of the man and morality of the writer: 600–02. Speaks of Berma and Racine: 603–5. His opinion of Norpois: 605–6. Favourably impressed by M; they leave together; his medical advice and malicious remarks about Cottard and the Swanns: 611–15. M's parents change their opinion of him: 617–18, 623–5. Sought after by Mme Verdurin: 645. M receives a letter from him at Balbec: 767–8. Charlus lends M one of his books: 822–3. M. Bloch's opinion of him: 826–30. Legrandin's opinion of him — "gamy stuff for the jaded palates of refined voluptuaries": 11 156. Admired by the Duchesse de Guermantes: 215–17, 228. Dr du Boulbon speaks of him to M's grandmother: 312, 316–17. His visits to M during his grandmother's illness; his own illness, his increasing fame, his indifference to the new: 336–40. Reputed to have written a satirical one-act play about the Prince de Guermantes: 700, 728. Mme Swann's salon crystallises round him: 770–74. Reported to be seriously ill: 1003. M still reads him: 111 50, 551. His death; "the little patch of yellow wall": 180–6. His instinctive attraction towards inferior women: 213. Charlus visits him on behalf of Morel: 218–19. M gives Albertine one of his manuscripts: 365. His one-time belief in table-turning: 539. His reaction to the *Figaro* article in M's dream: 604. His influence on Morel's style: 791–2. M's eventual disillusionment with his books: 922. The intricacy of his style now out of fashion: 929. The role he had played in M's love for Gilberte: 1040.

BERMA. Her rank as an actress: I 80. Admired by Bergotte: 105, 107. M's desire to see her perform: 427, 437. Her performance in *Phèdre*: 473–80; M's disappointment: 480–86. Norpois's opinion of her: 492–3. "What a great artist!": 517–18. M buys a photograph of her; her face and her loves: 525–7. Bergotte's opinon of her: 603–5. Swann's view: 610–11. M sees her again in *Phèdre*; an interpretation "quickened by the breath of genius": II 31–2, 39–54. Rachel's patronizing comments: 170. Françoise compared to her in histrionic virtuosity: 761. Gives a party in honour of her daughter and son-in-law; their selfishness and cruelty; failure of the party: III 887, 1045–50. Rachel's malicious remarks about her: 1054–5. Her daughter and son-in-law beg Rachel to receive them: 1066–7. Rachel's cruel disclosure of this proves a mortal blow to her: 1067–8.

BERNARD, Nissim. Rich great-uncle of Bloch. At dinner *chez* the Blochs at Balbec; the family butt; his lies: I 830–32; but he really did know M. de Marsantes: II 286. Grows mannered and precious with advancing age: 299–300. His relations with a young waiter at the Grand Hôtel: 871–4, 879 and with the tomato-faced waiters at the "Cherry Orchard": 883–4. Allusion to his death (?): 1137. Incurs Morel's enmity by lending him five thousand francs: III 47. Leaves money to the young waiter from the Grand Hotel, now manager of a restaurant: 758–9.

BERTHE. Friend of Albertine: III 559.

BIBI. Friend of the Prince de Foix, announces his engagement to Daisy d'Ambresac: II 419.

BICHE ("Master"). *See* Elstir.

BLANDAIS, M. Notary from Le Mans on holiday at Balbec: I 726–8, 739, 754, 815.

BLANDAIS, Mme. Wife of the above: I 728–9. Impressed by M. de Cambremer: 734. Annoys the barrister: 754. Not invited to the Cambremers': 758, 814–15. M tells a funny story about her: II 103.

BLATIN, Mme. Apparent friend of Gilberte; reads the *Journal des Débats* in the Champs-Elysées: I 431–2. Her affectation: 439–40. M's mother's poor opinion of her: 448. Mme Swann dreads her visits: 547–8. Resembles a portrait of Savonarola: 575–6. "Me nigger; you old cow!": 576–7.

BLOCH, Albert. Schoolfriend of M's. Recommends Bergotte to him; despises Racine and Musset, admires Leconte de Lisle: I 97. His neo-Homeric jargon: 97, 800–01, 826, 832 (cf. II 251, 865, 1137). Antagonizes M's family: 98–101. His likeness, according to Swann, to Gentile Bellini's portrait of Sultan Mahomet II: 105. Unwittingly helps M to gain access to the Swanns: 541. Greets Mme Swann in the Bois; she mistakes his name: 585 (cf. 834–5). Alters M's notions about women, and takes him to a brothel: 619–20, 764. His affectation of anti-semitism: 793 (cf. 802). His absurdity, his snobbery; his family; his ill breeding: 793–6, 799–804. M and Saint-Loup dine with him and his family: 824–35. His gaffe about Charlus: 834. Claims to have had carnal relations with Odette: 834–5. Sees Saint-Loup off at the station; his tactlessness: 926–7. Albertine's antipathy to him: 940–2. His Dreyfusism: II 104 (see also 307). Dislike of Stendhal: 106. At Mme de Villeparisis's reception, now a rising dramatist: 193–256. His exotic Jewishness: 194–5. Knocks over a glass of water: 221–2. His ambivalent remarks about Saint-Loup: 224 (cf. 234). His rudeness: 225–6. Introduced to Norpois: 227–8; discusses the Dreyfus Case with him: 239–41, 247–54. Snubbed by M. d'Argencourt and the Duc de Châtellerault: 254–5. Takes leave of Mme de Villeparisis, who feigns sleep: 256–7. His friendliness towards Saint-Loup, who invites him to dinner: 284–5 (cf. 414). Charlus's interest in him: 297–8. Snubbed by Charlus on being introduced to him by M: 396–7. Regular meetings with his Jewish friends to discuss the Zola trial in the restaurant where M and Saint-Loup dine one foggy night: 415. Behaviour on being introduced to Mme Alphonse de Rothschild: 525. His petition on behalf of Colonel Picquart: 738–9. His fondness for authentic Greek spelling: 865. Pretends not to recognize his sister: 879. Offended by M's reluctance to leave the little train to meet his father: 1137–40. Charlus questions M about him: 1140–44. Calls on M in Paris, without knowing that Albertine is in the house: III 1, 56. Arranges a loan for Morel and thereby incurs his enmity: 47. Sends M a photograph of his cousin Esther Lévy: 80–81, 106, 348. His taste in furniture: 174. Charlus wants to invite him to his house: 214. A poet "in my idle moments": 216. Fails to recognize Albertine dressed as a man: 340. Visits M after Albertine's departure and incurs his anger: 450–1. Ignores M's

Figaro article: 603. His noisy ostentation and pretentiousness in a Balbec restaurant: 697–8. During the war, chauvinistic before being passed fit for service, thereafter anti-militarist; "at once coward and braggart": 758–63, 766. Marries one of his daughters to a Catholic: 851. Bored by society novels: 915. After the war, M recognizes him in spite of his having aged: 968–9. His cult of his dead father: 972–3. Has adopted the name Jacques du Rozier; his English chic; his physical transformation: 995–6. Questions M about society figures of the past: 996–8. His own position in society; his fame as a writer: 1002, 1010–14. His new discretion: 1016. Refuses Berma's invitation: 1045–6. Compliments Rachel: 1053–4. His interest in M. de Bréauté: 1059–62. Steals M's ideas for articles: 1090.

BLOCH, M. Salomon, father of the above. Impressed by his son's acquaintanceship with Saint-Loup: I 803. His stereoscope: 803–4. M and Saint-Loup dine with him; his preposterous stories; his opinion of Bergotte; his avarice: 824–34. His admiration for Léa: 965. Impressed by Sir Rufus Israels: II 224. Charlus declines to be introduced to him; greets Mme Sazerat: 299. His post-chaise with postilions: 1137. His Stock Exchange connections: III 762. Dies of grief during the war: 968.

BLOCH'S cousin. *See* Lévy, Esther.

BLOCH'S sisters. At Balbec, introduced to M: I 793–4. Their admiration for their brother: 794, and imitation of his jargon: 826, 829–33. Their vulgarity: 964. One of them, with her cousin, attracts Albertine's attention in the Casino at Balbec: II 830–31, and causes a scandal in the Grand Hotel by her behaviour with an ex-actress: 871, 879.

BONTEMPS, M. Albertine's uncle. Chief Secretary to the Minister of Public Works: I 551–2. Dines with the Swanns: 562–3. At an official dinner with M's father: 674. Supports Albertine but anxious to be rid of her: 997. Considered somewhat "shady": 997, and a political opportunist: 999. Had been a counsellor in Vienna: II 1157. A "lukewarm" Dreyfusard: III 239. His election committee: 449. Chauvinist and militarist during the war, his Dreyfusism forgotten: 747–9. Mme Verdurin's telephone conversations with him: 754–5.

BONTEMPS, Mme. Albertine's aunt. Her visits to Odette; her vulgarity and snobbishness: I 547, 551–5, 642–4, 647–53.

Albertine's attitude towards her: 944. M's desire to meet her at Balbec: 989–91. Albertine conceals her assignation with M from her: 993–4. Her influence on Albertine: 11 369–70, 382. Her anti-Dreyfusism: 605. Takes a villa at Epreville: 808. Calls at the Grand Hotel to take Albertine home: 861. M's fears about her disreputable friend: 882. Strongly in favour of his marrying Albertine: 958. Her lunch party, attended by Bloch, at which M is praised: 1139–40. Her influence on Albertine's taste in music: 111 3. Raises no objection to Albertine's living *chez* M: 6, 41. Her pronunciation of "Béarn": 27. Gives Albertine a ring?: 57, 162. Placed on the Index by Charlus: 239. Unwittingly reveals to M one of Albertine's lies: 396. Saint-Loup's mission to persuade her to send Albertine back: 443, 448–9, 459, 480–83. Telegraphs M to inform him of Albertine's death: 485. Her schemes for Albertine to marry Octave: 627–9. Entertained by Gilberte: 684–5. One of the queens of war-time Paris: 743, 747. Firmly established in the Faubourg Saint-Germain: 749–50.

BORANGE. Grocer, stationer and bookseller at Combray: 1 90–91.

BORODINO, Prince de. Cavalry captain at Doncières: 11 71. Allows M to sleep in barracks: 76. Saint-Loup's poor opinion of him: 77. Refuses Saint-Loup leave: 125, then changes his mind at the instance of his hair-dresser: 127–8. His aloofness from Saint-Loup and his friends; his Imperial background; his social attitudes; differences between the two aristocracies: 129–33. He rides majestically by: 140–41. Mme de Villeparisis denounces him: 223–4. His invitations to M: 1137.

BOUILLON, Cyrus, Comte de. Father of Mme de Villeparisis: 1 761. His literary acquaintances: 763–4. Chateaubriand and the moonlight: 775–6. Visited by the Duc de Nemours: 778–9. (Somewhat confusingly, in *The Guermantes Way* Mme de Villeparisis's father is called Florimond de Guise: 11 550–51, cf. 11 196.)

BOUILLON, Comtesse de. Mother of Mme de Villeparisis. The Duchesse de Praslin's armchair: 1 779–80.

BOUILLON, Duc de. Outside the Duc de Guermantes's library; his timid, humble appearance: 11 595–6. Identified as the only genuine surviving member of the princely la Tour d'Auvergne family, Oriane's uncle and Mme de Villeparisis's brother: 706.

BOULBON, Doctor du. Admirer of Bergotte: I 102. His likeness to a Tintoretto portrait: 243. Recommended to M by Bergotte: 614. At M's grandmother's bedside: II 310–18. Provokes Cottard's jealousy at Balbec: 824–5, 1009. Compared with Louis XIV's physician, Fagon: III 1055.

BOURBON, Princesse de. *See* Mme de Charlus.

BRÉAUTÉ-CONSALVI, Marquis (or Comte) Hannibal de ("Babal"). At Mme de Saint-Euverte's; his monocle: I 355–6. Reputed lover of Odette: 387, 392 (cf. III 1075). Less witty than Bergotte: II 216–17. At the Guermantes'; his curiosity about M and extravagantly affable salutations: 445–7. His social assiduity, although he claims to loathe society; reputation as an intellectual: 468, 505, 508, 523. Discusses botany with Mme de Guermantes: 536. His mother a Choiseul and his grandmother a Lucinge: 556. Introduces M to the Prince de Guermantes: 678–9. His "improvements" to the Hubert Robert fountain: 683. His explanation for the alleged quarrel between Swann and the Prince de Guermantes: 700–01, 706. His malicious amusement at Mme de Guermantes's plan to avoid the Saint-Euverte garden party: 709. In Mme Swann's box: 773. An *habitué* of her salon; a changed man: 776. Regular visitor at Mme de Guermantes': III 30. Repeats Cartier's *mot* about Zola; his voice and pronunciation: 33–6. Refuses to know Odette and Gilberte: 588–9. Gilberte's interest in him: 600–01. "Dead!": 894. Oriane's reminiscences about him — "Bréauté was a snob": 1059–62 (cf. II 468). Odette's account of her love affair with him: 1075. His "provincialism": 1078, 1080.

BRÉQUIGNY, Comte de. Father of the ladies with the walking-sticks, Mme de Plassac and Mme de Tresmes: II 594, 597, 623.

BRETEUIL, Quasimodo. Friend of Swann and of Mme de Guermantes: III 600.

BRETONNERIE, Mme de la. Lady of Combray with whom Eulalie had been in service: I 74.

BRICHOT, Professor at the Sorbonne. Dines at the Verdurins': I 274. His pedantic witticisms: 275–6, 284–5. Admired by Forcheville: 276, 281. Swann's antipathy to him: 288–90. Bergotte's *mot* concerning him: 594–5. His anti-Dreyfusism: II 605 (*see also* 915). In the little train: 895–925. His near-blindness: 896–7. His liaison with his laundress torpedoed by Mme

attend Mme de Saint-Euverte's parties: II 694–5. Her social life
in the neighbourhood of Balbec: 792–5. Sends M notice of her
cousin's death: 814. Calls at the Grand Hotel; her elaborate
attire; her salivation; her worship of Chopin: 833–52. The
lift-boy's mispronunciation of her name: 833, 854. Her children:
944. Her relationship with her gardener: 948–9. Her letter to M;
the rule of the three adjectives: 977–8 (see also 1123). Her
influence throughout her family: 1123–4. "Queen of the
Normandy coast": 1129. Her grandson takes after her: III 690.
Lives to a very advanced age: 975–6.

CAMBREMER, Marquis de. Married to Legrandin's sister: I 73,
135. Calls at the Grand Hotel, Balbec, to collect guests for his
wife's weekly "garden party": 733–4. Lunches with the
barrister: 738–9. Nicknamed "Cancan": II 846. Invited to
dinner by the Verdurins: 913–16. His appearance, his nose, his
character; explanation of his nickname: 942–4. His two fables:
946, 956–7. Introduced to M: 947–8. His deference to Charlus:
949, 975, 978. Impressed by Brichot's etymological expertise:
952–3, 955–6, 960–61. His interest, not to say delight, in M's fits
of breathlessness: 957–8, 1008, 1133. Criticises the Verdurins'
taste in furniture: 976–7. His admiration for Cottard: 991–2.
Talks to him about drugs: 993–4. Explains a point in heraldry to
Mme Verdurin: 995–6. His anti-Dreyfusism: 998–9 (cf. III 236).
Fails to appreciate a Cottard pun: 1007. Tips the Verdurin
coachman: 1009–10. His ignorance of his native countryside:
1031. He and his wife quarrel with the Verdurins: 1124–32. Tries
to persuade M to remain at Balbec: 1163. His opinion on the
Dreyfus Case: III 236. Saint-Loup's favourable opinion of him
during the war: 761 (cf. II 488). M meets him at the Guermantes
matinée after the war, unrecognisably aged: 974–6.

CAMBREMER, Marquise Renée de. Wife of the above and sister of
Legrandin. Lives near Balbec: I 73. Legrandin avoids giving M
and his family a letter of introduction to her: 141–3. At Mme de
Saint-Euverte's *soirée*; a Wagnerian, despises Chopin: 361–2.
The candle incident: 366–7. Admired by Froberville: 367. Her
name discussed by Swann and the Princesse des Laumes: 371–2.
Introduced to Froberville by Swann: 373–5. Swann follows her
to Combray: 414. Said to have been "mad about" Swann: 575.
Aunts Céline and Flora refuse to mention her name: 696. Her

weekly "garden party" at Féterne: 733. Lunches with the barrister at Balbec: 738–40. At the Opéra: II 51–4. Ridiculed by Mme de Guermantes: 207–8, 238–9. Recommended to M by Saint-Loup: 780. Her rudeness and arrogance: 794. Introduced to M; her social and intellectual snobbery; contempt for her mother-in-law; avant-garde tastes in art and music: 835–46. Her pronunciation of Chenouville: 846–9. Her relations with Robert: 848. Invited to la Raspelière by the Verdurins: 913–17, 942–1011 *passim*. Her contempt for them; her "haughty and morose" demeanour; her pleasure at meeting Charlus; her irritating habits: 944–7. Criticises the Verdurins' alterations at la Raspelière: 953–4, 976–7. Conversation with M; his reflexions on her intellect, her aesthetic tastes, her snobbery, her vocabulary: 954–60. Her enthusiasm for Debussy and Scarlatti: 986–7. Her affected good-bye to M; mispronounces "Saint-Loup"; her impertinent teasing: 1010–11. Her social preoccupations; invitations to Morel and Cottard resented by Mme Verdurin: 1124–5. Brichot in love with her; Mme Verdurin intervenes: 1127–8. Dinner party for M. and Mme Féré at which Charlus fails to appear: 1128–30. Quarrel with the Verdurins: 1130–32. Reaction to her son's engagement to Jupien's niece: III 673, 678–9. Becomes indifferent to the friendly overtures of the Duchesse de Guermantes: 684. Criticised by Saint-Loup: 761. At the Verdurin reception after the war: 975.

CAMBREMER, Léonor de. Son of the above. Marries Jupien's niece (Mlle d'Oloron): III 672–4. An invert: 678. Deserts the minor nobility for the intelligent bourgeoisie: 679. His resemblance to his uncle Legrandin: 987, 1015–16.

CAMILLE. Servant of the Swanns: I 550.

CAMUS. Grocer at Combray: I 60–61, 73; his packing cases: 89; his pink sugar biscuits: 152.

CANCAN. *See* Cambremer, Marquis de.

CAPRAROLA, Principessa di. Visits Mme Verdurin: II 771. Visits Odette and mentions the Verdurins: 899–990.

CARTIER. Brother of Mme de Villefranche and intimate friend of the Duc de la Trémoïlle. His *mot* about Zola recounted by Bréauté, to the irritation of Mme de Guermantes: III 33–4. His later obscurity: 199.

CASHIERS. At the Rivebelle restaurant, "two horrible cashiers" like a pair of witches: I 868. At the Grand Hotel, Balbec, the cashier "enthroned beneath her palm": II 873. Hideous one in an unnamed hotel, regarded by the staff as a "fine-looking" woman: III 189.

CÉLESTE. *See* Albaret.

CÉLINE and FLORA. Sisters of M's grandmother. Share her nobility of character but not her intelligence; their aesthetic interests; their ingenious circumlocution: I 17, 23–8. Swann's present of wine: 23, 26–8, 37. Their provincial dogmatism; 106. Pupils of Vinteuil: 122. Disapproval of M's artistic taste: 160. Their revenge for Legrandin's insult: 696. Refusal to leave Combray to see their dying sister: II 336, 356. M's mother goes to visit one of them at Combray: II 50, II 59–60; III 6.

CHANLIVAULT, Mme de. Sister of "le vieux Chaussepierre", lives in the Rue La Pérouse: I 374. Aunt of M. de Chaussepierre, who later ousts M. de Guermantes from the Presidency of the Jockey Club: II 698.

CHARLUS, Baron de (Palamède, nicknamed "Mémé"). At Combray; reputed lover of Mme Swann: I 37, 107. Seen by M at Tansonville: "a gentleman in a suit of linen 'ducks' . . . stared at me with eyes which seemed to be starting from his head": 154–5. Friend of Swann: 210, 338. Go-between with Odette: 339, 344, 350. Chaperones her at Swann's request: 351. Suspected by Swann of writing an anonymous letter: 387–90. Expected at Balbec: 804. Saint-Loup's account of him; his social position; his arrogance, his reputation for womanising: 805–7. Visual encounter with M outside the Casino: 807–8. Mme de Villeparisis introduces him: 809. Studied sobriety of his clothes: 809. A Guermantes: 810. His title explained: 811. His intelligence and sensibility, aesthetic taste, obsession with virility, attitude to the nobility; 812–14; delights M's grandmother; 818–21. Invites M to tea: 814. His strange behaviour and enigmatic stare: 815–17. His voice: 820. Comes to M's bedroom and lends him a Bergotte novel: 821–3. Strange behaviour on the beach next day: 823–4. Bloch's derisive remarks about him: 834. Comes to call on Aimé at the restaurant where M is lunching with Saint-Loup and Rachel: II 171–2. At Mme de Villeparisis's; attaches himself to Odette; his relations with his aunt: 272, 276–9. Invites M to accompany him after the party: 286–7. Mme de Villeparisis seems upset by this: 293. Strange conversation with M; his views on high politics, the Jews, the Duchesse de Guermantes, Mme de Villeparisis; his sudden departure in a cab: 294–306. Mme de Guermantes pronounces him "a trifle mad": 393–5. His attitude to Bloch: 396–7 (cf. 297–9, 1138, 111 214). Through Saint-Loup, invites M to call on him: 427. "Teaser Augustus": 481–5, 504. "Knows Balzac by heart": 510. How he mourned his wife: 526–7. M's visit to him after dining at the Guermantes'; his strange welcome, violent rage followed by affectionate melancholy: 573–84. Accompanies M home: 584–8. His meeting with Jupien; his true nature suddenly revealed: 11 623–37, 650–56. At the Princesse de Guermantes's *soirée*; talks to the Duke of Sidonia: 662–4. His greetings to the guests: 672–3. Pretends to play whist: 676–7. Decline of his influence in society: 677–8. Refuses to introduce M to the Prince de Guermantes: 678, but talks to him about the gardens and the Hubert Robert fountain: 682–3. His conversation with M. de Vaugoubert: 688–90, 699 (cf. 666–8). Enveloped in the Comtesse Molé's skirt: 699 (cf. 717). In the card-room, gazes at the young Comte de Surgis: 713–14. Saint-Loup speaks of his womanising: 717–18. His attentiveness to Mme de Surgis, who introduces her two sons to him: 719–25, 729–33 (*see also* 1178). His outrageous diatribe against Mme de Saint-Euverte: 725–7. Swann's view of his sexual proclivities: 733–4. The Princesse de Guermantes's secret passion for him: 740–42 (*see also* 1082, 1179–87). Brotherly exchange with the Duc de Guermantes: 742–5. His first meeting with Morel at Doncières station: 889–92. His visit to la Raspelière announced by M. Verdurin: 931–2. Confused in artistic circles with another Charlus: 932–4. Arrives at la Raspelière with Morel; his mincing manner with the Verdurins: 936–47. Misinterprets Cottard's winks: 949–52. Impresses Mme Verdurin with a reference to the Comtesse Molé: 966–7. M. Verdurin's *gaffe*, Charlus's contemptuous laugh; he enumerates his titles: 973–4. Declines in a lordly manner M. de Cambremer's offer of his chair: 975–6. Expatiates on his family's heraldic situation: 978–80, 983–4. Accompanies Morel in a Fauré sonata; link between his artistic gifts and his nervous weaknesses: 985–6. Proposes a pilgrimage to Mont Saint-Michel: 989–90. Admiringly watches Morel playing cards: 990, 995–8, 1000.

Prefers strawberry juice; his feminine tone of voice: 999–1000. His first skirmish with Mme Verdurin: 1000–01. Dines at the Grand Hotel with a footman: 1019–22. His letter to Aimé: 1023–5. Motor-car excursions with Morel; their conversation in a restaurant at Saint-Mars-le-Vêtu: 1039–44. Becomes "the most faithful of the faithful"; conversations in the little train: 1070–70. His illusions about other people's knowledge of and attitude towards his proclivities: 1081–4. Cites Balzac on the subject of inversion: 1084–7. Admires Albertine's clothes, reminiscent of Balzac's Princesse de Cadignan: 1089–90, 1092–3. Relations with Morel: 1094–8. The fictitious duel: 1099–1110. Suspicions about Morel: 1110–13; spies on him with Jupien in the Maineville brothel: 1114–17. Instructs Morel as to the composition of the social hierarchy: 1125–6. Reveals Brichot's passion for Mme de Cambremer: 1127. Snubs the Cambremers: 1128–30. His interest in Bloch: 1138, 1140–41. His anti-Jewish tirade 1141–4. Tea with Morel at Jupien's; observations about Jupien's niece: III 37–8. Receives a love-letter from the doorman at a gambling club which he shows to Vaugoubert: 38–9. Approves of the idea of a marriage between Morel and Jupien's niece: 40–44. Fails to solve the mystery of Morel's algebra lessons: 159–60. His yellow trousers and the public urinal: 188–9. Encounter with M and Brichot on the way to the Verdurins' musical *soirée*; change in his appearance, development of his homosexual persona; the shady individuals in his wake; his deliberate "camping": 202–9. Discovers a strange letter from Léa to Morel: 211–14. Conversation in the street with M and Brichot; enquiries about Bloch; praises Morel's beauty, talent, writing ability (lampoons against Mme Molé); his relationship with Bergotte; discusses Albertine's taste in clothes: 214–23. At the Verdurins'; "forgets himself" with a footman: 227–8 (cf. 261). Lays down the law to Mme Verdurin about her guests; his quarrel with Mme Molé (cf. 218, 277): 231–6, 239. His desire to adopt an heir (Morel?): 244. Furtive exchanges with certain fellow-guests: 244–5. Rudeness of the society guests — the cause of his downfall: 246–9. His demeanour when Morel mounts the platform: 249–50. His indiscreet behaviour with the footmen: 261. Conversation with Mme de Mortemart and other guests after the concert: 267–75. Condescending remarks to Mme Verdurin; the Queen of

escaped being thrown out of the Jockey Club, according to Charlus: III 312. Asks for Gilberte's hand in marriage: 676. His appearance in old age: 960–61.

CHÂTELLERAULT, Prince de. Friend of the Prince de Foix; his matrimonial ambitions: II 419.

CHAUFFEUR. Hired by M at Balbec: II 1028–9. Charlus also a customer of his: 1039. Informs M of his recall to Paris: 1060–61. His intimacy with Morel: 1061 (cf. 1039, 1044) Conspires with Morel to oust the Verdurins' coachman and take his job: 1062–5. Lent to M by the Verdurins in Paris: III 9. Praises Morel to Jupien's niece: 60. M's doubts about his vigilance over Albertine; his account of the excursion to Versailles: 127–32. Albertine's accomplice in the invented trip to Balbec: 339–40. Extravagantly tipped by M: 373.

CHAUSSEGROS, Marquise de. Her supposed acquaintance with M: II 516–17.

CHAUSSEPIERRE, M. de. Nephew of "old mother Chanlivault": II 698. Ousts M. de Guermantes from the presidency of the Jockey Club: III 32–3.

CHAUSSEPIERRE, Mme de. Oriane refuses to recognise her at the Princesse de Guermantes's soirée: II 698. Her modesty; her musical parties: III 32–3.

CHENOUVILLE, M de. Referred to by the young Mme de Cambremer as "my uncle de Ch'nouville": II 846–7, 1131.

CHEVREGNY, M. de. Relation of the Cambremers; travels on the little train; his provinciality and lack of taste: II 1122–3. Turned away by Mme de Cambremer when Charlus expected to dinner: 1128–9. Invites M to lunch: 1137.

CITRI, Marquise de. At the Princesse de Guermantes's; her horror of high society and her all-embracing nihilism: II 712–13.

COACHMEN. Mme Verdurin's: see Howsler. Swann's: see Rémi.

COIGNET. One of Charlus's valets: II 574.

CONDUCTOR (of a tram or a bus) with whom Charlus has a rendezvous: II 742, 1181–6 (see also 632–4).

COTTARD, Doctor. Member of the Verdurins' "little clan": I 205–7. His artificial smile, naïve thirst for knowledge, obsession with figures of speech; his puns and his literal-mindedness: 217–21, 222–3, 275–8, 284. Failure to understand either Vinteuil's sonata or M. Biche's painting: 232–3. His stupidity and social inexperience: 235–7. Conversation with Forcheville: 285–8. Becomes "Professor Cottard": 465–6; his fame, prestige and diagnostic gifts: 467. His newly-acquired air of glacial impassivity: 468. Called in to attend M; his prescriptions; "we realised that this imbecile was a great physician": 536–7. Speaks favourably of M to Mme Swann: 541–2. Invited to dinner at the Swanns': 561–3. Bergotte's "mannikin in a bottle": 594, 614. Called in to attend M's grandmother: 11 308–9; has "something of the greatness of a general" in deciding on the right course of treatment: 333. "The most unfaithful and most attentive of husbands"; 340. Meets M at Incarville; his remark about Albertine and Andrée dancing together: 822–4. His professional jealousy and his failure to cure a grand-duke: 824–5. Narrowly misses the little train: 897–8. His new self-assurance: 901. Has a passenger ejected from the "little train's" compartment: 904. The importance of the Verdurin Wednesdays in his life: 905, 909–11. Excited by the idea of meeting the Cambremers: 913–15. Introduces M to Princess Sherbatoff: 921–2. Loses his ticket: 923–5. Introduced to Charlus: 942, who momentarily misinterprets his winks: 949–52. Criticises M. de Cambremer's clichés: 953. Questions M about his fits of breathlessness: 957. Discusses Charlus with Ski: 963–4. Plays a game of cards with Morel, interspersed with puns and witticisms: 990–92, 995–7, 1006–7. Mme Verdurin sings his praises for the benefit of M. de Cambremer: 991–2, 995. Teases his wife when she dozes off, and discusses drugs with M. de Cambremer: 992–5. His hand-rubbing and shoulder-shaking: 1007. Criticises Dr du Boulbon: 1008–9. With Charlus in the little train — his confused attitude to the Baron: 1072–5, 1085–7. Invited by Charlus to be his second: 1102, 1106–9. Refuses, on Mme Verdurin's instructions, an invitation to dine at the Cambremers': 1124–5. His death referred to prematurely: 111 242. Looks after Saniette, and informs M of the Verdurins' generosity to him: 329–32. Mentioned in the Goncourt pastiche: 730, 734–6. At the Verdurins' during the war, in a colonel's uniform with a sky-blue sash: 793. Dies from overwork: 794.

COTTARD, Mme Léontine. Wife of the above. At the Verdurins': I 205, 217, 221; her homely taste in painting and music: 232; the Japanese salad in *Francillon*: 279–81. Meets Swann in a bus;

discusses painting with him; assures him of Odette's affection: 407–10. Entertains her husband's colleagues and pupils: 467. Her visits to Odette: 547. Her modesty and good nature: 555–6. Her stately language: 642, 648–54. Her devotion to her husband: 644, 653. Calls on M's family during his grandmother's last illness, and offers to lend her "lady's maid": II 340. Her effeminate nephew: 937–8. At la Raspelière: 952–3, 970; falls asleep after dinner: 992–5; small talk with M. de Cambremer: 997–8. With Charlus in the little train; her mistake about his religion: 1071–4. Accused by her husband of being neurotic: 1086. Charlus's rudeness to her: 1108–9. Invited by an unsuspecting guest of the Verdurins to the luxury brothel at Maineville: IIII–12.

COURGIVAUX, M. de. M takes him for his son at the Princesse de Guermantes's *matinée*: III 986.

COURVOISIER, Vicomte Adalbert de. Nephew of Mme de Gallardon, "a young man with a pretty face and an impertinent air", introduced to Charlus at the Prince de Guermantes's *soirée*: II 677. An invert but a good husband; III 723. Frequents Jupien's brothel: 852–3.

COURVOISIERS, The. Relations and rivals of the Guermantes clan; their social ethos compared and contrasted with the latter's: II 458–69, 478–9, 484–7, 493–6.

COUSIN (female) by whom M is initiated into "the delights of love" on Aunt Léonie's sofa: I 622.

COUSIN of M's nicknamed "No flowers by request": II 353–4.

COUSIN (of Bloch). *See* Lévy, Esther.

CRÉCY, Pierre de Verjus, Comte de. Impoverished nobleman with a taste for good food and wine, cigars and genealogy, befriended by M at Balbec: II 1118–22. His patronym is Saylor, hence the family motto *Ne sçais l'heure*: 1121–22. Invites himself to dinner: 1146. M learns from Charlus that he was Odette's first husband, and lives on an allowance from Swann: III 304.

CRÉCY, Mme de. *See* Odette.

CRIQUETOT, M. de. "How goes it?": II 1149.

CRIQUETOT, Comtesse de. Cousin of the Cambremers; M receives notice of her death at Balbec: II 814.

CURÉ of Combray. His asparagus: I 59. His brother a tax-collector at Châteaudun: 62. His visits to Aunt Léonie; his knowledge of etymology: 74, 111–15, 129. "Touches" the Princesse des Laumes for 100 francs a year: 371. Transferred to Criquetot for a time; his pamphlet on the place-names of the Balbec district: 11 837–8. Brichot's criticisms of this work: 917–21, 952, 1026–8. Knew what was "right and proper": 111 7–8.

DAIRYMAID who brings M a letter at the Grand Hotel, Balbec: 1 767–8.

DAIRYMAID. "Startling towhead" glimpsed by M at the dairy: 111 135–6. Brought in by Françoise to run an errand: 137–40, 144.

DALTIER, Emilie. Pretty girl — "a good golfer" — known to Albertine: 111 415.

DANCER, back-stage in the theatre, admired by Rachel: 11 180–85.

DECHAMBRE. Pianist patronized by Mme Verdurin. Brichot announces his death; discussion about his age: 11 923–4. Effect of his death on the Verdurins: 925–31, 960. M. Verdurin speaks of him to Charlus: 973.

(See Pianist (young) patronized by the Verdurins.)

DELAGE, Suzanne. Mistakenly believed by Albertine and Mme Bontemps to have been a childhood friend of M's: 11 381–3.

DELTOUR, General. Secretary to the Presidency of the Republic. Approached by Charlus in connection with Morel's decoration: 111 281–2.

DIEULAFOY, Professor. See Index of Persons.

DRAWING-MASTER (of M's grandmother), who never saw his mistress without a hat: 1 918.

DUCRET. One of Charlus's valets: 11 574.

DURAS, Duc de. Mentioned by the Duc de Guermantes in connection with Saint-Loup's election to the Jockey Club: 11 246. Marries the widowed Mme Verdurin; dies two years later: 111 998.

DURAS, Duchesse de. At the Verdurins' musical soirée; praised by Charlus: 111 277–80; resented by Mme Verdurin: 315, 317–18.

DURAS, Duchesse de. See Verdurin, Mme.

DUROC, Major. Lecturer on military history admired by Saint-Loup: 11 76–7, 105–7; his Dreyfusism: 108.

E——, Professor. Distinguished doctor whom M persuades to

examine his grandmother after her stroke; his bad grace and his pessimistic (and accurate) verdict: 11 324, 327–8. M meets him again at the Princesse de Guermantes's *soirée*: 664–6.

EGREMONT, Vicomtesse d'. Assumes the role of parlour-maid *chez* the Princesse d'Epinay: 11 480–81.

ELSTIR. Painter, habitué of the Verdurin salon, where he is known as "Master Biche": 1 206, 217. His love of match-making: 220. Invites Swann and Odette to visit his studio; his portrait of Cottard: 221. His painting too advanced for the Cottards: 232–3. Swann finds him pretentious and vulgar, but admires his intelligence: 271, 273–4. His flashy dissertation on a fellow-painter: 277–9 much admired by Forcheville: 281. His (perhaps deliberate) gaffe in front of Swann: 310. Reputed lover of Odette: 387 (cf. 920, 111 447–8). Goes on a cruise with the Verdurins after an illness: 406–7. Appears in Swann's dream: 411–12. His art compared to that of Mme de Sévigné: 703. M and Saint-Loup meet him in the restaurant at Rivebelle — "the famous painter Elstir": 883–7. M's visit to his studio; his seascapes; visual "metaphors"; Balbec Church; his friendship with Albertine; the portrait of "Miss Sacripant"; Mme Elstir, "my beautiful Gabrielle!"; his ideals as a painter: 892–911. Walks with M along the front; meets the "little band"; is revealed as "M. Biche": 913–25. "We do not receive wisdom, we must discover it for ourselves": 923–4. His revelation to M of the poetry of "still lifes": 929. Gives a party at which M meets Albertine: 929–32. His good taste in dress; his influence on Albertine: 945–6 (*see also* 11 1089). Speaks of race-meetings, regattas, landscapes and seascapes, Venice, costume (Fortuny): 958–63. His influence on M's way of seeing things, and on his attitude to Berma's art: 11 23, 32, 41, 47. Saint-Loup's high opinion of his intelligence: 106. M's passion for his work — "my favourite painter": 125–7. Mme de Guermantes's Elstirs: 126–7, 143. Norpois and *The Bunch of Radishes*: 229. M sees the Guermantes's Elstirs at last: 434–8. Swann's attitude to him recalled ("an oaf", "balderdash"): 478. His work criticised by the Duc and Duchesse de Guermantes: 518–21. His portrait of Oriane: 543. His work disliked by the Kaiser: 543, 546, 979. Admired by Albertine and Mme de Cambremer: 838–9. Compared with Ski: 902. His breach with the Verdurins: 970–75. His opinion of the church of Marcouville-l'Orgueilleuse: 1047 (cf. III 165). M visits the scene of two of his landscapes: 1062. His austere taste in women's clothes: 1089. His paintings of a little boy on the sands at Saint-Pierre-des-Ifs: 1145. His passion for violets: III 135, 137. In contradiction with his own impressionism: 165 (cf. II 1047). Brichot describes his "buffooneries" in the old days at the Verdurins': 201. The uniqueness of his art: seeing the universe through other eyes: 257, 259–60. His views on the furnishing of yachts, on old silver, on Fortuny gowns: 375–6 (cf. I 960). Compared to Dostoievsky and Mme de Sévigné: 385. Two of his pictures sold to the Luxembourg by Mme de Guermantes: 412. Significance of his portrait of Odette: had he been her lover?: 447–8. His intellectual charm: 505, 507. His paintings of naked girls in a wooded landscape remind M of Albertine and the laundry-girls: 537–8. His work becomes fashionable: 595. Mentioned in the Goncourt pastiche; Mme Verdurin claims to have taught him how to paint flowers ("he was always known simply as Monsieur Tiche"): 733–4, 740. His grief at M. Verdurin's death: 794.

ELSTIR, Mme. M meets her in the artist's studio at Balbec; "My beautiful Gabrielle!": I 908–10. Albertine admires her taste in clothes: 945. Denounced by Mme Verdurin as a "trollop": II 971–2. Embodies the kind of "heavy", "Venetian" beauty Elstir sought to capture in his painting: III 794, 1037.

ENTRAGUES, Mlle d'. Daughter of the Duc de Luxembourg, sought in marriage by Saint-Loup and by the Duc de Châtellerault: III 676–7.

EPINAY, Victurnienne, Princesse d'. Entertains the Duc and Duchesse de Guermantes; admires Oriane's witticisms ("Teaser Augustus"): II 479–85.

EPINOY, Princess d'. Astonished at the brilliance of Odette's *salon*: II 771–2.

EPORCHEVILLE, Mlle d'. Name wrongly thought by M to be that of the girl of good family recommended by Saint-Loup as a frequenter of brothels: III 574–8, 584–5.
  (*See* Orgeville, Mlle de l'; Gilberte.)

ESTHER. *See* Lévy, Esther.

EUDOXIA, Queen. Wife of King Theodosius: III 247.

EUDOXIE, Grand Duchess. Friend of Princess Sherbatoff: II 905–7.

EUGÈNE, M. Deputy of the Liberal Action party, an habitué of Jupien's brothel: III 844. Re-elected after the war: 885.

EULALIE. Retired domestic servant at Combray; confidante of Aunt Léonie: I 74–6. Visits Aunt Léonie with the Curé: 110–15. Her rivalry with Françoise: 115–17, 127–8. Praised by Françoise after her death: II 20–21. M remembers a week spent in her room in early childhood: III 914–15.

FAFFENHEIM-MUNSTERBURG-WEINIGEN, Prince von. German Prime Minister. Visits Mme de Villeparisis; poetry of his name belied by his persona; his efforts to persuade Norpois to get him elected to the *Institut*: II 264–72. Introduced to M by Norpois: 282–3. Praises Mme de Villeparisis's painting: 283–4. At the Guermantes's dinner-party; his vice-like German handclasp; his nickname "Prince Von": 448. Speaks to M about Rachel, and invites him to come home with him: 528–30. His ironical praise of the Kaiser's intelligence and taste in art: 546–7. His hatred of the English: 547–8. A Dreyfusard: 703.

FARCY, Mme de. American wife of the Comte de Farcy, an obscure relation of the Forchevilles; friend of Bloch: III 1005, 1059.

FATHER of the narrator. His interest in meteorology: I 11 (*see also* 99, 180–81; III 72–3). Annoyed by the "good-night kiss": 14, and by his wife's pleas on behalf of Swann's wife and daughter: 24. His arbitrariness; his unexpected indulgence; his resemblance to Benozzo Gozzoli's Abraham: 37–40. His fondness for chocolate cream: 77. M resembles him, according to Uncle Adolphe: 82. The "lady in pink" (Odette) finds him "exquisitely charming", to M's surprise: 83–4. Quarrels with Uncle Adolphe: 86. Irritated by Bloch: 99. Evening walks round Combray: 123–4. Doubts about Legrandin: 129–30, and vain efforts to elicit from him information about his relations at Balbec: 141–4. His influential position: 189. Discusses M's proposed visit to Venice: 425–6. Unaware of M's passion for Gilberte Swann: 447–9. Dismisses Swann as a "pestilent" fellow: 465. His relations with Norpois: 470–72 and their effect on his attitude to M's career: 473–4. Invites Norpois to dinner: 480, discusses M's career with him: 486–92, and talks to him about international affairs: 495–501. Proposed trip to Spain with Norpois: 500 (cf. 694). Resigns himself to M's abandonment of diplomacy for literature: 519–20. His opinion of Norpois: 521. Discusses restaurants with Françoise: 523. His reactions on hearing of M's meeting with Bergotte: 617–18. Mme de Villeparisis speaks of him and his trip with Norpois; his admiration for El Greco: 753–4. His naïvety: 1002–3. His liking for thin toast exasperates Françoise: II 21–2. His relations with the Duc de Guermantes; 28, 151–2. His candidature for the *Institut*; will Norpois support him?: 152–3 (*see also* 231–2). "Cut" by Mme Sazerat because of his anti-Dreyfusism: 153–4. Norpois speaks about him to M: 231–2. During the illness of M's grandmother: 353–7. Appears in M's dreams about his grandmother: 788–9, 806–7. M's increasing resemblance to him: III 72–3, 86, 103–4. His sensibility concealed behind a cold exterior: 104. His brusque manner: 105.

FÉRÉ, M. and Mme. Fashionable friends of the Cambremers, who give a dinner in their honour: II 1028–9. M plays chess with them: 1148.

FIERBOIS, Marquis de. His "complicated and rapid capers" condemned as ridiculous by Charlus: II 463. His illness: 624.

FISHER-GIRL approached by M at Carqueville: I 769–70.

FLORA. *See* Céline and Flora.

FOGGI, Prince Odo. Discusses Italian politics with Norpois in Venice: III 647–51.

FOIX, Prince de. Habitué of the restaurant where M dines with Saint-Loup; his wealth, arrogance and secret sodomy: II 417–22. Saint-Loup borrows his cloak: 425–6. At the Guermantes': 448, 528–9. Inherits his sexual tastes from his father: III 856–7.

FOIX, Prince de. Father of the above. Habitué of Jupien's brothel, where his death is regretted: III 856–7.

FOOTMAN (young). Favourite of Françoise. *See* Périgot.

FOOTMAN at the Guermantes'. *See* Poullein.

FOOTMAN of Mme de Chevregny. Invited to dinner at the Grand Hotel, Balbec, by Charlus: II 1019–21.

FOOTMAN at the Verdurins'. Object of Charlus's attention: III 227–8.

FOOTMEN (other). At the Guermantes': II 29–30; Georges: 502; Saint-Loup gives one of them some cynical advice: III 479–80.

FOOTMEN at the Swanns': I 549–67.

FOOTMEN of M. de Charlus. *See* Burnier; Charmel.

FOOTMEN at Mme de Saint-Euverte's: I 352–5.

FORCHEVILLE, Comte (later Baron) de. Introduced to the Verdurin circle by Odette; his snobbery and vulgarity: I 273–89. Becomes one of the "faithful": 294–5. Brutally insults Saniette (his brother-in-law): 301–2. Letter addressed to him by Odette deciphered through its envelope by Swann; his intimacy with Odette and Swann's jealousy: 307–10, 312–13, 325–31, 346, 387, 402–3. Swann dreams of him: 411–13. Marries Odette and adopts Gilberte: III 586–7, 594–5.

FORCHEVILLE, Mme de. *See* Odette.

FORCHEVILLE, Mlle de. *See* Gilberte.

FORESTELLE, Marquis de. Friend of Swann, who visits him at his house near Pierrefonds: I 320–21. At Mme de Saint-Euverte's; his monocle: 356.

FORESTIER, Robert. Playmate of M in the Champs-Elysées: II 381–3.

FRANÇOISE. Aunt Léonie's cook at Combray: I 11, 19. Her code: 30–31. Takes a note from M to his mother: 31–2. Her devotion to M's family; her qualities as a servant; her family; conversations with Aunt Léonie: 55–63, 109–11. Her artistry and largesse as a cook: 76–7. Her kitchen-maid: 86–9. Conversation with the gardener on war and revolution: 95–6. Her attitude to money; hatred of Eulalie; relations with Aunt Léonie; her Saturday routine: 115–21, 126–8. In her kitchen; cruelty and sentimentality; policy towards other servants; harshness to the kitchen-maid: 131–5 (cf. 118). Resembles the figures in the porch of Saint-André-des-Champs — a "mediaeval peasant": 164–5. Her wild grief at the death of Aunt Léonie: 167–8. Her malapropisms: 168 and her colourful idiom: 180. Enters into service with M's family after Aunt Léonie's death; takes M to the Champs-Elysées: 416, 427–9, 431, 439, 443, 445, and accompanies him in pursuit of the Swanns: 451, 453–4. Prepares dinner for Norpois; compared to Michelangelo: 480–81, 494. Her views on Norpois and on Paris restaurants: 521–4. Visits the water-closet in the Champs-Elysées; the "Marquise": 530–31. Reactions to M's illness: 534, 538. Praised by Odette: "your old nurse": 547. Her "simple but unerring taste" in clothes; her natural distinction; "the élite of the world of the simple-minded": 698–9. Her social connections in the Grand Hotel,

Balbec: 744–6. Her pride; attitude towards the aristocracy; forgives Mme de Villeparisis for being a marquise: 747–50. Her opinion of Bloch and of Saint-Loup: 835–7. M mocks her sentimentality: 843–4. Her resentment of M's reproaches, discontent with Balbec and dislike of the "little band": 956–8. Wants to leave Balbec: 1013–14. In the family's new flat in Paris; regrets at leaving Combray: 11 3–4. Her preoccupation with the Guermantes: 10–11. Holds court below stairs; invocation to Combray: 11–12. Relations with Jupien ("Julien"): 13–16. Reflections on the Guermantes: 16–19, and further reminiscences of Combray, Méséglise, Aunt Léonie: 19–21. Conversations with the Guermantes footmen; cult of the nobility: 29–30. Her relations with M; disapproval of his pursuit of Mme de Guermantes; her intuition, her moods and idiosyncrasies: 60–64. "The very language of Saint-Simon": 66. Visits to her relations: 149–50. Her sympathy for the Guermantes' lovesick footman: 149, 155, 317–18. During M's grandmother's illness; her irritating reflections at the bedside: 311; her devoted care for the patient despite her tactlessness and insensitivity: 330–32, 341–7, 356–7. Interrupts M and Albertine making love; her knowledge of M's doings: 371–4. Her peasant sense of propriety: 381. Admires Charlus and Jupien: 654. Entertains her daughter; her highly individual French; her dialect: 752–5. Refuses to use the telephone: 756–7 (see also 111 96, 152). Her dislike of Albertine: 761–4. Reveals to M the circumstances that had caused his grandmother to have her photograph taken by Saint-Loup: 803–4. The servant's lot; M's pity and affection for her; 805–6. Prophesies that Albertine will make M unhappy: 815–16. Complaints about money-grubbers: 818. Disapproves of Céleste and Marie: 877–8. Shocked at seeing Charlus arm in arm with a servant: 1021. With M and Albertine in Paris; makes Albertine observe the rules of the house: 111 2, 3, 7–8. Her regrets at not having said good-bye to the housekeeper at Balbec: 8–9. Her hatred of Albertine: 93 (see also 150–51). Listens to M's telephone conversations: 96. Fetches a dairymaid to run an errand for M: 135–7. Sent to bring back Albertine from the Trocadéro; her vocabulary contaminated by her daughter's slang; her inability to tell the time correctly: 148–54. How Aunt Léonie thwarted her secret plans for an outing: 361. Unable to contain her jealousy of Albertine: 367. Her innuendoes; her curiosity about money: 371–3. Announces Albertine's departure: 421–2. Discovers the rings left behind by Albertine: 471–3. Alarmed at the possibility of Albertine's return: 475–6 (cf. 450). Makes no pretence of sorrow at Albertine's death: 490–91. Her attitude to her "masters"; despises them so as not to feel despised herself: 578–9. Her persistent errors in grammar and pronunciation: 585. Her attitude to liaisons between men: 719–20. In 1914, tormented by the butler about the war news: 769–72 (*see also* 872–7); her concern to get the butcher's boy exempted from military service: 779. Unimpressed by Saint-Loup's bravery: 871–2; her pacifism: 875. Her nephew killed at Berry-au-Bac; the noble behaviour of her cousins, the Larivières: 875–7. Her grief at Saint-Loup's death: 879–80. Speaks of M's "paperies": 947; M compares his work with hers: 1090–91.

FRANÇOISE's cousins. *See* Larivière.

FRANÇOISE's daughter. *See* Marguerite.

FRANÇOISE's nephews. One of them tries to get exempted from military service during the war: 111 769–80, 871; another killed at Berry-au-Bac: 876.

FRANÇOISE's niece. "The butcheress": 11 149, 753.

FRANÇOISE's son-in-law. *See* Julien.

FRANQUETOT, Vicomtesse de. Cousin of the dowager Marquise de Cambremer. At Mme de Saint-Euverte's: 1 357–66; 11 694.

FRÉCOURT, Marquis de. Owner of a coach-house with a red-tiled turret: 11 595, 623.

FROBERVILLE, General de. At Mme de Saint-Euverte's; his monocle: 1 355–6. Conversation with the Princesse des Laumes; admires the young Mme de Cambremer: 366–70, who is introduced to him by Swann: 373–5. Exchanges ironical looks with Swann at the Elysée Palace: 111 688.

FROBERVILLE, Colonel de. Nephew of the above. At the Princesse de Guermantes's: 11 699–700; his social position; ingratitude and envy vis-à-vis Mme de Saint-Euverte: 701–2; hopes for the failure of her garden-party and is delighted to hear that Mme de Guermantes will not attend: 708–11. Described as "gaga" by the Duc de Guermantes: 766.

G——. Writer; visits Mme de Villeparisis; frequently invited to the Guermantes': 11 211.

GALLARDON, Marquise de, *née* Courvoisier. At Mme de Saint-Euverte's; her obsession with the Guermantes family: 1 358–9. Unrewarding exchange with her cousin the Princesse des Laumes; snide remarks about Swann's Jewishness: 362–5. Her Courvoisier snobbery and conventionality: 11 458, 494. Despised by Mme de Guermantes: 521. Introduces her nephew to Charlus, in spite of her doubts as to the latter's morals: 677 (*see also* 932). Encounter with Oriane on the staircase at the Princesse de Guermantes': 745, 747–8.

GALLARDON, Dowager Duchesse de, mother-in-law of the Princesse de Gallardon. Her Courvoisier ignorance of literature: 11 464.

GALOPIN. Pastrycook at Combray: 1 61; his dog: 63.

GARDENER at Combray. Aligns the garden paths too symmetrically for M's grandmother: 1 12, 69, 93. His views on war and revolution: 95–6.

GARDENER at la Raspelière. Groans beneath the Verdurins' yoke; his mixed feelings about Mme de Cambremer: 11 948–9.

GAUCOURT, Mme de. Sister of M. de Cambremer. Suffers from fits of breathlessness: 11 957–8, 1008, 1010, 1133, 1146; 111 975.

GIBERGUE. Friend of Saint-Loup at Doncières: 11 106.

GILBERT. *See* Guermantes, Gilbert, Prince de.

GILBERTE. Daughter of Swann and Odette. (Later Mlle de Forcheville, then, through her marriage to Robert, Marquise de Saint-Loup.) Remembered by the narrator (as Mme de Saint-Loup): 1 7. Worshipped by her father; M's mother speaks to him about her: 24–5. Bergotte "her greatest friend"; M's reflections on learning this: 107–8, 149. M's first sight of her, at Tansonville; her indelicate gesture; the name Gilberte: 153–5. M's obsession with her: 157–9. In the Champs-Elysées, the little girl with reddish hair playing battledore and shuttlecock: 428. M's love for her; games of prisoner's base; the agate marble and Bergotte's monograph on Racine; her indifference, her absences; waiting for a letter from her: 429–47. Before her parents' marriage, Odette would blackmail Swann by refusing to let him see his daughter: 503. Swann's ambition to present her to the Duchesse de Guermantes: 507–8. Norpois's opinion of her: 513–14. New Year's Day: M writes her a letter which remains unanswered: 524–7. She returns to the Champs-Elysées: 528. Her parents "can't stand" M: 529. Amorous wrestle behind the clump of laurels: 531–3. Writes to the convalescent M inviting him to tea; her signature: 538–41. Her tea-parties: 542–7, 550–52. Her kind-heartedness and apparent devotion to her father: 577–8. Her strange behaviour to him: 586–7. Her resemblance to both her parents; the two Gilbertes: 607–10. M's doubts as to her true character: 612–13. Why he dare not invite her to his home: 618–19. Beginnings of the rupture with M; her sulks; M writes her mutually contradictory letters to which she does not reply; his feigned indifference: 625–36, 642–3. Another New Year's Day; M's efforts to extinguish his love; his letters: 654–61, 668–70. The two walkers in the Elysian gloom: Gilberte and a young man — later identified as Léa in male costume (III 714): 671–4. M's dream about her: 677–8. Further progress towards forgetting her: 680–82. Brief recrudescence of his love for her, extinguished by habit: 691–3. Later, M declines Swann's invitation to meet her again: II 739. He gives the turquoise-studded book-cover she had had made for him to Albertine: 764–5 (see 756). He writes to her, without emotion; her name depoeticised: 765–6. She inherits a fortune; the Faubourg Saint-Germain begins to take an interest in her and her mother: 774. M interrogates Albertine about her: III 15–16 (cf. II 764). He learns from her maid that at the time when he used to visit her every day, she was in love with another "young man": 130–31. Albertine admits to having kissed her: 383. Her resemblance to Albertine: 512. M meets her without recognising her; she gives him a furtive glance that arouses him; he wrongly identifies her as Mlle d'Eporcheville: 573–8. Reintroduced to M at Mme de Guermantes'; she has become Mlle de Forcheville: 584–7. Responds with alacrity to Mme de Guermantes's advances; lunches at her house: 589–94; prefers to forget her father; conceals her origins; her snobbery: 594–602. Failure to fulfil her father's hopes: 604–5. Sends M a telegram in Venice which he imagines to be from Albertine: 656–9 (cf. 670–71). Her marriage to Robert de Saint-Loup: 670–72, 676–7, 679–80. Changes in her attitude to society after her marriage: 684–8. M renews his friendship with her, and visits her at Tansonville: 694. Robert's infidelity: 695–7. Her pregnancy: 698. Jealous of Rachel, whom she seeks to imitate: 700–01. Her avarice: 702–3. Walks with M at

Combray; her surprising revelations about the two "ways": 709–11. Confesses her love for him as a child; the meaning of her indelicate gesture: 711–12. It was with Léa that she had been walking in the Champs-Elysées: 712–14 (cf. I 671). Her love for Robert: 715, and her relations with him at Tansonville: 717–22. Discusses Albertine with M: 725–7. Reads Balzac's *La Fille aux yeux d'or*: 725, 728. Lends M a volume of the Goncourt Diaries: 728. In September 1914, leaves Paris for Combray; writes to M about the German invasion: 773–4. In 1916, writes him another letter with a new interpretation of her departure: 777–8. Her face becomes a perfect replica of Odette's: 978. At the Princesse de Guermantes's, M takes her for her mother: 1028–9. Conversation about Robert: 1029–31. Her friendship with Andrée: 1032–3. Her disdain for the new Princesse de Guermantes (Mme Verdurin) and even for Oriane: 1033–4. Her ironic and fanciful reply to Mme de Morienval: 1053–4. Vilified by Mme de Guermantes: 1080–83. Introduces her daughter to M: 1083–8.

GINESTE, Marie. Sister of Céleste Albaret; lady's maid at Balbec: II 824, 874–5. Her friendship with M; her colourful language: 875–8. Her grief at M's departure: 1163.

GIRL (tall and handsome) admired by M as she serves *café au lait* to the passengers on the train to Balbec: I 705–7.

GIRL ("glorious") with the cigarette who joins the little train at Saint-Pierre-des-Ifs: II 912.

GIRL (with blue eyes) whom Swann meets in a brothel: I 405–6.

GIRL (blonde) who gazes at M in the restaurant at Rivebelle: I 875; his obsession with her: 880–81.

GIRL resembling Albertine getting into a car in the Bois: III 573.

GIRL (little poor) taken home by M after Albertine's departure: III 440. Her parents bring a charge against him: 451–2.

GIRL (little) with a bicycle in the Bois: III 170.

GIRL (little) with the sharp voice, a friend of Gilberte's, in the Champs-Elysées: I 428, 433, 440.

GIRLS (two), friends of Léa, whom Albertine stares at in the mirror in the Casino at Balbec. In Vol. II they are identified as Bloch's sister and cousin (pp. 830–31); in Vol. III they are differentiated from the Bloch girls: 80. M fears that Albertine may meet them with Léa at the Trocadéro: III 141,

144–8. Said to frequent the bathing establishment of the hotel: 501.

GIRLS (three) in the Bois, sitting beside their bicycles; how Albertine stares at them: III 167.

GIRLS at Balbec (the little band). First appearance on the esplanade: I 845–56, 858–9, 865, 874. M sees a photograph of them as little girls, an amorphous, undifferentiated group: 881–3. M's anxiety to meet them: 888–91. Elstir knows them; their social background: 902–6. M sees them with Elstir on the front — "a few spores of the zoophytic band" — but his hopes of being introduced to them are disappointed: 914–16, 924–5. Hopes of making their acquaintance through Albertine; her reluctance: 936–8, 946–50. M finally gets to know them all; their flowering-time: 951–4. Games in the Casino: 954. Excursions and picnics: 956–8, 965–6. Their faces: 966–7. Their conversation, voices, mannerisms: 969–72, A subject for French composition: 972–6. M's collective love for them; the confrontation of memory with an ever-changing reality: 976–80. The game of "ferret": 980–83. Their faces differentiated: 1007–9. From fabulous beings to ordinary girls: 1011–13. On his second visit to Balbec, M longs to see them again: II 808. That summer, he enjoys the "ephemeral favours" of thirteen of them, not counting Albertine: 817. The picnics resumed: 866. Still a race apart: 1150. A grove of budding girls: III 62–3. Their impenetrable solidarity as liars: 177–8. M's love divided among them all: 515–16. Andrée denies that any of them had Sapphic tastes: 559. Their attitude to Albertine: 621.

GISÈLE. Member of the little band at Balbec. Makes a sarcastic remark in a rasping voice when Andrée jumps over the old gentleman: I 849 (cf. 947–9). "The cruel one": 853. Joins M and Albertine on the beach: 947–8. Hated by Andrée (cf. 956) and considered "boring" by Albertine: 948–9. Leaving Balbec to "swot" for her exams: 949. M attempts to accompany her: 950–51. Andrée speaks of her with affection: 956. A letter from her; her French composition: 972–6. Mistakenly referred to as the girl who jumped over the old gentleman: II 376–7. M meets her in Paris; her lies: III 175–8. Accused by Andrée of treachery: 560. Andrée's "best friend": 610.

GLASS-VENDOR (young Venetian). M's liaison with her and plan to take her back to Paris: III 655. A "new Albertine": 659.

GOUPIL, Mme. At Combray: Did she get to Mass before the Elevation?; has company for lunch: I 59–61, 73, 117. Her new silk dress: 109. Gossips with M's family after Mass: 135. Writes to congratulate M on his article in the *Figaro*: III 602–4.

GOVERNESS (Gilberte's). In the Champs-Elysées; her blue feather: I 428–9, 432. Goes shopping with Gilberte: 440, 445–6. Goes to a concert with Gilberte: 586–7.

GRANDFATHER of the narrator (Amédée). His house in Combray: I 6–7. Encouraged by his cousin to take a sip of brandy, though forbidden to do so: 12–13. A great friend of Swann's father: 15–16. His interest in Swann's social contacts: 22–9. His refusal to answer a letter from Swann about his relations with Odette: 37 (cf. 211–12). Disapproval of Uncle Adolphe's philandering: 81; violent "words" with him: 86. Distrusts M's Jewish friends: 98–9. Walk by Swann's way with M and his father: 148–56. Refuses to further Swann's amatory intrigues: 211–12, or to introduce him to the Verdurins, with whom he was acquainted: 217. Invites Swann to his daughter's wedding: 338. Suspected by Swann of writing an anonymous letter: 389. Appears in Swann's dream: 411. His daughter has inherited something of his cast of mind: 555. His love of the Army: II 154. During his wife's last illness: 353–6. Mme Verdurin speaks contemptuously of him and his father: 940. His social rigidity, passed on to his daughter: 1060. His loathing for the Germans: III 103.

GRANDMOTHER of the narrator (Bathilde or Mme Amédée). Evenings at Combray; her walks in the garden; her love of fresh air and of naturalness; her worries (M's lack of will-power and delicate health, her husband's brandy-drinking); her sweetness and humility: I 11–13, 15, 20. Visits Mme de Villeparisis, a childhood friend of hers (cf. 112); finds the Jupiens charming and the Prince des Laumes "common": 21. Admires Swann's taste: 23. Her principles in the matter of upbringing: 38–40. Her ideas on literature; gives M the pastoral novels of George Sand: 42. Her choice of presents: 42–4. Her love for the steeple of Saint-Hilaire: 68–9. Her opinion of Legrandin: 73 (cf. 137). Begs M to go out of doors: 90. Displeased by Bloch: 99. Criticised by

Françoise — "a bit off her head": 110. Her remark about Mlle Vinteuil: 122. Plan for her to accompany M to Balbec: 141–4. Concern for M's health: 473–4. Accompanies him to see Berma in *Phèdre*: 480, 484, 492. During M's illness, her loving care; her anxiety about his taking alcohol, even as medicine: 534–6 (cf. 700–01). Reproaches M for not working: 624. Accompanies M to Balbec: 691, 695–6; her "beloved Sévigné": 695, 698–703 (*see also* I 21, 746, 749, 818–19; II 311, 322, 797–8; III 9, 672); her concern about M's drinking: 700–01. Arrival at Balbec: 711–15. Her loving tenderness; the knocking on the wall: 718–20. Opens the dining-room window: 724–6. Meets Mme de Villeparisis, whom she avoids at first, then resumes her friendship with her: 735–8, 746–54. Excursions with Mme de Villeparisis: 756–7; sings her praises: 780–81. M tells her that he couldn't live without her: 781–2. Introduced to Saint-Loup: 786, who makes a conquest of her: 788–90. Introduced to Charlus: 809, whom she finds delightful: 812–23. Photographed by Saint-Loup: 843–5. Her concern for M's moral and physical welfare: 850–51, 856, 866–7. Reproaches M for not visiting Elstir: 888, 891–2. Her nature and M's: 911. Presents Saint-Loup with a collection of Proudhon's letters: 925–6. Move to a flat in the Hôtel de Guermantes for the sake of her health: II 4. Her voice on the telephone: 133–9. Her changed appearance on M's return from Doncières: 141–3. Refuses invitations from Mme de Villeparisis on the grounds of health: 152. Her attitude to the Dreyfus Case: 154. Her health deteriorates; Cottard called in; Dr du Boulbon's visit: 308–18. Goes to the Champs-Elysées with M and has a stroke: 319–23. M takes her to see Professor E—: 324–8. Her last illness and death: 328–35, 343–8, 351–7. Professor E— seeks confirmation of her death: 664–6. Her resurrection in M's memory on his second arrival at Balbec — "the intermittencies of the heart": 783–7. M dreams of her: 787–90. Memories and meditations concerning her; the truth about the Saint-Loup photograph: 802–7, 810, 812–13. M's mother talks to him about her; her literary purism: 864–6. Would have thought M. de Cambremer "very common": 944. Her life in her daughter's memory, like "a pure and innocent childhood": 1159. Their resemblance: 1166–7, 1169. Her influence on her daughter: III 6, 9; and on M: 72–3, 104–5. M wakes up thinking of her: 120. He has inherited from her a lack of self-importance: 293. Her death juxtaposed with Albertine's; "a double murder": 506, 511. Appears with Albertine in a dream: 550. Invoked by M's mother in the train from Venice apropos of the marriages of Gilberte and Jupien's niece: 672–6, 690–91.

GREAT-AUNT of the narrator. Cousin of M's grandfather and mother of Aunt Léonie: I 53. Reads the "accompanying patter" of the magic lantern: 10. Teases M's grandmother: 12–13. Underestimates Swann and misconstrues his social position: 14–19. A trifle "common": 18. Her ideas on *déclassement*: 21–5. Finds Swann aged: 36. Her "indictment" of M's grandmother: 44. Leaves her fortune to a niece from whom she had been estranged for years: 100. Slandered by Bloch: 101. Her ideas on Sunday observance: 108–9. Her concern for her invalid daughter: 129. Her straightforwardness: 615–16.

GREAT-GRANDFATHER of the narrator. Referred to contemptuously by Mme Verdurin; his stinginess: II 940.

GREAT-UNCLE of the narrator. Pulls M's curls: I 4.

GRIGRI: *See* Agrigente, Prince d'.

GROUCHY, M. de. Late for dinner with the Guermantes: II 450. Offers Mme de Guermantes some pheasants: 501–2.

GROUCHY, Mme de. Daughter of the Vicomtesse de Guermantes: II 450, 501.

GUASTALLA, Albert, Duc de. Son of the Princesse de Parme: II 440, 538; Charlus's cousin: 586.

GUASTALLA, Duc de. Son of the Princesse d'Iéna: II 538. Visited on his sick-bed by Mme de Guermantes: 540–41. His title ridiculed by Charlus: 586.

GUERMANTES, The. Legrandin suffers from not knowing them: I 138–40. The Guermantes way: 146–7, 180–202. Mme de Gallardon's obsession with them: 358–9. The "witty Guermantes set" as represented by the Princesse des Laumes: 363–4, 367–73. Odette adopts some of their verbal mannerisms through Swann: 550, 562 who has imbibed their combination of taste and snobbishness: 553–4, 611. The magic of the name Guermantes: II 6–10. Françoise's interest in them: 10–11, 16–19. Their position in the Faubourg Saint-Germain: 23–7. Their characteristic features: 77–8, 210 (*see also* 447–8). Their attitude to distinguished commoners: 211–14, 259. Charlus speaks of "these

powerful Guermantes": 296, 303. Their reliance on Dr Dieulafoy in grave cases: 349. Their house "forbidden territory" to M;
his invitation to dinner: 389–91. Vulgar arrogance and ancient
grandeur: 431, 434, 451–3. Their physical characteristics: 454–6.
The family genie; the Guermantes and the Courvoisiers; the wit
of the Guermantes: 456–69, 475–87, 492–7. Their earthiness, as
exemplified by the Duchess: 513. M. de Bréauté follows the
Guermantes style: 523. Poetry and reality; family history;
cousins galore: 545, 551–4, 563–4, 568, 591–2, 596. The
Guermantes style as exemplified by Swann: 601–5 and by
Charlus: 624–5 (see also 1073, 1094, 1097, 1107–8, 1125–6, III
207, 261, 267). Party-giving à la Guermantes: 671–2, 677–9,
686–7. M earns credit from the Guermantes for his discreet bow:
687. Mme de Saint-Euverte tries to emulate them: 693–6, 701,
709. People beginning to lose interest in them: 773–4. Cottard's
low estimate of them: 909–10. The noblest family in France,
according to Charlus: 1125–6 (see also III 43, 234). Discussed by
the Cambremers: 1130–31. Their contempt for the opinion of
commoners: III 207. The Guermantes tone: 261. Attitude to
Mme de Villeparisis: 296. Adopt a German style: 626–7 (cf. 774).
Indifference to wealth: 655. Inherited characteristics — Saint-
Loup, Charlus and the Duke: 704–5, 719, 722–3. Gilberte adopts
something of the Guermantes spirit: 774. Saint-Loup a true
Guermantes: 881–2. The old magic of the name Guermantes
revived for M: 887–8, 919, 922–3. A profound transformation:
1000, 1013–17. Their roots deeply embedded in M's past life:
1023–4. Their superstitious respect for old-fashioned protocol:
1043. Oriane epitomises the decline of the Guermantes: 1055–62,
1083. Time and the Guermantes "way": 1084–8.

GUERMANTES, Basin, Duc de. (Prince des Laumes before
inheriting the dukedom on the death of his father.) M's
grandmother finds him "common": I 21. Consistently unfaithful to his wife: 368. Suspected by Swann of writing an
anonymous letter: 387–90. Brother of M. de Charlus: 805.
Present owner of the Château de Guermantes: 810. His ducal
habits; his appearance; his horses; his affability to M's father: II
27–9 (cf. 230). At the Opéra: 49. Praised by Norpois: 151–2.
Plays a joke on Mme de Villeparisis: 197, 215. His entry chez
Mme de Villeparisis: 229–30; his looks, his wealth and vanity:

230 (*see also* 294); his weird vocabulary: 233 (cf. 242–6); acts as "feed" to his wife: 237–8, 246–7; deplores Saint-Loup's Dreyfusism: 241–6. Calls on M's family during his grandmother's illness: 348–51. Rumour of a separation between him and his wife: 384, 389. Vulgar arrogance and ancient grandeur: 431. M dines at his house; his old-world courtesy: 432–4, 438–42, 451–3. A bad husband but a trusty friend in Oriane's social activities: 470–71, 480–83, 489–90. Member of Parliament when Prince des Laumes; his political flair: 491–3. His mistresses: 497–501, 511. Conversation at dinner: 501–31; his views on literature, art and music: 509–10, 519–21, 544; genealogical talk — "But he's Oriane's cousin!": 550–72 *passim*. M's visit to ask him about an invitation from the Princesse de Guermantes; Amanien's illness and the fancy dress ball; his "Velazquez"; Swann's view of him; more genealogy; the Duchess's red shoes: 593–620. Breaks off his liaison with Mme d'Arpajon: 676. Compared unfavourably by M with his cousin the Prince: 679. Appreciates M's discreet bow: 687–8. His suspicion of authors: 691–2. Reproaches his wife for snubbing Mme de Chaussepierre: 698. Deplores Swann's Dreyfusism and his marriage: 702–5. His furious bow to M. d'Herweck — "Jupiter Tonans": 707–8. His relationship with Mme de Surgis: 711, 732–3. Affectionate but gaffe-ridden exchange with his brother Charlus: 742–5. His bad French: 746, 750–51 (cf. 985). His impatience to get to the ball; reaction to the news of Amanien's death ("They're exaggerating"): 751–2. His change of mind on the Dreyfus Case: 766–7. Fails to be elected President of the Jockey Club: III 32–3. Irritated by any mention of the Dreyfus Case (two years after): 33–5. The world of the arts closed to him: 205. Encourages his wife to see Gilberte: 592–5. Reads M's *Figaro* article: 595–6; his qualified compliments: 601–2. Hints that Mlle d'Oloron is the natural daughter of Charlus: 682. Physical mannerisms similar to Charlus's: 704–5. Rumours of his being sued for divorce in 1914; "a dreadful husband", in Saint-Loup's opinion: 759–60. Anglophile and anti-Caillautist during the war: 808–9. At the Prince de Guermantes's reception, "as majestic and handsome as ever": 1058–9. His liaison with Odette, now Mme de Forcheville: 1068–70. His appearance in old age — "a magnificent ruin": 1070–74, 1106.

GUERMANTES, Oriane, Duchesse de. Married to her cousin; M refuses to believe that she is related to Mme de Villeparisis: I 112. Having caught a glimpse of her, M asks Legrandin if he knows her: 138. M's daydreams about her along the Guermantes way: 188, 199. Her appearance in Combray Church: 190–94. A friend of Swann's: 295, 304. As Princesse des Laumes, at Mme de Saint-Euverte's; snubs Mme de Gallardon; conversations with Froberville and with Swann; a preliminary sketch of her character: 358–73. Swann's longing to present his wife and daughter to her: 507–8 (cf. II 260–61). Swann adopts some of her social attitudes: 553–4. Niece of Mme de Villeparisis and aunt of Saint-Loup: 810–11. Her Elstirs: 893 (cf. II 125–7, 143). The magic and mystery of her name: II 5–10. "The highest position in the Faubourg Saint-Germain": 23. M speculates about her life: 23–31. At the Opéra: 49–55. Her morning walks, and M's obsession with her: 55–60; "I was genuinely in love with Mme de Guermantes": 65–7. Her photograph in Saint-Loup's room at Doncières: 72, 77–8. M speaks of her to Robert, and asks him in vain for the photograph: 98–102. M's longing for her: 119–21. Robert agrees to persuade her to show M her Elstirs: 125–7; she fails to do so: 143. Her clothes and her appearance out walking: 145–6. At Mme de Villeparisis's tea-party: 204–72. Her chilly demeanour on being introduced to M and the historian of the Fronde: 205. Ridicules Mme de Cambremer: 207–8, 238–9. M's reflections on her appearance, her eyes and voice, her "smiling, disdainful, absent-minded air", her manner of treating intellectuals and other distinguished commoners: 209–15. Her witticisms on the subject of the Queen of Sweden: 216. Refers appreciatively to Bergotte: 216–17, 228. Ridicules Rachel: 229–30, 233–7. Her views on the Dreyfus Case: 241–6. Refuses to meet Odette: 260–61, 272. Addresses M for the first time: 262–3; offers him tea and cake: 272. Charlus's view of her: 302–3. The end of M's love for her: 385–7. Change in her attitude towards him; a new friendliness and an invitation to dinner: 388–96. Dinner at her house: 431–568. M takes her in to dinner: 450–51; her character as a Guermantes; the family genie; her social style, studied unconventionality, wit, imitations: 455–80. "Teaser Augustus": 481–5. Her perverseness of judgment: 486–9. Relations with her husband: 489–90. "Oriane's latest":

494–7. Relations with her husband's mistresses: 497–501. Hypocritical cruelty to her servants (the lovesick footman): 501–2 (cf. 149, 155, 318, 438, 610). Conversation at dinner: 502–32; views on Wagner: 509; Victor Hugo: 512; Zola: 517–18; Elstir: 519–21 (cf. 543; III 595); Mme de Villeparisis: 523–6; Charlus: 526–7; Saint-Loup: 528–9. Refuses to intercede on Saint-Loup's behalf with General de Monserfeuil: 531, 534–5. Views on botany: 535–7; on the Empire style: 537–42 (cf. I 568–9; III 1079–80); on Manet and Frans Hals: 542–6. Her "musical moments": 566–7. Her red dress and her rubies admired by Swann; her views on the Prince and Princesse de Guermantes; her "card" for Mme Molé; Swann's illness; the red shoes: 606–19. At the Princesse de Guermantes's reception: 683–713; her party expression: 685–6, 692; snubs Mme de Chaussepierre: 697–8; her refusal to meet Swann's wife and daughter: 705–6; intends to avoid Mme de Saint-Euverte's garden-party: 708–11; her unexpected politeness to Mme de Gallardon: 745–8. In the carriage on the way home, indignantly refuses to introduce M to Mme Putbus: 749–50. Her gradual withdrawal from the social scene brings Mme Molé to the fore: 773. Her opinion of Mme de Montmorency: 776–7 (cf. 591–2). M consults her about Albertine's clothes; more attractive than in the days when M was in love with her; the purity of her speech; her anecdotes; her views on the Dreyfus Case: III 23–36. Gives M some syringa: 48. Her attitude to the Dreyfus Case in its social aspects: 236. Fails to turn up at the Verdurins' musical *soirée*: 279. Her Fortuny dresses: 375–6 (*see also* 26). M calls on her and meets Gilberte, now Mlle de Forcheville: 584. Her change of attitude towards Gilberte after Swann's death: 587–91; invites her to lunch and talks to her about Swann: 592–4. Repeats some of her anecdotes, with variations: 596–7, 600–01. Becomes friendly with Mme de Cambremer: 684. Rumours of her suing for divorce in 1914: 759. Her unexpected grief at the death of Saint-Loup: 882. Her sympathy for the Russian imperial family after the Revolution: 883. Greets M, at the Prince de Guermantes's *matinée*, as her "oldest friend": 967, 969–70; dyes her hair: 977; her cheeks, "like nougat": 980; her new position in society: 1004–5; would have sworn that Bloch had been born in her world: 1019; friendship with Rachel; antipathy to Gilberte:

1041–5. Decay of her wit and social decline: 1055–8. Speaks to M and Bloch hazily about the past; her husband and his mistresses: 1058–9; Bréauté and Mme Varambon: 1059–62; her red dress: 1063–4. Claims to have discovered Rachel: 1065–6 (cf. II 229–37). Her unhappiness with her husband, because of his liaison with Odette: 1068–9, 1077. Her legendary chastity called into question by Charlus: 1077–8. Her lies and changeability: 1078–80. Savage attack on Gilberte: 1081–3.

GUERMANTES, Gilbert, Prince de. Cousin of the Duc de Guermantes: II 30. Violently anti-semitic, according to Oriane: 241–2. Described as "feudal" by the Duke: 245. His contempt for M. de Grouchy as husband for a Guermantes: 450. Allusion to his future marriage to Mme Verdurin: 450 (cf. III 998). His antiquated ideas: 456. His grave and measured steps: 463. Mocked by his aunt, Mme de Villeparisis: 466. An "animated gravestone", in Oriane's words: 543. His obsession with rank and birth: 550–51, 592 (see also 607–8). Swann talks of his anti-semitism: 603–4 (cf. 600 and 693). The soirée at his house; M introduced to him; his stiff and haughty greeting (but M detects a genuine simplicity beneath his reserve): 679–80. Leads Swann off to the far end of the garden, reputedly "to show him the door": 680, 697, 700–01. Swann's account of their conversation: how the Prince, and his wife, had become persuaded of Dreyfus's innocence: 728–31, 734–8. Revealed as an invert: 1020. Spends a night with Morel at Maineville: 1113; failure of subsequent assignations: 1117–18. Charlus gossips about his homosexuality: III 310. Referred to by the name of his country house, Voisenon: 593. Gives an afternoon party in his new house in the Avenue du Bois: 888–9. A bibliophile: 922. Aged almost beyond recognition: 960. Bloch introduced to him by M: 996–7. His marriage to Mme. Verdurin: 998.

GUERMANTES, Princesse Marie de, née Duchesse en Bavière, known as Marie-Gilbert or Marie-Hedwige (cf. II 236). Wife of the above, sister of the Duke of Bavaria: II 30. In her box at the Opéra; her beauty and her finery: 36–40. Her elegance compared to that of her cousin the Duchess: 49–55. Her name: 236. Her beauty and distinction praised by Charlus: 587. M invited to her house: 590. Her royal birth; the exclusiveness of her salon: 592–3. Oriane's description of her: 606–7. Her grandeur

ISRAELS, Lady. Wife of the above, aunt of Swann. Norpois refers (without naming her) to her campaign to ostracise Odette socially: I 502–3. Her wealth; Swann presumed to be her heir; jealous of Swann's social position: 557–8. Meets, and ignores, Odette *chez* Mme de Marsantes: 558 (*see also* 1025–6). Her social position: 688. Mme de Marsantes turns against her, on account of the Dreyfus Case: II 261. Her nephew "Momo": 393. Gilberte denies knowing her (here Proust refers to her as "Israel"): III 597.

JOURNALISTS in the theatre: II 181; Saint-Loup strikes one of them: 183–5.

JULIEN. Françoise's son-in-law; lives near Combray: I 58.

JULOT. One of the men M overhears in Jupien's brothel: III 839.

JULOT ("Big"). Another habitué of Jupien's brothel, now at the front, of whom there has been no news; is he or isn't he a ponce?: III 841–2.

JUPIEN. Tailor (or waistcoat-maker) who keeps a shop in the courtyard of Mme de Villeparisis's house; praised by M's grandmother: I 21. A new friend for Françoise: II 13–16 (*see also* 342, 353, 1021). M's unfavourable first impression of him, later dispelled; his appearance, his cultured speech: 15–16. Claims compensation from the Duc de Guermantes for damage to his shop-front: 27–8. His indiscretion; reveals to M Françoise's criticism of him: 64. His fits of ill-humour: 143–4. His respect for the laws of syntax: 319. Expands his shop: 585–6. His meeting with Charlus in the courtyard: 623–35, 651–3. Charlus engages him as his secretary: 654. Accompanies Charlus to the brothel at Maineville to spy on Morel: 1114–17. Morel asks him for his niece's hand: III 45. An ex-convict, according to Mme Verdurin: 282–3. Tells Charlus of Morel's maltreatment of his niece: 315. Odette's first cousin: 689. Informs M in indignant terms of Saint-Loup's relations with Morel: 695–6. M comes across him during the war in a brothel which he has bought on behalf of Charlus; his conversation with the latter: 843–6. His astonishment at finding M in his establishment: 852. His dealings with the "gigolos", whom he encourages to be "more vicious": 853–9. Explains his position to M: 859–62. His intelligence and sensibility: 868. Looks after the Baron in his old age: 891–3, 895–7.

JUPIEN, Marie-Antoinette. Niece of the above (although M's grandmother takes her for his daughter, and Proust occasionally makes the same mistake): I 21. Seamstress in Paris: II 14–15. Introduced to Morel; their mutual attraction: 274–5. Recommended by Charlus to the aristocracy: 653–4. Seems to be enamoured of Morel: 891, 1041–2. His sadistic plans in relation to her: 1041–2. Attitude towards her of Charlus; "stand you tea"; her charming manners; received in society; had once been "in trouble": III 37–44. Morel asks Jupien for her hand: 45–6. Alters her opinion of Morel and Charlus: 60–61. Brutally insulted by Morel: 161; his guilt and shame, and his decision to break with her: 192–6. Adopted by Charlus under the title of Mlle d'Oloron: 315. Marries the young Léonor de Cambremer: 673–5. Her death, a few weeks after her marriage: 688.

'KING' of a South Sea island, staying with his mistress at the Grand Hotel, Balbec: I 727–8, 734.

KITCHENMAID at Combray. Her resemblance to Giotto's "Charity": I 86–9; her confinement: 118; Françoise's cruelty to her; allergic to asparagus: 131–5.

LAMBRESAC, Duchesse de. At the Princesse de Guermantes's; her way of greeting people: II 706–7.

LARIVIÈRES, The. Rich cousins of Françoise; their self-sacrificing behaviour during the war; "the only real people in the book": III 875–6 (cf. II 343).

LAU D'ALLEMANS, Marquis du. Mme de Guermantes speaks of his informality with the Prince of Wales: III 29, 600. A friend of Swann; Gilberte's desire to meet him: 600–01.

LAUMES, Prince and Princesse des. See Guermantes, Duc and Duchesse de.

LAUNDRESS, Brichot's mistress; Mme Verdurin breaks up his relationship with her: II 897–8; he has a daughter by her: 1128 (cf. III 283).

LAUNDRY-GIRL in Touraine; her relations with Albertine, reported by Aimé: III 534–40.

LAUNDRY-GIRLS (two) whom M brings to a house of assignation; their love-making: III 561.

LAVATORY ATTENDANT. See "Marquise".

LAWYER friend of the Cambremers: II 833. His passion for Le Sidaner: 834, 839–40. His wife and his son: 849. Invites

M to see his collection in Paris and to meet Le Sidaner: 850.

LÉA, Mlle. Actress; Elstir speaks of her elegance at the races: I
960. Admired by Bloch's cousin; her Gomorrhan tastes: 965.
Lives with Bloch's cousin: II 830. Mme de Cambremer alludes
to her obliquely in connection with Albertine: 1133. Billed to
appear at the Trocadéro on the occasion of Albertine's visit: III
140–41. M's anxiety about her possible relations with Albertine:
141–8. Her letter to Morel: 212–13, 380. Albertine admits to
having visited her in her dressing-room: 351–2; and to having
gone on a three-week trip with her: 357–9. It was she who,
dressed as a man, had been walking with Gilberte in the
Champs-Elysées (cf. I 671): 714.

LEBLOIS DE CHARLUS, Comte. Confused with the Baron de
Charlus in professional and artistic circles: II 933.

L'ÉCLIN, Mme de. Nicknamed "Hungry belly": II 448.

LEGRANDIN. Engineer and man of letters; his character and
appearance; tirades against the nobility; flowery speech: I 72–3.
Strange behaviour to M's father: 129–30. His snobbery and
affectation; his wink; M dines with him: 135–41. His lyrical
descriptions of Balbec; refuses to introduce his sister, Mme de
Cambremer: 141–5 (see also 417). M meets him in Paris, and is
rebuked for his social zeal: II 155–7. At Mme de Villeparisis's;
obsequious to her, furious with M: 204–9, 219, 283. Raises his hat
to M's grandmother as she drives back with M from the
Champs-Elysées after her stroke: 325–6. His sister's displeasure
when M claims acquaintance with him: 848–9. Assumes the name
Legrand de Méséglise: 1120. His kindness to M's great-aunt: III
6. Discussed by Charlus and the Princesse de Parme in
connection with his nephew's marriage to Jupien's niece; the
Princess invites him to call; changes in his appearance and sexual
proclivities; of his two vices, snobbery now giving way to the
other: 680–84. Becomes Comte de Méséglise: 689. His relations
with Théodore: 719. A journalist during the war: 800. In old age,
ceases to use cosmetics, becomes gloomy and taciturn: 976–7.
Resemblance to his nephew: 987. His new civility towards
Bloch: 1022.

LÉON, Prince de. Nephew of Mme de Guermantes, brother-in-
law of Saint-Loup. Mme de Guermantes's anecdote about him:
III 28–9.

LÉONIE, Aunt (Madame Octave). Her habit of giving M a piece of *madeleine* dipped in tea or tisane: I 50–51. Bedridden since her husband's death; her bedroom, her way of life: 53–6. Relations with Françoise: 58–63, and with Eulalie: 74–6. Conversations with Françoise, Eulalie and M. le Curé: 109–17. Her "little jog-trot": 117–19. Occasional longing for change; her "counter-pane dramas"; plays Françoise and Eulalie off against one another; terrorises Françoise: 125–9. Vague plan to visit Tansonville: 156–7. Her death: 167–8. Leaves her fortune and her furniture to M: 489. M gives some of her furniture to a brothel-keeper; sells her silver to buy flowers for Mme Swann: 622, and her Chinese vase to buy flowers for Gilberte: 670. Françoise sings her praises: II 21. M begins to resemble her more and more: III 72–3. Analogy between one of her ploys with Françoise and M's with Albertine: 361.

LEROI, Mme Blanche. A snob; "cuts" Mme de Villeparisis: II 190, 192. Her superior social position: 192–3 compared to Mme de Villeparisis: 198–9. Her witticism about love: 199. The daughter of rich timber merchants; Mme de Villeparisis affects to despise her: 282–3. After the war, her name is all but forgotten: III 1008–9.

LÉTOURVILLE, Duchesse de. Meets the aged Charlus with M in the Champs-Elysées and is shocked by his appearance: III 894–5.

LÉTOURVILLE. Young relative of the above; M meets him on his way into the Princesse de Guermantes's afternoon party; just out of Saint-Cyr; regards M as an elderly gentleman: III 968.

LÉVY, Esther. Cousin of Bloch; her unconcealed admiration for Léa: I 964–5, 1004. Lives with Léa; she and Bloch's sister attract Albertine's attention in the Casino at Balbec: II 830–31. Her amorous intrigue with a young married woman whom she meets in the Grand Hotel: 881. M's suspicions as to her relations with Albertine; he asks Bloch for her photograph: III 80–81. Albertine denies knowing her: 106, but later confesses to having given her a photograph of herself: 348, 371.

LIFT-BOY at the Grand Hotel, Balbec. M's first introduction to him and his esoteric craft: I 715–16. M puzzled by his vocabulary: 857–8. A know-all: 859–60. The manager gives M his opinion of him: II 782. Glows with pleasure on seeing M again: 791. Go-between with Albertine; his inability to shut doors, his verbal mannerisms, false veneer of intelligence, democratic pride, physical appearance: 818–22. "Camembert" for "Cambremer": 833, 854, 886. His anxiety over his tip: 853–6. Cycles to Doncières station with a telegram for M: 884. His whooping cough: 1058–9. Saint-Loup had made advances to him, according to Aimé: III 698–700. Joins the air force in 1914: 769.

LOISEAU, Mme. Her house beside the church at Combray; her fuchsias: I 67.

LONGPORT, Mme Barbe de. Star attraction at one of Mme Verdurin's Wednesdays at la Raspelière: II 1003.

LOREDAN. Nickname of Swann's coachman. See Rémi.

LUXEMBOURG, Grand Duke of. Formerly Comte de Nassau, nephew of the Princesse de Luxembourg. His high qualities; writes to M during his grandmother's illness: II 341. Malicious stories about him retailed by the Prince de Foix and his friends: 426, and the Guermantes and their friends, including Oriane and the Turkish Ambassadress: 554, 558–60.

LUXEMBOURG, Princesse de. At Balbec; her stately appearance; introduced to M and his grandmother by Mme de Villeparisis; her presents; her little negro page: I 750–53. Mme Poncin takes her for an elderly tart: 754–5. Saint-Loup describes her as "an old trout": 837. In the restaurant at Rivebelle: 872. Presents her negro page to her nephew the Grand Duke: II 554.

MAMA. See Osmond, Amanien, Marquis d'.

MAMMA (M's mother). Her good-night kiss at Combray: I 13–14, 29–39 (see also 199, 201–2). Speaks to Swann about his daughter: 24–6. Spends a night in M's room; reads him François le Champi (cf. III 918–24). Her practical wisdom tempers the ardent idealism of her mother: 40–46. Gives M a madeleine soaked in tea: 48. Holidays at Combray; her relations with Françoise: 57–8. Her resemblance to M, according to the "lady in pink": 81–2. Her kindness to M. Vinteuil: 122. Her admiration for her husband: 123–4. Amused by Legrandin's snobbery: 141. Finds M in tears on the little path near Tansonville: 158. Pities Mlle Vinteuil after her father's death 174–5. Swann invited to her wedding: 388. Her black hair and beautiful plump white hands:

438. Her unfavourable opinion of Mme Blatin: 448. Meets Swann at the Trois Quartiers: 448–50. Disapproves of make-up: 467. Her opinion of Norpois, a reflection of her own modesty, delicacy and wifely devotion: 471–3. Entertains Norpois to dinner: 480, 491, 494–5, 500–01. Her doubts about M's literary career: 519. Discusses Norpois with her husband: 521. Talks to Françoise about cooking and restaurants: 522–3. Quarrels with Cottard's prescriptions; her concern for M: 537–8. Ridicules Odette and her friends: 555. Her reaction to M's acquaintance with Bergotte: 617–18. Refuses to meet Mme Swann: 619 (cf. 449). Remains in Paris when M and his grandmother go to Balbec: 694; sees them off at the station: 697–700. Incapable of rancour, and absolutely unspoiled: 801. "Cut" by Mme Sazerat: II 153–4; her impartiality over the Dreyfus Case: 154. Her deference to Dr du Boulbon: 313–14, 317–18. At her mother's death-bed; her grief and devotion: 329–31, 334–5, 341, 345–56. Her respect for her mother's memory: 359. Cures M of his obsession with Mme de Guermantes: 385. Joins M at Balbec; her cult of grief for her mother, and her increasing resemblance to her, including her veneration for Mme de Sévigné: 795–9, 803, 807. Avoids M's visitors: 835–6. Reminiscences of her mother; gives M both French versions of the *Arabian Nights*: 864–6. Her views on Albertine's suitability as a wife: 958, and her anxiety about M's intimacy with her: 1051–2. Congenitally attached to the rule of caste: the "Combray spirit": 1060. Gratified to learn that M has decided not to marry Albertine: 1150. Plans to visit Combray to look after one of her aunts: 1159–60. M mistakes her for his grandmother: 1166–8. He informs her of his decision to return to Paris and marry Albertine: 1169. Writes daily to M from Combray; disapproves of his living with Albertine; quotes Mme de Sévigné: III 5–9, 136–7, 363. Teaches M to distinguish between sensibility and sentimentality: 102–3. Reserves her love and generosity for those close to her: 326. Brings M the *Figaro* containing his article: 578. Lunches with Mme Sazerat: 609. Visits the Princesse de Parme, who ignores her: 610. The Princess returns her visit next day: 626–7. Takes M to Venice: 637–40, 643. Invites Mme Sazerat to dinner: 644. In the baptistery of St Mark's; compared to the old woman in Carpaccio's *St Ursula*: 660–61. Refuses to postpone their departure from Venice; M

rebels, but joins her in the train at the last minute: 666–70. Her views on the marriages of Jupien's niece and Gilberte: 671–6, 690–92.

MANAGER of the Grand Hotel, Balbec. Receives M and his grandmother; his appearance and character, alien ancestry, malapropisms: I 711–16, 734, 749, 856–7, 926, 1014–16. Welcomes M on his second visit to Balbec; more malapropisms: II 778–9. Complains of his staff: 782–3. Brings M a message from Albertine: 790–92. Displeased with Albertine and her friends: 803. Tells M of his grandmother's "sincups": 806. Carves the turkeys himself: 1119–20. Interned as a "Boche" in 1914: III 769.

MANCHESTER, Consuelo, Duchess of. Takes Oriane shopping in London; now dead: III 36.

MARIE-AYNARD. See Marsantes, Comtesse de.

MARIE-GILBERT or MARIE-HEDWIGE. See Guermantes, Princesse Marie de.

MARGUERITE. Françoise's daughter. Lives near Combray: I 57–8. Moves to Paris; Françoise's visits to her; her trendy slang and contempt for the country: II 149–50, 353. Recommends a "radical" cure for M's grandmother: 342–3. Entertained by Françoise; more Parisian slang: 754. Her deplorable influence on Françoise's vocabulary: III 151–2, 771.

"MARQUISE", The. Keeper of the water-closets in the Champs-Elysées. Françoise regards her as "a proper lady"; her partiality towards M: I 531. Discusses her customers with the park-keeper; her exclusiveness; M's grandmother compares her to the Guermantes and the Verdurins: II 320–22.

MARSANTES, Comte or Marquis de. Saint-Loup's father; contrasted with Robert: I 787–8. Nissim Bernard claims to have been a friend of his: 831–2 (cf. II 286). Was President of the Jockey Club for 10 years: II 242. Killed in the war of 1870–71: 1131.

MARSANTES, Comtesse de (Marie-Aynard). Widow of the above, Saint-Loup's mother, and sister of Basin de Guermantes and Charlus. Her relations with Mme Swann and Lady Israels: I 558 (cf. 502: a possible allusion in Norpois's conversation with M's family, 1025, and II 261). Niece of Mme de Villeparisis: 785. How she brought up her son: 786. Anti-Dreyfusist: II 167 (cf.

243, 245, 261, 604). *Mater semita*: Rachel's anti-semitic etymology of the name Marsantes: 182 (cf. 246 and III 680). At Mme de Villeparisis's; her character and looks: 257–60 (cf. 424). Her joy at seeing Robert: 262–3, 279–80, and possessive love and concern for him: 286, 289–93. Her deference to M: 285–6, 293 (cf. 259). Hypocritical and mercenary (finding a rich wife for Robert): 424 (cf. 260, 467, 724, III 677). Old-fashioned purity of her vocabulary: 514 (cf. III 27). Furthers Odette's social ascent: 773–4 (cf. III 588–9). Charlus's resemblance to her: 938. Brings off the marriage of Robert and Gilberte: III 677. Condescends to dine with the Cottards and the Bontemps *chez* Gilberte: 684–5. Brings about a reconciliation between Robert and Gilberte: 696. Robert resembles her more and more: 722.

MAURICE. One of the "gigolos" in Jupien's brothel. Flogs Charlus: III 840, 843. His resemblance to Morel: 845–6. His kindheartedness: 849–50. His virtuous principles disappoint Charlus: 855.

MÉMÉ. Charlus's nickname (Palamède).

MOLÉ, Comtesse. Leaves an envelope instead of a card on Mme de Guermantes: II 612–13, who replies in kind: 617. Envelops Charlus in her huge skirt; his professed admiration for her: 699, 717. Goes to the Swanns': 700. In Odette's box at the theatre: 773. Her exalted position in society: 773. Mme Verdurin's interest in her: 966–7, 1000–01 (cf. III 234–5). The object of slanderous newspaper articles by Morel inspired by Charlus (an allusion to her death that does not accord with subsequent references to her): III 218. The mystery of Charlus's furious rancour against her: 234; he denounces her to Mme Verdurin: 235; 277–9. During the war, defends Charlus against Mme Verdurin: 789. Admires Brichot but disowns him: 818. M refuses an invitation to dine with her: 1097–8.

MONK, brother-in-law of M's grandmother. Surreptitiously observes M while praying by her death-bed: II 351.

MONSERFEUIL, General de. Mme de Guermantes refuses to speak to him on behalf of Saint-Loup; his failures at the polls: II 531–2, 534.
   (*See* Beauserfeuil.)

MONTERIENDER, Comtesse de. At Mme de Saint-Euverte's; her absurd remark about Vinteuil's sonata: I 383–4.

MONTMORENCY-LUXEMBOURG, Duchesse de. Contrasted by M, as a friend, with Mme de Guermantes: II 591–2; her opinion of Oriane, and Oriane's of her: 776–7. M's pleasure in visiting her; her town-house: 777–8. Charlus's response to an invitation from her: III 268.

MONTPEYROUX, Comtesse de. Sister of the Vicomtesse de Vélude; nicknamed "Petite" because of her stoutness: II 448 (cf. Hunolstein, Mme d').

MONTPEYROUX, Marquis de. Comes to meet the little train at Incarville; recommends his son to M: II 1146.

MOREAU, A. J. Friend and colleague of M's father. Provides a ticket for Berma at the Opéra: II 31. Gives M's father some information about Norpois: 150. Referred to by Norpois: 229.

MOREL, Charles. Violinist, son of Uncle Adolphe's valet. Calls on M at his father's instigation; his conceit and ambition; attracted to Jupien's niece: II 272–5. His first meeting with Charlus, at Doncières station: 890–92. Mme Verdurin's favourite violinist: 913, 922, 931. Arrives with Charlus at la Raspelière: 936. His obsequious request to M, followed by rudeness towards him: 939–41. His vile nature and his gifts as a musician: 941. Plays Fauré's violin sonata, followed by Debussy and Meyerbeer: 985–6. Plays cards with Cottard: 990, 995–1000, 1006–7. Motor-car trips with Charlus; his friendship with the chauffeur; conversation with the Baron in a restaurant at Saint-Mars-le-Vêtu: 1039–43. Pursuit of young girls: 1044. His machinations with the chauffeur to displace Mme Verdurin's coachman: 1062–5. Was he on friendly terms with Albertine?: 1065 (cf. III 612–13). His contradictory character: 1065–7. The nature of Charlus's relations with him: 1081–4, 1087–8, 1093–8. His affectionate allusions to M's Uncle Adolphe: 1091–2. His attitude to M and his cruelties to Charlus; pride in his musical career: 1094–8. His behaviour over Charlus's sham duel: 1099–1109. His requests for money: 1110. The bogus algebra lessons: 1113. His assignations with the Prince de Guermantes in the Maineville brothel; spied upon by Charlus and Jupien: 1112–18. Takes Charlus's social precepts too literally: 1125–6. Declines an invitation to dine with the Cambremers: 1126; on another occasion accepts, but turns up without the Baron: 1128–30. His hostility to Bloch: 1144. Tea with Charlus at

Jupien's: III 37–41. His ambivalent feelings vis-à-vis Jupien's niece and cynical intentions towards her: 42–5 (cf. II 1040–42). Asks for her hand in marriage: 45–6. Borrows money from Nissim Bernard through Bloch and fails to repay it; his anti-semitism: 47–8. Jupien's niece becomes aware of his malevolence and perfidy: 60–61. The algebra lessons: 159–60. Neurotic outburst against his fiancée (*grand pied de grue*): 161. His madness: 180. His remorse, and his decision to break with the Jupiens: 192–6. His relations with Léa: 211–14 (*see also* 380). Charlus admires his successes with women and his talents as a writer: 214–17; the lampoons against Mme Molé: 218. Refuses to perform for Mme Verdurin's friends; she resolves to separate him from Charlus: 229–31, 245–6. Plays Vinteuil's septet: 249–53, 258–9. Reactions to his performance: 270–75, 277–8, 281–2, 289–90. Refuses to play Bizet: 291. The Verdurins persuade him to break with Charlus: 313–27. Charlus recites poetry to him: 611. His illicit relations with Albertine, according to Andrée: 612–13. His liaison with Saint-Loup (the letter signed "Bobette"): 695–6, 700, 702–4, 719–24, 780. A deserter during the war: 751. Pursues Charlus with a venomous hatred; attacks him in newspaper articles; his Bergottesque style: 790–92. Joins up at last: 792. Meets Charlus in the street and teases him; the latter threatens revenge: 805. Turns heterosexual: 806. His justified fear of Charlus; the latter's posthumous letter: 830–33. Arrested as a deserter, sent to the front, decorated for bravery: 883–4. After the war, a distinguished and respected public figure; M meets him at the Guermantes *matinée*: 1001, 1042.

MORIENVAL, Baronne de. At the Opéra, compared unfavourably to the Princesse and the Duchesse de Guermantes ("eccentric, pretentious and ill-bred"): II 37, 51. Her ignorance of La Fontaine: III 1053–4.

MORTEMART, Duchesse de. Conversation with Charlus at the Verdurins': III 268–73.

MUSICIAN (eminent), friend of Ski's, invited to la Raspelière; furthers Morel's career and his relations with Charlus: II 1081–2.

NASSAU, Comte de. *See* Luxembourg, Grand Duke of.

NASSAU, Princesse de. Aged society courtesan; greets M at the Princesse de Guermantes's *matinée*: III 1027–8. (She and the Princesse d'Orvillers (q.v.) are clearly the same person.)

NIÈVRE, Princesse de. Cousin of Mme de Guermantes; has designs on Gilberte for her son: III 591.

NOÉMIE, Mlle. Attendant in the "house of pleasure" at Maineville; arranges for Charlus and Jupien to spy on Morel: II 1115–16.

NORPOIS, Marquis de. Ex-Ambassador; his career and character: I 468–74. Dines with M's family; his physical appearance, manner and voice; advice on M's career and investments: 486–90. His opinion of Berma: 492–3. Appreciates Françoise's cooking: 494–5. King Theodosius's visit: 495–500. Opinions on Balbec and the Swanns: 500–04; on the Comte de Paris, Odette, Bergotte, M's prose poem, Gilberte: 508–14. Reasons for his failure to inform the Swanns of M's admiration for them: 514–17 (cf. II 280–82). Reactions to his visit of M's parents: 521, and of Françoise: 522. His views (in the matter of art) compared with Bergotte's; the latter's opinion of him, and those of Swann and Odette: 605–7. Allusion to his liaison with Mme de Villeparisis: 606. Visits Spain with M's father: 694 (cf. 500, 753). His social diplomacy: the art of "killing two birds with one stone": 1002–3. Likened by M to Mosca in La Chartreuse de Parme: II 107. M's father's discovery of his friendship with Mme de Villeparisis: 150–51. M's father's hopes of his support as a candidate for election to the Institut: 152–3. His relations with Mme de Villeparisis: 187–8, 225–7. At Mme de Villeparisis's reception; introduced to Bloch; views on art: 227–9. Declines to support M's father's candidacy: 231–2. Discusses the Dreyfus Case with Bloch: 239–41, 247–54. His tortuous diplomatic manoeuvrings with Prince von Faffenheim: 264–71. Calls M "a hysterical little flatterer": 280 (cf. 549). Attends M's grandmother's funeral: 355. Meets M in the street and gives him no sign of recognition: 386–7. In favour of an Anglo-French rapprochement: 547–8. Mme de Guermantes talks about him (and his liaison with Mme de Villeparisis) at dinner: 548–50 (see also 1177–8). Widower of a La Rochefoucauld: 551. Fails to introduce any of his Institut colleagues to Mme de Villeparisis: 1090–91. His amnesia about his false prognostications: III 31. In Venice with Mme de Villeparisis: 644–54 (cf. 1116–19). His war-time articles: 754, 800, ridiculed by Charlus: 804–10, 824, 836.

NORPOIS, Baron and Baronne de. Nephew and niece of the Marquis: 11 28.

NOTARY from Le Mans. *See* Blandais, M.

OCTAVE. Young toff at Balbec, consumptive, dissipated, gambling son of an industrialist: 1 728, 734. Friend of Albertine and the little band; his golf-playing; "I'm a wash-out": 938–40. Related to the Verdurins: 944. His views on Mme de Villeparisis and Mme de Cambremer: 991–3. Maligned by Andrée: 111 54 (cf. 616–17). His liaison with Rachel: 617; marries Andrée: 618. His artistic genius: 618–21. Previously in love with Albertine: 627–30 (cf. 93 — a vague allusion by Françoise), 618, 751). His friendliness towards M: 635–6. One of the stars of Mme Verdurin's war-time salon: 751. His illness; a poor friend: 752.

OCTAVE, Madame. *See* Léonie, Aunt.

OCTAVE, Uncle. Husband of Aunt Léonie; already dead when M used to spend his holidays at Combray: 1 53, 60, 110, 118.

ODETTE (Mme de Crécy, then Mme Swann, and finally Mme de Forcheville). M's family refuse to receive her at Combray: 1 14; "a woman of the worst type": 22; Charlus's mistress, according to Combray gossip: 37 (cf. 107, 154–5). The "lady in pink" at Uncle Adolphe's: 81–5 (cf. 11 275). The "lady in white" at Tansonville: 154–5. As Odette de Crécy, a member of the Verdurins' "little clan": 205. Beginnings of her liaison with Swann; introduces him to the Verdurins; her looks; "I'm always free": 208, 213–17. The little phrase of Vinteuil, "the national anthem of their love": 231, 238–9, 258–60. Her house in the Rue La Pérouse; entertains Swann to tea: 239–42. Resemblance to Botticelli's Zipporah: 243–5. The letter from the Maison Dorée: 246. Swann's anguished search for her through the night: 247–52. The cattleyas; becomes Swann's mistress: 253–60. Her discomfiture when she lies: 260–61 (cf. 306). Her vulgarity and bad taste: 263–70. Introduces Forcheville to the Verdurins: 273, 276–7, 284–9. Her money troubles; Swann's presents; a "kept woman": 291–3. Swann's jealous suspicions: 297–300. A cruel smile of complicity with Forcheville: 301–2. Lies to Swann: 302–7. Her letter to Forcheville, which Swann reads: 307–8. Acquiesces in Swann's exclusion from the Verdurins': 310–11. Expeditions with the Verdurins; progress of Swann's jealousy: 315–24. Her soothing words: 325–6. The trip to Bayreuth: 327–31. Her confidence in Swann's devotion to her: 332–6. Friendship with Charlus: 339, 344, 349–51 (cf. 811; III 302–4). Quarrels with Uncle Adolphe: 339–40. Swann's jealousy, and her feelings towards him: 341–50. The little phrase reminds Swann of the early days of their love: 375–8. An anonymous letter about her love life: 387. Swann's suspicions; he interrogates her about her illicit relations with women and dealings with procuresses; her admissions: 390–402. Confesses to having been with Forcheville on the evening of the cattleyas: 402–3. Her suspect effusions: 405. Cruises with the Verdurins; thinks constantly of Swann, according to Mme Cottard: 406–9. Proof that she had indeed been Forcheville's lover: 411. "A woman who wasn't even my type": 415. Married to Swann; Gilberte's mother; still not received by M's family: 447–51. Walks or drives in the Allée des Acacias: 452–6, 459–62. Her social position as Swann's wife: 465–6. Norpois reports on a dinner-party in her house: 501–4. Scenes she made to Swann before their marriage; has now become "angelic": 504–8. Receives M at last; her house, her "at home" days, her social mannerisms, development of her *salon*: 542–62. Her Anglomania: 559 (cf. 84, 208, 213–14, 242, 547, 566–7, 576, 578, 586, 588, 625, 627, 638, 686, 689; II 192, 282; III 815, 993). Change in Swann's feelings towards her: 563–6. Plays Vinteuil's sonata: 570–75. Walks in the Zoological Gardens: 582–7. Invites M to lunch with Bergotte: 587–9. Criticises Norpois: 605–7 (cf. II 280). M's visits to her after his breach with Gilberte; her flowers, her "tea"; her indoor elegance: 636–41. Entertains Mmes Cottard, Bontemps and Verdurin: 641–54. Changes in her furniture and clothes: 662–3. Her new style of beauty; "an immortal youthfulness": 664–5. The embodiment of fashion; "a period in herself": 665–8. Walks in the Bois: 683–90. Bloch claims to have enjoyed her favours in a train: 835. Her portrait as "Miss Sacripant", by Elstir: 906–8, 919–22 (*see also* II 275; III 302, 447). Oriane's view of her: II 235. Gains an entrée into aristocratic society through anti-Dreyfusism: 260–61. At Mme de Villeparisis's: 272; Charlus pays court to her: 276–8; she and Oriane ignore one another: 282. Her salon crystallised round Bergotte; her social rise: 770–77. Denies and then admits her former intimacy with the Verdurins: 899–900. Photographs of her — "touched-up" portraits and Swann's snapshot: III 202 (cf. I 664). Charlus's account of her life before meeting Swann; his own relations with her; her lovers; *was* married to M. de Crécy: 302–4 (cf. II 1121). Said to have been Elstir's mistress: 447 (cf. I 922). Sincerely grieved by Swann's death; marries Forcheville: 586–9. A first cousin of Jupien: 689. Changed attitude to Gilberte's marriage; finds a generous protector in her son-in-law Saint-Loup: 701–2. During the war, Mme Verdurin fails to win her back: 753. Her remarks about the war; admiration for the English: 815. Her appearance in old age "defies the laws of chronology": 990–93; less than three years later "a bit gaga": 994–5. Her love for Gilberte: 995. M mistakes Gilberte for her: 1028–9 (cf. 993). Listens to Rachel's poetry recital: 1051. Her liaison with the Duc de Guermantes: 1068–74. Regales M with anecdotes about her former lovers; had been "desperately in love" with Swann: 1074–7.

OLORON, Mlle d'. *See* Jupien, Marie-Antoinette.

ORGEVILLE, Mlle de l'. Girl of good family said by Saint-Loup to frequent brothels: II 719. M's desires focus on her: 749; III 81, 524. Confused with Mlle de Forcheville (Gilberte): III 574–8, 584–5.

(*See* Éporcheville, Mlle de.)

ORIANE. *See* Guermantes, Oriane, Duchesse de.

ORSAN, M. d'. Friend of Swann, suspected of having written an anonymous letter: I 387–9.

ORVILLERS, Princesse d' (Paulette). Makes advances to M in the street: II 387. Late arrival at the Princesse de Guermantes's *soirée*; said to be a natural daughter of the Duke of Parma; her ambiguous social position: 746–7. "Rather a prude", according to Oriane and her husband: 750.

(*See* Nassau, Princesse de.)

OSMOND, Amanien, Marquis d' ("Mama"). Cousin of the Guermantes; his imminent death and its potential effect on the Guermantes' social arrangements: II 597, 600–01, 609–11, 686. The Duc de Guermantes's reaction to his death: "They're exaggerating": 751. Ran off with Odette, according to Charlus: II 304.

PAGES at the Grand Hotel, Balbec.

"Arborescent" page: I 758–9, 777; goes off with a Polish countess: II 800.

"Squinting" page (brother of the above): II 801; his vulgar sister: 1012.

"Hat-doffing" page: II 800.

Handsome page whom the lift-boy claims to resemble: II 820.

"Chorus" of pages: I 759; II 801–2, 1019.

PALANCY, Marquis de. His resemblance to a Ghirlandaio: I 243. At Mme de Saint-Euverte's; his monocle: 356–7. At the Opéra; his fish-like appearance: II 39, 49.

PARK-KEEPER in the Champs-Elysées: I 531; conversation with the "Marquise" (q.v.): II 319–22.

PARME, Princesse de. Gives the most splendid parties in Paris: I 293. Swann sends her a basket of fruit for her birthday: 337. Her shadow theatre show and her box at the Opéra: II 29–31. 34. Her philantrhopy and lack of snobbishness: 51. M presented to her at the Guermantes'; her affability; "She thinks you're charming": 440–41 (cf. I 753). Reasons for her amiability; her pedigree and upbringing as a "daughter of kings": 443–5. Her admiration for the Guermantes style: 453–4. Her *salon*; her enraptured curiosity and wonderment at Oriane's doings: 469–75, 483–4, 487, 490, 496–7. The Guermantes dinner-party; Oriane shows off in front of her; her naïvety; intercedes on behalf of Saint-Loup: 501–42. The leave-taking ceremonial; her lady-in-waiting; M's snow-boots: 565–8. Visits Balbec; her royal politeness; her tips: 816–17. M's mother pays a call on her and is ignored: III 610. Her return visit next day: 626. Arranges the marriage of young Cambremer with Jupien's niece: 680–82.

PASTRY-COOK. Stared at by Albertine, whom she ignores: III 416–17.

PERCEPIED, Doctor. His malicious jokes about the Vinteuils: I 161. Mme de Guermantes attends his daughter's wedding: 190. M composes his first literary essay in his carriage: 196–8.

PÉRIGOT, Joseph. Françoise's young footman in Paris; his pleasure at moving house: II 3–4; his deference to Françoise: 11–12, 19–22; his taste for poetry; "borrows" M's books: 332–3, 571; his letter: 588–9.

PERUVIAN (young). Conceives a violent hatred for Mme de Mortemart: III 272.

PHILOSOPHER, Norwegian. Guest of the Verdurins at la Raspelière; his deliberation of thought and diction and rapidity of departure: 11 960–61, 966. Mystery of his disappearance: 1008. Quotes Bergson on soporifics; his belief in the immortality of the soul: 1016–18.

PIANIST (young) patronized by the Verdurins: 1 205–6; his aunt: 205–7, 222, 283, 318; plays Vinteuil's sonata: 224–5, 230–32, 238–9, 287. (Is this pianist Dechambre? q.v.)

PIERRE, Monsieur. Historian of the Fronde. Visits Mme de Villeparisis; "solemn and tongue-tied": 11 193; his insomnia: 197, 221; his ignorance of social customs and of botany: 218–20; mocked by the Duc de Guermantes: 244–6 (see also 203–5, 232–3, 236–7).

PIERRE. Club doorman, writes M. de Charlus an intimate letter: 111 38–9.

PIPERAUD, Dr. Combray doctor: 1 59.

PLASSAC, Walpurge, Marquise de. Her town-house: 11 594–5. Calls on her cousin the Duc de Guermantes, with her sister Mme de Tresmes, to report on Amanien d'Osmond's state of health; her walking-stick: 597–8. Brings news of Amanien's death: 751.

POICTIERS, Duchesse de. Cousin of Saint-Loup, who recommends her to M as a substitute for his aunt Oriane — "a very good sort": 11 148–9.

POIRÉ, Abbé. Dreyfusist priest confided in by both the Prince and the Princesse de Guermantes: 11 735–7.

POIX, Princesse de. Intimate friend of Oriane de Guermantes, attends Alix's "Fridays": 11 200. Visits Gilberte de Saint-Loup: 111 685.

POMMELIÈRE, Marquise de la. Nicknamed "la Pomme"; the Princesse de Guermantes's inane remark about her: 11 683–4.

PONCIN, M. Senior judge from Caen, on holiday at Balbec: 1 726–8, 739, 742, 754–5. Becomes Commander of the Legion of Honour: 11 779. His delight on hearing of M's arrival at Balbec: 782, 791. Condoles with M's mother: 798. His mistake as to the identity of the Princesse de Parme: 814. Doffs his hat to the Marquise de Cambremer: 833. His frustrated snobbery: 850–53, 1069 (cf. Toureuil, Judge).

PONCIN, Mme. Wife of the above. Her social resentment and disapproval: 1 728–9, 738–9. Her misapprehensions about Mme de Villeparisis and the Princesse de Luxembourg: 755. Observes the passers-by on the esplanade: 846. Regards M. de Cambremer as a man of supreme aristocratic distinction: 11 943.

PORTEFIN, Berthe, Duchesse de. Helps Mme de Villeparisis with her theatricals: 11 221. Admired by Morel: 111 320.

POULLEIN. Guermantes footman, prevented from going to see his fiancée; Françoise's sympathy for him: 11 149, 155, 318, 386, 438. Mme de Guermantes changes his day off out of jealousy and spite: 502, 511, and insists on his staying in when the Duke allows him a night out: 609–10.

POUSSIN, Mme. Lady from Combray on holiday at Balbec with her daughters; nicknamed "Just You Wait"; her absconding son-in-law: 11 798–9.

PUBLISHER from Paris. Visits la Raspelière; "not smart enough for the little clan": 11 934.

PUPIN, M., daughter of. Schoolgirl at Combray: 1 60–61.

PUTBUS, Baroness. Patient of Dr Cottard: 1 287. Described by Mme de Guermantes as "the dregs of society": 11 750. Invited to la Raspelière: 779–81. Friend of Princess Sherbatoff: 907. No longer expected at la Raspelière: 963. Extremely prudish: 111 201. Arrives in Venice on the day of M's departure: 666.

PUTBUS, Maid of Mme. Said by Saint-Loup to frequent brothels, to be partial to women, and to be "wildly Giorgionesque": 11 719, 721. M's desire for her: 749, 779–81. M dreads her arrival in Balbec, because of Albertine: 870, 885. Sister of Théodore, of Combray: 111 310.

RACHEL. M meets her in a brothel and nicknames her "Rachel when from the Lord": 1 620–21. Mme de Villeparisis's allusion to her liaison with Saint-Loup: 782. Saint-Loup's love for her: 790; he telegraphs her every day: 804; her influence over him; her mercenariness; their quarrels: 837–41. Her performance *chez* Oriane: 841–3 (cf. 11 229 sqq.; 111 1064–5). Rupture and reconciliation with Saint-Loup: 11 121–5. Saint-Loup invites M to meet her; her house on the outskirts of Paris; M's stupefaction on discovering that Robert's mistress is "Rachel when from the Lord": 155–63. Her two different selves: 163–6. In the restaurant; her literary talk; her Dreyfusism; ogles the waiters and other customers; Robert's jealousy; her maliciousness; quarrel and reconciliation: 166–75. In the theatre; her appearance on the stage: 177–9; the ballet-dancer; Robert's jealousy; the promised necklace: 177–84. Remarks about her at Mme de Villeparisis's reception: 223–45 *passim*. Robert's gloom and remorse about their quarrel; she refuses the necklace; her generosity; Robert's ignorance of her infidelities: 287–92. Final breach: 360–62. Prince Von talks to M about her: 528–9. She and her friends make fun of Robert: 721. Robert's dialect borrowed from her: 848. Her liaison with Octave: 111 617, and her despair when he leaves her to marry Andrée: 618. Her continued influence over Robert: 696–8, 703. Her resemblance to Morel: 700, 704. Gilberte tries to look like her: 700–01, 720–21. After the war, becomes a famous actress and an intimate friend of the Duchesse de Guermantes; invited to recite poetry at the Princesse de Guermantes's: 1043–5. Berma's low opinion of her: 1045–8. Her recital and its reception: 1050–52. Makes eyes at M, who fails to recognize her: 1052–3. Her malicious remarks about Berma: 1054–5. Oriane's opinion of her: 1064–5, 1081. Her reception of Berma's daughter and son-in-law: 1066–8.

RAMPILLON, Mme de. At Mme de Saint-Euverte's — "that appalling Rampillon woman", says Oriane: 1 373. At the Princesse de Guermantes's — "old mother Rampillon" ridiculed by Oriane: 11 710.

RAPIN, M. Chemist at Combray: 118, 67.

RÉMI. Swann's coachman: 1 237–8. His resemblance to Rizzo's bust of the Doge Loredan: 243. Helps Swann in his nocturnal search for Odette: 250–52. Odette takes against him: 349–50. Suspected by Swann of writing an anonymous letter: 389.

RESTAURATEUR. Proprietor of restaurant in Paris where M dines with Saint-Loup; his rudeness and servility: 11 416–17, 421–3, 425.

ROSEMONDE. Member of the little band at Balbec: 1 950, 952, 958. Her "incessant japing"; her northern face and voice: 971–2. Games on the cliff: 972, 975, 977, 983, 988. Her mother: 997. Her features and colouring — "a geranium growing by a sunlit sea": 1008. Her parents take Albertine "en pension" at Incarville: 11 808, 813. Her remark to M about his attitude towards Albertine: 833, 853. Albertine kisses her on the neck: 1155 (cf. 111 559).

ROUSSEAU, Mme. Her death at Combray: 1 60.

SAINT-CANDÉ. At Mme de Saint-Euverte's; his monocle: 1 356.

SAINT-EUVERTE, Marquise de. Gives a musical *soirée* attended

by Swann, the Princesse des Laumes and others: I 351–84. Gives
a dinner-party attended by the Guermantes: II 609, 618–19,
which is followed by the reception at the Princesse de
Guermantes's, to which she comes to recruit guests for her
garden-party next day: 693–4. Changes in the composition of her
salon: 694–6. Colonel de Froberville's ambivalent attitude to her
garden-party: 701–2. Oriane announces her intention not to go,
much to Froberville's delight: 708–11. Overhears Charlus's
scatological remarks about her; her craven reaction: 725–8. Mme
de Surgis's portrait in her house: 733. Mme d'Arpajon declines to
introduce her to Odette: 775. Further Charlus insults: 1178.
During the war, her *salon* "a faded banner": IIi 746. After the
war, greeted with obsequious respect by Charlus: 891–2. At the
Guermantes *matinée*: 1026. Oriane denies ever having known
her: 1078–9.

SAINT-EUVERTE, Mme de. Wife of a great-nephew of the above,
née La Rochefoucauld; M comes across her at the Guermantes
matinée listening to music in a Mme Récamier pose: III
1078–80.

SAINT-FERRÉOL, Mme de. Mme de Guermantes proposes to
visit her; Saint-Loup pretends not to know who she is: II 263,
272. (Françoise claims that the lavatory attendant "marquise" in
the Champs-Elysées belongs to the Saint-Ferréol family: I 531.)

SAINT-FIACRE, Vicomtesse de. At the Guermantes *matinée*;
prematurely aged from drug addiction: III 986.

SAINTINE. Once "the flower of the Guermantes set", now
déclassé through marriage: III 231–3.

SAINT-JOSEPH, General de. Saint-Loup hopes Mme de Guermantes will use her influence with him to get a transfer from
Morocco: II 428, 535. Françoise despairs of his help in getting
her nephew exempted from war service: III 770.

SAINT-LOUP-EN-BRAY, Marquis Robert de. Son of Aynard
and Marie de Marsantes. Comes to Balbec on leave to visit his
great-aunt Mme de Villeparisis: I 782. His dashing aristocratic
elegance; his apparent coldness and arrogance, then his immedi-
ate friendship and regard for M; his intellectual tastes and
advanced ideas: 783–92. His tact with Bloch: 793–5. He and M
invited to dinner by Bloch: 800–04. Speaks to M of his uncle
Charlus: 804–7, and of the Guermantes: 810–11 (cf. II 8–9). His

fashionably slangy vocabulary: 806, 819–20. Regards genealogy and heraldry as "rather a joke": 810–11. Prefers modern furniture: 813 (cf. 11 572). Dinner with the Blochs: 824–34. His egalitarianism, contempt for high society, gift for friendship: 836–7. His liaison with Rachel; her influence on his character and behaviour; their quarrels: 837–43. Photographs M's grand-mother: 843–4. Dinners with M at Rivebelle: 865–7, 872, 875–7, 883–6. His departure from Balbec; writes to M: 925–9. Rumours of his engagement to Mlle d'Ambresac: 945–6, (cf. 11 30, 103–4). M visits him at Doncières: 11 67–141. His welcome; his idiomatic turns of phrase; his contempt for the Prince de Borodino (cf. 129–32); his resemblance to his aunt Oriane: 68–78. His solicitude for M: 87–9. His popularity: 91–3. Conversation about Oriane; agrees to recommend M to her but refuses to give him her photograph: 98–102, 125–7. Dinners with his mess-mates; conversations on military strategy; his Dreyfusism: 109–19. His unhappiness because of Rachel: 121–5. His relations with the Prince de Borodino; the two aristocracies: 127–32. His strange salute: 139 (cf. 179–80). Brief visit to Paris; offers to introduce M to his cousin Mme de Poictiers instead of Oriane as being a more "liberal" representative of the aristocracy: 148–9. Invites M to lunch with Rachel: 155. His tender feelings for her and illusions about her: 158–66 (cf. 177–9). In the restaurant; his jealousy; quarrel and reconciliation: 166–75. In the theatre; another quarrel; he hits a journalist and an "impassioned loiterer": 181–7. Remarks about him and his mistress at Mme de Villeparisis's: 223–45 *passim*. Arrives *chez* Mme de Villeparisis: 261–4. Refuses to be introduced to Mme Swann: 272. Irritation with his mother: 278–80, 289–91. His friendship with Bloch: 284–5. His remorse about Rachel; the promised necklace: 287–9. His ignorance of Rachel's life: 291–2. Writes M a letter of bitter reproach: 318 (cf. 360–61). Calls on M's family during his grandmother's illness: 350. Posted to Morocco; writes to M about Mme de Stermaria. Final breach with Rachel: 360–62. Calls on M in Paris and takes him out to dinner: 409–31; his tactless remark concerning M and Bloch: 414; borrows the Prince de Foix's cloak for M; his nimble circumambulation of the restaurant; his physical grace and effortless good breeding — epitome of the best qualities of the aristocracy: 423–31. Oriane mocks his mannerisms of speech and refuses to speak to General de Monserfeuil or General de Saint-Joseph on his behalf: 527–31, 534–5. Elected to the Jockey Club in spite of his Dreyfusism: 604–6. At the Princesse de Guermantes's; speaks to M about Charlus, recommends brothels and Mlle de l'Orgeville and Mme Putbus's maid; no longer interested in literature: 716–21. No longer Dreyfusist: 724, 738. Recommends M to the Cambremers: 780. Mme de Cambremer-Legrandin adopts his vocabulary (borrowed from Rachel); alleged to have been Mme de Cambremer's lover: 848. Meets M and Albertine at Doncières station; ignores Albertine's flirtatious advances: 887–9 (cf. 1137–9, 1144–5). Albertine discusses him with M: 893–4. Rumour of his engagement to the Princesse de Guermantes's niece: 959 (cf. 1130; III 760). M's fear of his meeting Albertine at Balbec or *chez* the Verdurins; S-L has no wish to meet the latter: 1054–5. His Dreyfusism discussed by the Cambremers: 1130–31. Visits M on the little train; Albertine avoids him: 1137–9, 1144–5. M employs him to search for Albertine after her flight: III 441–50, 452–6, 459–61. Strange conversation with a Guermantes footman overheard by M: 479–80. Reports on his abortive mission: 480–84. Consulted by M about Mlle d'Eporcheville (de l'Orgeville): 576–8. His marriage to Gilberte: 670–72, 676–80, 687–8. Turns out to be "one of those": 678. Unfaithful to Gilberte; Jupien's revelations; his liaison with Morel: 695–7. Visit to Balbec with Gilberte; Aimé's revelations; the development of his inversion; Rachel's influence still visible; her resemblance to Morel; gives her an enormous income: 697–701. Bribes Odette with expensive presents to obtain her complicity: 701–2. M's reflections on the new Robert; when did it date from?: 702–6. At Tansonville; his relations with his wife; changes in his personality; his love for Charlie: 717–27. During the war, dines with M one evening while on leave: 756. Feigns cowardice but secretly does everything he can to be sent to the front; comparison with Bloch; his undemonstrative courage and patriotism: 758–69. His "delightful" letter from the front: 773–7. Visits M on leave from the front; discussion about aeroplanes at night; opinions on the war; compared with Charlus: 779–85. M sees him emerging from Jupien's brothel: 838. The lost *croix de guerre*: 849, 871–2. Killed in action: 877. M's grief; memories of him, linked to those of Albertine; effect of his death on Françoise and on Oriane; buried at Combray: 877–83. "If he had lived. . . .": 884–5. M talks to Gilberte about him at the Guermantes *matinée*: 1029–32.

SAINT-LOUP, Mlle de. Daughter of Robert and Gilberte. Introduced to M by her mother at the Guermantes *matinée*; memories and reflections she awakens in M; her beauty; her resemblance to her parents and grand-parents: III 1084–8.

SANIETTE. Palaeographer; member of the Verdurins' "little clan"; his shyness, simplicity and good nature: I 221–2. Forcheville's brother-in-law: 273. Scolded by Mme Verdurin: 284. In an endeavour to amuse, makes up a story about the La Trémoïlles: 285. Attacked by Forcheville and driven from the house: 301–2. Dreyfusist, in spite of being a practising Catholic: II 605. His social awkwardness aggravated by his efforts to correct it: 900–03. Upset by Cottard's behaviour in the little train: 905. The Verdurins' whipping-boy: 930–31, 961, 963 8. His failed witticisms: 968–70. Unable to play whist: 990. Mme Verdurin's views on him: 1006–9. M's analysis of his social deficiencies: 1055–7. His pedantic phraseology: III 226, 229 (*see also* 1114–15). His bankruptcy and his stroke; the Verdurins' generosity to him; M attends his funeral some years later: 329–31 (cf. 1114–15).

SANILON. Surname of Théodore (q.v.)

SANTOIS, Bobby. Proust's original name for the violinist Charlie Morel: *see* I 1130–32; III 695.

SAUMOY, Guy. Friend of the "little band" at Balbec, retrospectively evoked by M: III 620.

SAXONY, Prince of. Is he the blond young man who joins the Princesse de Guermantes in her box at the Opéra?: II 32–3, 49.

SAYLOR. Patronym of M. de Crécy (q.v.).

SAZERAT, Mme. Neighbour of M's family at Combray: I 61. Her dog: 62–3. In church: 64. Eulalie's belief that her name is Sazerin: 75. Comments on Odette's make-up: 107. Her son: 189. Her mauve scarf: 191. Her attitude to servants: II 62. Her Dreyfusism separates her from M's family: 153–4, 336. Meets Bloch *père*: 299. M's mother's opinion of her lunch-parties: III 9, 609. Her Wednesday voice; her restricted life, the result of her father's indiscretions with a duchess: 609–10. M's mother invites her to dinner in Venice: 644. Her emotion on hearing the name Villeparisis; reveals that Mme de Villeparisis was the duchess who ruined her father: 648–9. Death of her son: 1097.

SERVING-GIRL seduced by M in an inn at Doncières: II 411.

SHERBATOFF, Princess. In the little train at Balbec; M's mistake as to her identity: II 887. A model member of the Verdurins' "faithful"; impresses her fellow-members of the "little clan"; reality of her social position; her three friends: 903–11. M recognizes her as the fat, vulgar lady he had seen alone on the train: 921–2. Her pronunciation: 923. Her obligingness: 924–5. Her concern about the effect of Dechambre's death on Mme Verdurin: 926, 928–9. Mme Verdurin uses her as a screen to hide her mock laughter: 987. Rebuffed by Cottard in the little train: 1074–5. Her proclaimed anti-snobbery the result of wounded snobbery; quarrels with M: 1077–80. Appreciates a Cottard pun: 1085. Her death announced by Saniette: III 228. Mme Verdurin's indifference to the event: 240–41. Referred to in the Goncourt pastiche as having perhaps been the murderer of the Archduke Rudolph: 730.

SIDONIA, Duke of. Spanish grandee and formidable talker; competes with Charlus at the Princesse de Guermantes's: II 662–3.

SILISTRIE, Princesse de. Calls on the Guermantes to discuss Amanien d'Osmond's illness: II 597. Seeks to marry her son to Gilberte: III 676–7.

SIMONET. See Albertine.

SKI, diminutive of Viradobetski. Polish sculptor, friend of the Verdurins. In the little train: II 896–7; his character and appearance; superficially gifted in all the arts; his affectations: 902–3. His opinion of Mme de Cambremer: 916. Warns Mme Verdurin against Charlus: 932–4. Teases Brichot about his "eye for the ladies": 953. Reveals Charlus's vice to Cottard: 964. His affected flight of fancy about the colour of food: 971. Mistaken about Charlus's background: 987–9. His witticisms at the Baron's expense: 1075. Discusses Bizet with Morel; his affected laugh: III 291. Charlus ridicules Brichot's suggestion that he might be homosexual: 305. Fascinated by Morel's tears: 324. In old age, has become like a dried fruit or flower: 978.

SOUVRÉ, Marquise de. Friend of the Princesse de Parme, but not received by Oriane de Guermantes: 11 470–71. Her social manner: 673. Half-hearted attempt to introduce M to the Prince de Guermantes: 674, 676, 679. Conversation with Odette about the Verdurins: 900. Evoked by M at the Guermantes *matinée*: 111 1021.

STERMARIA, Mlle (later Mme, and finally Vicomtesse Alix) de. At Balbec with her father, a Breton squire: 1 730–31. Her aristocratic looks: 735. M's dream of love on a Breton island with her: 740–42 (cf. 11 400–01). Saint-Loup meets her in Tangier (divorced after three months of marriage) and arranges for M to dine with her in Paris: 11 360–63. A letter from her agreeing to dine on the island in the Bois: 384. M's pleasurable anticipation; she cries off at the last moment: 397–408.

STERMARIA, M. de. Breton squire, father of the above, on holiday at Balbec: 1 730. His contemptuous arrogance: 731, 735. Introduces himself to the barrister as a friend of the Cambremers: 739–42.

SÛRETÉ, Director of the. M receives a summons from him for having corrupted a little girl; his cynicism: 111 451–2.

SURGIS-LE-DUC, Marquise or Duchesse de. Mistress of the Duc de Guermantes: 11 511. At the Princesse de Guermantes's; her statuesque beauty: 676, reproduced in her two sons: 711, 714–15. Charlus's unwonted friendliness towards her; her portrait by Jacquet; introduces her sons to the Baron: 719–33. Swann gazes concupiscently at her bosom: 730–31, 733. Origin of her name; her social position: 732–3. Later, forbids her sons to visit Charlus: 111 203–4.

SURGIS-LE-DUC, Victurnien and Arnulphe de. Sons of the above; their "great and dissimilar" beauty derived from their mother: 11 711–12. Admired by Charlus: 714–15. Introduced to him by their mother: 722–3. Conversation with him: 723–5, 729–30. Their subsequent visits to him, eventually forbidden by their mother: 111 203–4.

SWANN, Charles. His evening visits at Combray; his brilliant social life unsuspected by M's family: 1 14–29. Why he might have understood M's anguish at having to go to bed without a good-night kiss from his mother: 32–4. His habit, inherited from his father, of rubbing his eyes and drawing his hand across his forehead in moments of stress: 37 (cf. 264, 293, 322, 346, 377,

390, 411). "Giotto's Charity": 87. His Jewish origin: 98. Speaks to M about Bergotte and Berma: 105–7. "Swann's Way" (the Méséglise way); his estate at Tansonville: 146 sqq. Meets Vinteuil in Combray: 162–3 (cf. 233). *Swann in Love*: 205–415. His womanising: 208–13. Introduced to Odette; his initial indifference to her: 213–17. His essay on Vermeer: 215–16 (cf. 262–3, 325, 384, 505, 575; II 733). Introduced by Odette to the Verdurins: 217. His social ease and courtesy: 220–22. Hears Vinteuil's sonata: 227; the "little phrase": 228–31, "the national anthem of their love": 238 (cf. 258–60, 288). Visits to Odette's house: 239–42. His penchant for comparing people to figures in the old masters: 243–5 (cf. 87, 105, 352–4, 357, 576; III 390). His nocturnal search for Odette: 249–52. The cattleyas; Odette becomes his mistress: 253–6. Progress of his love: 256–70. His enthusiasm for the Verdurins: 270–72. Dines at the Verdurins' with Forcheville: 273–88. The beginnings of his jealousy; he taps on the wrong window: 297–301. Odette lies to him: 302–7. He reads her letter to Forcheville: 307–8. Rejected by the Verdurins; his tirade against them: 310–15. Progress of his jealousy: 315–50. At Mme de Saint-Euverte's: 351–84; conversation with the Princesse des Laumes: 370–73; the little phrase again, reminding him of the early days of his love for Odette: 375–84. Abandons hope of happiness with Odette: 384–6; hopes for her death: 386 (cf. III 485). The anonymous letter: 387–90, and the suspicions it arouses in him: 390–93. Interrogates Odette: 393–403. Visits brothels: 405–6. Conversation with Mme Cottard on a bus: 407–10. Dreams of Odette and Forcheville: 411–14. "A woman who wasn't even my type": 415. Speaks to M of Balbec church: 417–18. His need for gingerbread: 436. Comes to fetch his daughter from the Champs-Elysées; his prestige and glamour in M's eyes: 440–42, 447–8. Meets M's mother in the Trois Quartiers: 449–50. His new persona as Odette's husband: 465–7. Norpois's remarks about the Swann *ménage*: 501–4. How the marriage came about: 504–8. His suspicions of M: 529–30. M becomes a regular visitor to his house: 542. His library: 548–9. His changed attitude to society: 552–63. His indifference to Odette; in love with another woman (Mme de Cambremer?): 563–6 (cf. 414, 575, II 946). His love for his daughter: 610. Bergotte's remarks about him: 615. Relations with Mme

Verdurin: 645–6. Has "a separate life of his own": 650. His
photograph of the Botticellian Odette: 664 (cf. III 202).
Persuades the Guermantes to buy Elstirs: II 519–20. Oriane
recalls her botanical expeditions with him: 536–7. Inculcates in
her a taste for Empire furniture: 539, 541. His researches into the
Templars: 596. M meets him at the Guermantes'; his changed
appearance; his illness; his Dreyfusism; his comment on the
Duke's "Velazquez"; has only three or four months to live:
600–20. At the Princesse de Guermantes's; said to have
quarrelled with the Prince: II 680, 697, 700–01, 728. His
grandmother, a Protestant married to a Jew, was the Duc de
Berry's mistress: 693. The Duc de Guermantes, supported by his
wife, deplores his Dreyfusism and his marriage — a double
betrayal of the Faubourg Saint-Germain: 702–5. His desire to
introduce his wife and daughter to Oriane before he dies: 705 (cf.
I 507–8; III 587–9). His face grotesquely changed by illness; his
Jewishness more pronounced: 715–16, 725. His preoccupation
with the Dreyfus Case: 723–4, 738–40; but nevertheless desires
to be buried with military honours: 739. Talks to M about
jealousy: 728–9. Concupiscent gaze at Mme de Surgis-le-Duc's
bosom: 730–31, 733. Reports to M his conversation with the
Prince de Guermantes: 731–8. Effect of his Dreyfusism on his
wife's social aspirations: 774. Casual allusion to his death: 899.
Vilified by Mme Verdurin: 1003–4. Charlus cites his views on
Balzac: 1084, 1086–7, 1093. His death in retrospect: III 197–200.
Allusion to the Tissot picture of Charles Haas, of whom there are
"some traces in the character of Swann": 199. Charlus's
reminiscences concerning him; madly attractive to women;
fought a duel with d'Osmond; had been the lover of Odette's
sister: 302–4. Recalled patronizingly by the Duc and Duchesse
de Guermantes in conversation with Gilberte: 592–5. How
mistaken he had been in pinning his hopes of survival on his
daughter: 604–5 (cf. II 610). Referred to in the Goncourt
pastiche: 730, 735–6. The many different Swanns: 950. How the
raw material of M's experience, and of his book, came from S:
953–5.

SWANN *père*. Stockbroker; close friend of M's grandfather; his
behaviour on the death of his wife ("often, but a little at a time");
his familiar gesture when faced with a perplexing problem: I

15–16. Recalled by M's mother apropos of his grand-daughter's marriage: III 674, 692.

SWANN, Mme. *See* Odette.

SWANN, Gilberte. *See* Gilberte.

TAORMINA, Princess of. Hears Morel play at the Verdurins': III 290.

TELEGRAPH-BOY. Protégé of a colleague of Brichot's, then of M. de Charlus, who finds him a post in the colonies: III 334–5.

THÉODORE. Choirboy and grocer's boy at Combray: I 60, 63. He and his sister show visitors the crypt of the church: 66, 114. His encyclopaedic knowledge of local affairs: 73–4. A scapegrace, but nevertheless helps Françoise to tend Aunt Léonie; the spirit of Saint-André-des-Champs: 165. Coachman to a friend of Charlus; his sexual misbehaviour; his sister is Mme Putbus's maid: III 310. Writes to M to congratulate him on his *Figaro* article; his surname is Sanilon: 604, 720. Gilberte's revelations about his escapades with the girls; becomes chemist at Méséglise: 712. His liaison with Legrandin: 719.

THEODOSIUS II. East European sovereign on a state visit to Paris: I 442, 449. His conversation with Norpois: 471, 495. Norpois's comments on his speech at the Elysée: 495–500. Charlus and Vaugoubert discuss his possible inversion: II 690. Return visit to Paris with Queen Eudoxia: III 247.

THIRION, M. Second husband of Mme de Villeparisis: II 303–4.

TICHE (Monsieur). *See* Elstir.

TOUREUIL, Judge. Presumably the senior judge from Caen, elsewhere referred to as Poncin (q.v.): II 958.

TOURS, Vicomtesse de (*née* Lamarzelle). At the Princesse d'Epinay's; remarked by the Duc de Guermantes: II 480.

TRANIA, Princesse de. Visits Odette at the time of her liaison with the Duc de Guermantes: III 1069–70.

TRESMES, Mme Dorothée de. Cousin of the Duc de Guermantes: II 594. Calls on the Duke, with her sister Mme de Plassac, with news of Amanien d'Osmond; her walking-stick: 597–8. She and her sister bring news of Amanien's death: 751.

TROMBERT, Mme. Regular visitor to Odette's *salon*: I 547; M's mother's joke at her expense: 555; her hats: 650.

USHER (or "barker") at the Princesse de Guermantes's. His adventure with the Duc de Châtellerault: II 657–8, 660–61.

VALCOURT, Mme Edith de. At the Verdurins'; excluded from Mme de Mortemart's musical evening: III 271–3.

VALET, M's father's. *See* Victor.

VALET, Uncle Adolphe's: I 81. Charlie Morel's father; his veneration for Uncle Adolphe's memory: II 272–5. Described to the Verdurins, at Charlie's request, as "intendant" in M's family: 939, 945. Charlie has inherited his conviction of Uncle Adolphe's grandeur: 1091–2.

VALLENÈRES, M. Archivist, occasional secretary to Mme de Villeparisis: II 193, 196–8; helps with the management of her estates: 220. A strong Nationalist and anti-Dreyfusard: 225, 244, 255–6. The "daughter of the house": 237. Explains the word "mentality" to M. de Guermantes: 243–4. His influence over Mme de Villeparisis: 255–6.

VARAMBON, Mme de. Lady-in-waiting to the Princesse de Parme. Her stupidity; insists that M is related to Admiral Jurien de la Gravière: II 516–17. Irritates the Princess: 566, 568. Mme de Guermantes's anecdote about her: III 1061–2.

VATRY, Colonel the Baron de. Tenant of M's Uncle Adolphe: II 1092.

VAUDÉMONT, Marquis Maurice de. One of two young noble-men who, with an actress and her lover, form an exclusive group at Balbec: I 731–3. Invites M to dinner: 1015. M and Charlus discuss him and his friends in the context of sexual inversion; the actress's lover an invert: III 310–11.

(*See* Actress from the Odéon.)

VAUGOUBERT, Marquis de. Ambassador of France at the court of King Theodosius; praised by Norpois: I 496–7, 499. Has the same tastes as Charlus: II 666. His mediocrity does not prevent him from being one of the best representatives of the French Government abroad: 667–8. Introduces M to his wife at the Princesse de Guermantes's: 669. Manifestations of his vice; conversation with Charlus: 688–90, 699. His excessive polite-ness: 699, 701. Further homosexual exchanges with Charlus: III 39. Forcibly retired from the service: 247–8. Loses his son in the war; his extreme grief: 775–6.

VAUGOUBERT, Mme de. Wife of the above. Her masculine air; her considerable intelligence: II 668–71. Brings about her husband's disgrace: III 247–8.

VÉLUDE, Vicomtesse de. Sister of the Comtesse de Montpeyroux (q.v.), nicknamed "Mignonne" on account of her stoutness: I I 448.

VERDURIN, M. The "little clan": I 205–6. His subordinate role vis-à-vis his wife: 208. M's grandfather knew his family: 217. His laugh and his pipe: 223–4, 234, 286. His opinion of Swann and Odette: 247–9, 272–3. His hostility to Swann: 289–90. Organizes a Mediterranean cruise for the "faithful": 406–7. Despised by Octave, who is a relative of his — "an old fellow in a frock coat": 944 (cf. II 900). At la Raspelière; his attitude towards the death of one of the "faithful": II 926, 928–31. Uses Saniette as a whipping-boy: 930 (cf. 961, 963 sqq., 1009). His irony at Brichot's expense: 932 (cf. 981–2). His enthusiasm for la Raspelière: 935–6. His ignorance of the hierarchy of social rank: 947 (cf. 973–4). Bullies Saniette: 965–8, 970, 990, 1006. His ineptitude with Charlus ("one of us"): 973–4. Pride in his intimacy with Cottard: 991–2. The evening of the concert organized by Charlus; further brutality to Saniette: III 228–9 (see also 1114–15). Abets his wife's despotic behaviour towards the "faithful". 230–31. Reaction to Princess Sherbatoff's death: 241. Takes Morel aside to warn him against Charlus: 313–14. His name is Gustave: 318 (cf. 733) His generosity to the sick and penurious Saniette: 329–32. His contradictory nature: 332. Eulogised in the Goncourt diary; art critic in his younger days and author of a book on Whistler: 728–30; addressed by his wife as "Auguste": 733. Praises Morel's satires: 791. Dies soon after Cottard; mourned by Elstir, who saw him as the man who had had "the truest vision" of his painting: 794.

VERDURIN, Mme. "Mistress" of the "little clan": I 205–8. Reactions to music: 206, 224–5, 231–2. Dislocates her jaw from laughing so much: 206. Her new, less dangerous way of showing her hilarity: 223–4. Distressing effect on her of the discovery of Swann's grand connections: 236–7 (cf. 273, 282–4). Attitude to Swann and Odette: 248–9, 271. Gives a dinner-party attended by Swann, Odette, Forcheville, Brichot and others: 274–89. Her hostility to Swann: 289–90; breaks with him: 310–15. Excursions with Odette: 318–22. Her strange behaviour with Odette (Les Filles de marbre): 392–3. Mediterranean cruise with Odette and the "faithful": 406–9. Her relations with Odette after her

marriage to Swann; their rival *salons*; entertains the idea of
"Society" as her final objective: 645–52. Instals electricity in her
new house: 653. M "makes a conquest" of her: 654. M
unintentionally pursues her in the street: 767. Her latent
bourgeois anti-semitism awakened by the Dreyfus Case [this is
entirely inconsistent with what follows]: II 260. An extreme
Dreyfusard and anti-clerical: 605. Successful development of her
salon; the Russian Ballet: 770 (cf. III 236–8). The little clan an
active centre of Dreyfusism: 771, 774 (cf. 914–15). Rents la
Raspelière from the Cambremers: 779. Her "Wednesdays":
884–6. Compels Brichot to break with his laundress: 897–8.
Evolution of her *salon* towards Society; a Temple of Music:
898–900. Her recruits to the little clan — Ski (replacement for
Elstir) and Princess Sherbatoff (the ideal member of the
"faithful"): 902–10. Ambivalent attitude to the Cambremers;
plays down her Dreyfusism: 913–16 (cf. III 236–7). Her attitude
to the death of one of the faithful: 925–6, 929–30. Her delight in
la Raspelière: 934–5. Physical changes produced in her by years
of listening to music: 936 (cf. III 230, 250). Hatred of family life;
anecdote about M's great-grandfather: 940. The changes she has
made at la Raspelière: 948–9. Impressed by Mme Molé, on whom
she bestows a nobiliary particle: 966–7. Disparages Elstir and
eulogises Ski: 970–73. Shows M Elstir's flowers: 974–5.
Disparages Brichot: 980–83 and Saniette: 983. Her new
technique for showing her amusement: 987–8 (cf. I 223–4).
Attempts to annex Charlus to the little clan; suppresses her
outraged anti-clericalism: 989. Praises Cottard: 995. Her first
skirmish with Charlus: 999–1001. Her advances to M; disparages
the Cambremers and Féterne; vilifies Swann: 1001–6. Jeers at
Saniette: 1006, then coaxes him to return: 1007, 1009. Her
assiduity as a hostess; excursions with her guests; knows the
neighbourhood better than the Cambremers: 1030–31. Her
Monday tea-parties: 1032–3. Visited by M and Albertine:
1034–6. Charlus becomes for her "the faithfullest of the
faithful"; her tolerance of his relations with Morel: 1077–9.
Deterioration of her relations with the Cambremers: 1124–5.
Compels Brichot to forswear his passion for Mme de Cambremer: 1128. M goes to a musical party organised by Charlus at her
new house in the Quai Conti; Brichot describes to him her

former *salon* in the Rue Montalivet: III 197, 201–2. Infuriated by Charlus's dictatorial attitude, determines to separate him from Morel: 229–34. Social development of her *salon*; influence of the Dreyfus Case; her genuine love of art; the Russian Ballet: 235–8 (cf. II 770). Her indifference to the death of Princess Sherbatoff: 240–41. Takes rhino-gomerol to counteract the effects of Vinteuil's music: 242–3. Rudeness of Charlus's guests to her, apart from the Queen of Naples: 246–9, 267–75. How she listens to the music: 250, 252–3. Enraged by Charlus's insolence: 275–81. Persuades Brichot to co-operate in her plan of revenge: 282–4. Her slanderous attack on Charlus convinces Morel: 314–21. Humiliated by the Queen of Naples: 325–7. Supports her husband's generosity to Saniette: 329–31. Wanted Albertine to meet her nephew Octave: 629–30. Her *salon* described in the Goncourt pastiche; Fromentin's "Madeleine": 728–36. One of the queens of war-time Paris: 743. Visits Venice during the war: 746. Thoroughly at home with the Faubourg Saint-Germain; no longer dreads "bores"; constant mention of G.H.Q.: 749–51. Overtures to Odette: 753. Her telephonings, her receptions: 754–5. Her aversion to Charlus: 787–9. Tries to persuade the faithful not to join up: 793. Her life little changed by the war; her *croissants* and the sinking of the *Lusitania*: 796–7. Her relations with Brichot; ridicules his articles: 816–20. After the war, and M. Verdurin's death, marries first the Duc de Duras and then the Prince de Guermantes: 998–9. At her *matinée*; her false teeth and monocle; still as indefatigable as ever: 1033. Reaction to Rachel's recital: 1051–2.

VICTOR. Butler to M's family (sometimes referred to as valet). Peppers his conversation with the latest witticisms: II 16. His cynical view of politicians: 22. Purloins writing-paper from M's bedroom: 23 (cf. 332). A Dreyfusard: 306–7. Quarrels with Françoise: III 121. His mispronunciation of *pissotière* (Charlus's yellow trousers): 188–9 (cf. 772). Teases Françoise by pretending to read unpleasant news in the newspaper: 476. His familiarity with the nicknames of sovereigns: 750. Terrifies Françoise during the war with tales of disasters and atrocities: 770, 871–7, 880.

VILLEBON, Mme de. A Courvoisier and stickler for social distinctions: II 459–60.

VILLEMANDOIS, Marquis de. Asks to be introduced to M at the Princesse de Guermantes's *matinée*, having totally forgotten their old feud: III 1011–12.

VILLEMUR, Mme de. Introduced to the painter Detaille at the Princesse de Guermantes's: II 658–9.

VILLEPARISIS, Marquise de, *née* Mlle de Bouillon, aunt of the Duc and Duchesse de Guermantes. Visited by M's grandmother, a friend from convent days: I 21 (cf. 112). Likened by Odette to a "lavatory attendant": 266. Allusion to her by Norpois: 501. Allusion by Swann to her liaison with Norpois: 606. At the Grand Hotel, Balbec; her entourage; ridiculed by the barrister and his friends: 728–30. Pointed out to M's grandmother; "the fiction of a mutual incognito": 735–8. Their accidental meeting and renewed friendship; her kindness to M and his grandmother: 746–51. Introduces them to the Princesse de Luxembourg: 751–3. Her knowledge of the movements of M's father: 753–4 (cf. II 187–8). Takes M and his grandmother for drives; her aristocratic erudition, "liberal" views, literary anecdotes, acquaintance with the great: 757–80. Introduces her great-nephew Saint-Loup: 785–6. Introduces her nephew Charlus: 809–10. A Guermantes! — transformed in M's eyes: 810 (cf. 1026–8 and III 296–7). Tea with Charlus in her room at the hotel; critical of Mme de Sévigné: 815–16, 818–21 (cf. 749). Complains about diabolo: 992. Neighbour of M's family in Paris: II 10, 29. M. de Norpois's regular visits; he speaks of her in glowing terms to M's father: 150–51. Her "School of Wit": 152. Her intimacy with Norpois: 187–8, 226–8. Her "at home": 187–293. Vicissitudes of her social situation; her *salon*; her *Memoirs*: 187–200. Her rivalry with the three Parcae: 200–07. Her flower painting: 193, 208, 219–22, 283–4. Her *grande dame* act with Bloch: 256–7. Receives Mme Swann: 260. Her relations with her nephew Charlus: 276–8. Alarmed by his interest in M: 293. Origin of the Villeparisis name explained by Charlus: 303–4. Gives a reception at which M arrives late; invites him to dinner: 384, 388–9. Influenced by the Guermantes family genie: 457, 466–7. Discussed by Oriane; the horrors of her dinner-table; her morals; known as "aunt Madeleine": 523–6. Oriane ridicules the idea of her marrying Norpois: 549–50 (cf. 1177–8). Praised by the Turkish Ambassadress: 560–61. Charlus calls on her at an unusual hour: 624–6. M talks to her on the little train, to the disgruntlement of Princess Sherbatoff: 1079–80. Premature allusion to her death: III 296. Her true social situation: 296–7 (cf. II 187–93; I 810). In Venice with M. de Norpois in old age: 644–9 (cf. 1116–19). Had been the ruin of Mme Sazerat's father: 648–9 (cf. 610). Dies in isolation: 788, survived by Norpois: 807.

VINTEUIL. Musician, former piano-teacher to M's grandmother's sisters; living in retirement at Montjouvain, near Combray: I 26. His prudishness and modesty; his passion for his daughter: 121–3. Pain which she causes him: 160–62. Meets Swann: 162–3. His death; his compositions: 174–5. His daughter's sacrilegious gesture: 175–8. His sonata played at the Verdurins': 224–34. The "little phrase" becomes the "national anthem" of Swann's love for Odette: 238–9, 258–9, 287–8. Swann hears the sonata again at Mme de Saint-Euverte's, and it reminds him of his lost happiness: 375–83. Odette plays the little phrase to M; M's reflections on the work, Swann's comments on it: 570–75. Vinteuil the pianist: II 43. His extraordinary prestige — "the greatest of contemporary composers": 899. M mentions his name to Albertine: II 51–2. M plays his sonata; reflections on artistic creation; Vinteuil and Wagner: III 154–8. Effect of his music on Mme Verdurin: 242–3. His septet played at the Verdurins': 250–66. His work transcribed by his daughter's friend: 263–6. Albertine plays his music on the pianola: 379–83. "Expressing the inexpressible": 380–82, 388. The little phrase and Albertine: 570–71.

VINTEUIL, Mlle. Daughter of the above. Her boyish appearance: I 122–3. Her bad reputation; causes her father unhappiness: 160–2. Scene of sadism with her friend at Montjouvain; profanes her father's memory: 173–80. Gilberte's disapproval of her: 577–8. Shattering revelation of Albertine's intimacy with her and her friend: II 1152–68. She and her friend expected at the Verdurins' (in fact they fail to appear): III 223–5. M interrogates Mme Verdurin and Morel about her: 243. Her penitence and veneration for her father; her sadism merely a pretence of wickedness: 263–4. M interrogates Albertine, who denies being on terms of intimacy with her and her friend: 388, 341–2 (cf. 403). The truth concerning her relations with Albertine, according to Andrée: 628–9.

VINTEUIL, Friend of Mlle. Comes to live at Montjouvain; her bad reputation; Vinteuil regards her as "a superior woman", with great musical gifts: I 160-61. Her part in the scene at Montjouvain: 175-80. Albertine reveals that she had been a mother or a sister to her: 1152-3, 1156-60, 1167-8. Expected at the Verdurins': III 223-5, 243. Her patient and dedicated labour transcribing Vinteuil's works: 263-7. Albertine denies having been more or less brought up by her: 341-2. Andrée's version of the story: 628-9.

VIRADOBETSKI. *See* Ski.

VIRELEF, Mme de. Invites the Guermantes to the Opéra with Gilberte: III 591.

VLADIMIR, Grand Duke. His delighted amusement at the inundation of Mme d'Arpajon: II 681-2.

VON, Prince. *See* Faffenheim.

WAITERS at the "Cherry Orchard". Twin brothers resembling tomatoes; Nissim Bernard's relations with them: II 883-4.

WAITERS in the hotel at Doncières; their breathless speed; the "reserve of cherubim and seraphim": II 97-8.

WAITERS in the restaurant at Rivebelle; their gyrations round the "astral tables": I 867-9; one of them fascinates Albertine: II 1048-9; two of them, transferred to the Grand Hotel, Balbec, whom M fails to recognize: 1021-2.

WAITERS in Aimé's restaurant in Paris, like superannuated actors: II 168, 171.

WAITERS in the restaurant in Venice: III 644-5.

WARWICK, Lady. English friend of Mme de Guermantes: III 36.

YOURBELETIEFF, Princess. Sponsor of the *Ballets russes*; appears at the theatre in the company of Mme Verdurin: II 770; III 238.

WOMAN ("beautiful young") with the flashing eyes who seems to recognize Albertine and strikes up a Gomorrhan relationship with Bloch's cousin: II 880-81.

WOMAN (young Austrian) who attracts M in Venice because of her resemblance to Albertine: III 663-5.

INDEX OF PERSONS

ARNAULD, Antoine, Jansenist theologian (1612–94): III 692.

AROUET. *See* Voltaire.

ARVÈDE BARINE (Mme Charles Vincens), French writer (1840–1908). Saint-Loup reads a book of hers on a train, and mistakes the author's sex and nationality: I 928.

ASSURBANIPAL, King of Assyria 668–626 BC: I 516.

AUBER, Esprit, French composer (1782–1871). References to his operettas, *Les Diamants de la Couronne, Le Domino noir* and *Fra Diavolo:* I 79; II 465–6, 509–10; III 890.

AUDIFFRET-PASQUIER, Duc d', French politician (1823–1905): I 22.

AUGIER, Emile, French playwright (1820–89): I 832; II 213; Oriane de Guermantes ascribes to him a line of Musset's: 235.

AUGUSTUS III of Poland, Elector of Saxony (1696–1763): III 821.

AUMALE, Henri d'Orléans, Duc d', French general and historian, fourth son of Louis-Philippe (1822–97). Cottard's euphemism for lavatory: I 286. M. Bloch *père* referred to as his double: 828. The Guermantes visit him at Chantilly: II 29 (cf. 608–9). In a box at the Opéra: 35; frequents Mme de Villeparisis's *salon*: 198. He and Princesse Mathilde brought together by Oriane: 486, 538. His liaison with Mme de Clinchamp: 1129.

AVENEL, Vicomte Georges d', French historian and economist (1855–1939): II 219.

BACH, Johann Sebastian, German composer (1685–1750). Conversation of the inhabitants of Françoise's native village has the "unshakeable solidity" of a Bach fugue: II 754. Charlus's laugh and Bach's "small high" trumpets: 974. Morel plays a Bach air and variations on a walk with the Verdurins: 1064. A "sublime aria" by Bach: III 650.

BAGARD, César, sculptor and cabinet-maker from Nancy (1639–1709). Executed the panelling in the apartments of Mme de Villeparisis's father in the Hotel de Bouillon: I 779, and in Charlus's apartments: II 583.

BAKST, Léon, Russian painter and designer (1866–1924). His decors for the *Ballets russes:* I 1009; II 770; III 376. Andrée disapproves of his decoration of the Marquis de Polignac's house: 752.

BALTHY, music-hall singer (1869–1925), whom Mme de Guer-

mantes hesitates to cultivate, though finding her "adorable": III
1043.

BALZAC, Honoré de, French novelist (1799–1850). His "tigers"
now "grooms": I 352. Disparaged by Mme de Villeparisis: 764,
776, 781. Parodied by Saint-Loup: 805. "Adored" by the Duc de
Guermantes, who attributes to him a novel by Dumas, *Les
Mohicans de Paris*: II 510. Charlus "knows him by heart": 510.
Discussed by Charlus with Victurnien Surgis-le-Duc, who has
the same Christian name as d'Esgrignon in *Le Cabinet des
Antiques*: 723–5. Charlus reads him in the little train: 1072–3.
The Baron's favourite volumes of *La Comédie humaine*: 1084.
Discussed by Charlus and Brichot: 1084–8. The Princesse de
Cadignan: 1089–90, 1092–3. The Cambremers as Balzac charac-
ters: 1127. Clothes of his heroines: III 26 (cf. II 1089–90).
Retrospective unity of the *Comédie humaine*: 157–8. The
"spoken newspaper of Paris": 218. Construction of his novellas:
510. The marriage of Mlle d'Oloron and the young Cambremer a
"marriage from the end of a Balzac novel": 673. Gilberte reads
La Fille aux yeux d'or: 725. His genius, in spite of his vulgarity:
740.

BARBEDIENNE, Ferdinand, bronze founder (1810–92): II 949;
III 174.

BARBEY D'AUREVILLY, French novelist (1808–89): I 800;
"key-phrases" in his work: III 382.

BARRÈRE, Camille, French diplomat, Ambassador in Rome from
1897 to 1924: III 651.

BARRÈS, Maurice, French writer (1862–1923): I 470. Swann
revises his opinion of his work in the light of the Dreyfus Case,
comparing him unfavourably to Clemenceau: II 605. His
denunciation of parliamentary corruption: III 301. His views on
art and the nation: 822–3, 917.

BARRY, Mme du, mistress and favourite of Louis XV (1743–93):
III 286, 375, 571, 731.

BARTOLOMMEO, Fra, Florentine painter (1469–1517). Mme
Blatin resembles his portrait of Savonarola: I 576.

BAUDELAIRE, Charles, French poet (1821–67). Allusion to his
poem *L'Imprévu* — the epithet "delicious" applied to the sound
of the trumpet: I 194. Allusions to poems about the sea: 724, 746,
760. The antithesis of the kind of writer approved of by Mme de

Villeparisis and her like: 763, 781, and of Mme de Guermantes's type of mind: 11 522, 592 (cf. 111 27). Mme de Cambremer quotes a line from *L'Albatros*: 842. Denounced by Brichot: 988. Quotation from *Les Fleurs du Mal* XLI ("like a dulcimer"): 1017. Quoted by M on murder: 111 386. Allusion to *La Lune offensée* — the "yellow and metallic" moon: 414. Saint-Loup quotes from *Le Balcon*: 782. M finds in his work reminiscences, transposed sensations, which for him are the foundation of art; quotations from *La Chevelure* and *Parfum exotique*: 959.

BEETHOVEN, Ludwig van (1770–1827). The Ninth Symphony one of Mme Verdurin's "supreme masterpieces": 1 278. The Moonlight Sonata in the Bois: 310, 313. The late quartets: 572 (cf. 806; 11 662, 987, 1042). Allusion to one of the Razumovsky quartets by Mme de Guermantes: 11 542. The Pastoral Symphony played in Charlus's house: 584. Charlus's ogling glances at Jupien likened to Beethoven's "questioning phrases": 627. Mme de Citri finds him "a bore": 713. Mme de Cambremer inhales the sea air like the prisoners in *Fidelio*: 846. Invoked by Brichot in connection with Dechambre's death: 927. Charlus on the piano transcription of Quartet No. 15: 1042–3. The "Bonn Master": 111 314–15. His "terrible ravaged face": 943. The Kreutzer Sonata played at the Princesse de Guermantes's *matinée*: 1080.

BELLINI, Gentile, Venetian painter (1429–1507). Bloch resembles his portrait of the Sultan Mahomet 11: i 105 (cf. 386). His painting of the portico of St Mark's: 181.

BELLINI, Giovanni, Venetian painter (c. 1430–1516). The "little band" play upon their vocal instruments "with all the application and ardour of Bellini's angel musicians": 1 969–70. Vinteuil's music evokes "a grave and gentle Bellini seraph strumming a theorbo": 111 262.

BENOIS, Alexander, Russian painter and ballet designer (1870–1960): 11 770; 111 376.

BERGSON, Henri, French philosopher (1859–1941). On the effect of soporific drugs on the memory: 11 1016–17.

BERLIOZ, Hector, French composer (1803–69). The *Childhood of Christ*: 11 1141–2; as a writer: 111 218.

BERNARD, Samuel, French financier (1651–1739): 1 802; 11 271.

BERNARDIN DE SAINT-PIERRE, French writer, author of *Paul et Virginie* (1737–1814). Cited by Charlus: III 279.

BERNHARDI, General Friedrich von, German military historian (1849–1930): III 112.

BERNHARDT, Sarah, French actress (1844–1923): I 80, 219; II 1105, 1120; III 235, 854–5, 1004.

BERRY, Duc de, grandson of Louis XIV (1686–1714). Cited by Saint-Simon as living his life among his lackeys: III 860.

BERRY, Duc de, son of Charles X (1778–1820): II 557. Swann's grandmother said to have been his mistress, hence the legend (subscribed to by the Prince de Guermantes) that Swann was his natural grandson: II 600, 693.

BEYLE, Henri. *See* Stendhal.

BIDOU, Henry, French writer, military commentator of *Le Journal des Débats* during World War I: III 1029.

BILLOT, General, French Minister of War between 1896 and 1898: II 307.

BING, Siegfried. Franco-German art collector, pioneer of Art Nouveau (1838–1905): II 573.

BISMARCK, Prince Otto von (1815–98). Rates Norpois's intelligence highly: I 471, 510 (cf. II 228, 231). Struck by the Prince de Borodino's resemblance to Napoleon III: II 130.

BIZET, Georges, French composer (1838–75). Disliked by Morel: III 291.

BLACAS, Duc de, Restoration politician (1771–1839). Contrasted by Mme de Villeparisis with Chateaubriand: I 775–6.

BLANCHE DE CASTILLE, wife of Louis VIII and mother of St Louis (1188–1252). Subject of one of Brichot's rodomontades: I 275.

BOIELDIEU, François-Adrien, French composer (1775–1834): I 788; II 509.

BOIGNE, Mme de (1781–1866). Friend of Sainte-Beuve, famous for her *salon* and for her *Memoirs*: II 431; III 581.

BOILEAU-Despréaux, Nicolas, French poet and critic (1636–1711):I 470; quotation from *L'Art poétique* in Gisèle's essay: 973.

BOISDEFFRE, General de, French Army Chief of Staff 1893–98: II 105, 249; III 803.

BOISSIER, Gaston, antiquarian and permanent secretary of the *Académie Française* (1823–1908): II 1091; III 335.

BONAVENTURE, Saint (1221–74). Quoted by Charlus: II 578.

BORELLI, Vicomte de, society poet of the late 19th century: I 263; II 219, 257; III 83.

BORNIER, Vicomte Henri de, French writer, author of *La Fille de Roland* (1825–1901): II 507–9.

BORODIN, Alexander, Russian composer (1833–87). Allusion to the Polovstian Dances from *Prince Igor*: III 238. Albertine plays *In the Steppes of Central Asia* on the pianola: 388.

BOSSUET Jacques-Bénigne, French prelate, writer and orator (1627–1704): I 313; III 302, 893.

BOTHA, General (1862–1919). Boer leader, quoted by Prince Von on the subject of English ineptitude: II 547, 569, 588.

BOTTICELLI (Sandro di Mariano), Italian painter (c. 1445–1510). Odette's resemblance to the figure of Zipporah in "The Life of Moses" in the Sistine Chapel: I 243–6, 254, 260; and to the women in some of his other paintings, including the "Madonna with the Pomegranate": 306; the Primavera, La Vanna, and the Venus: 341; the Virgin in the "Magnificat": 665.

BOUCHARD, Charles, French physician (1837–1915): II 991, 1086.

BOUCHER, François, French painter (1703–70): I 812; II 9; III 94, 200.

BOUFFE DE SAINT-BLAISE, French obstetrician: II 992.

BOUFFLERS, Duc de, Marshal of France (1644–1711). One of Charlus's list of alleged 17th-century inverts: III 306.

BOULLE, André-Charles, French cabinet-maker (1642–1732). The Guermantes' "marvellous Boulle furniture": II 572.

BOURGOGNE, Duc de, grandson of Louis XIV and father of Louis XV (1682–1712): II 453, 984.

BOUTROUX, Émile, French philosopher (1845–1921). Quoted by the Norwegian philosopher: II 962, 1016–17.

BRESSANT, 19th-century French actor. Swann adopts his hair-style: I 15.

BREUGHEL the Elder, Peter, Flemish painter (c. 1520–69). Soldiers in the streets of Doncières resemble Breughel peasants: II 97.

BRISSAC, Henri-Albert de Cossé, Duc de, brother-in-law of Saint-Simon (1644–99). One of Charlus's 17th-century inverts: III 306.

BROGLIE, Victor-Claude, Prince de (1757–94). Posthumous connection with Mme de Staël: III 1014.

BROGLIE, Duc Victor de (son of the above), French statesman (1785–1870): I 22; II 198; his daughter marries the Comte d'Haussonville 593; he himself had married the daughter of Mme de Staël: III 1014.

BROGLIE, Duc Albert de (son of the above), French statesman and historian (1821–1901). Author of *Le Secret du Roi*: III 553.

BROGLIE, Duchesse de, daughter of Mme de Staël and wife of Duc Victor de B; her letters: II 284, 510–11, 514; her daughter and son-in-law: III 1014.

BRONZINO, Angiolo, Florentine painter (1503–63). Morel "so beautiful", according to Charlus, "he looks like a sort of Bronzino": III 215.

BRUANT, Aristide, Montmartre *chansonnier* (1851–1925): III 247.

BRUNETIÈRE, Ferdinand, French literary critic, Professor at the Sorbonne (1849–1906): II 258, 847; III 929.

BRUNSWICK, Duke of, German prince and soldier (1624–1705). Another of Charlus's alleged inverts of the 17th century: III 306.

CAILLAUX, Joseph, French politican (1863–1944). His foreign policy "severely trounced" in the *Echo de Paris*: II 779. His trial for treason: III 808.

CALLOT, dress designer. Approved of by Elstir: I 961, and by Mme de Guermantes: III 36.

CAPET, Lucien, French violinist (1873–1928): III 289.

CAPUS, Alfred, French dramatist (1858–1922). Reference to his *La Châtelaine*: II 1122.

CARNOT, Lazare, mathematician and revolutionary, "the organiser of victory" (1753–1823): II 608.

CARNOT, Sadi, President of the French Republic from 1887 until his assassination in 1894: I 737; II 608.

CARO, Elme Marie, French philosopher (1826–87): II 847.

CARPACCIO, Vittore, Venetian painter (1450–1525). Tender sweetness in pomp and joy expressed in certain of his paintings: I 194. San Giorgio degli Schiavoni: 475 (cf. III 656). Elstir on his paintings of regattas on the Grand Canal: 959–60 (cf. III 375). "Speaking likenesses" of his friends or patrons: II 436. His reliquaries: 557. His courtesans: III 384. M and his mother admire his pictures in Venice; his *St Ursula* and *The Patriarch of Grado* (Albertine's Fortuny cloak): 661–2. War-time Paris as exotic as his Venice: 786.

CARRIÈRE, Eugène, French painter (1849–1906). Admired by Saint-Loup (portrait of his Aunt Oriane at Guermantes): I 810 (cf. II 572).

CARVALHO, Mlle, French opera singer (1827–95): II 483.

CASTELLANE, Mme de, Mme de Villeparisis's Aunt Cordelia (*née* Greffulhe). Admired by Chateaubriand, married Colonel (later Marshal) Comte Boniface de Castellane: II 284.

CAVAIGNAC, Jacques Godefroy, French politican, extreme anti-Dreyfusard, twice Minister of War during the Dreyfus Case (1853–1905): II 249.

CELLINI, Benvenuto, Italian sculptor and metalsmith (1500–71). A Saint-Euverte footman resembles his statue of an armed watchman: I 354; his *Perseus*: 486.

CHABRIER, Emmanuel, French composer (1841–94). Quoted by Mme Verdurin: III 318.

CHAIX D'EST-ANGE, French lawyer and politician (1800–76): II 615.

CHAMBORD, Comte de, Pretender to the throne of France under the name Henri V (1820–83): II 296; 1143; III 28 (allusion to Frohsdorf, where he lived in exile from 1841 until his death).

CHAMISSO, German writer (1781–1838), author of *Peter Schlemihls wundersame Geschichte*: I 830.

CHAPLIN, Charles Josuah, French society portrait-painter (1825–91): III 742.

CHARCOT, Dr Jean Martin, French neurologist (1825–93): II 311, 910, 991, 1123.

CHARDIN, Jean-Baptiste, French painter (1699–1779): I 698. Elstir and Chardin: II 435–6 (cf. III 1102); III 640.

CHARLES VI, King of France (1368–1422): I 64.

CHARLES X, King of France (1757–1836): II 732, 1143; III 32.

CHARTRES, Duc de, grandson of Louis-Philippe and younger brother of the Comte de Paris (1840–1910). Friend of Swann: I 338, 559 (cf. II 702, 704). His attitude to the Dreyfus Case: II 250. M. de Bréauté lunches with him: 447. Charlus his cousin: 1143.

CHATEAUBRIAND, François-René de, French writer and statesman (1768–1848). His genius; "marvellous pages of Chateaubriand": I 518–19; 560. Bergotte's opinion of him: 598. Mme de Villeparisis's reminiscences of him: 763, 775. Quoted by M: 775. His ready-made speech on moonlight: 776 (cf. III 414). *Chez* Mme Récamier at L'Abbaye-aux-Bois: II 906. Attacked by Brichot, defended by Charlus: 1085–6. Local legends related in the *Mémoires d'Outre-tombe*: III 28. His writings "insufficiently confidential" (Sainte-Beuve quoted by Brichot): 334. The moon in Chateaubriand: 414. M. de Guermantes finds traces of his "antiquated prose" in M's *Figaro* article: 602. Reflections on the *Mémoires d'Outre-tombe*; examples of involuntary memory such as will inspire M's own book: 749, 958–9.

CHÂTELET, Mme du, friend and patroness of Voltaire (1706–49): II 906.

CHERBULIEZ, Victor, French novelist and Academician (1829–99). Norpois compares him favourably to Bergotte: II 228.

CHEVREUSE, Marie de Rohan, Duchesse de (1600–79), formerly married to the Connétable de Luynes: II 206.

CHEVREUSE, Charles-Honoré d'Albert, Duc de (1646–1712), son of the Duc de Luynes and grandson of the Connétable: II 452 (cf. 561).

CHOISEUL, Duchesse de. *See* Praslin.

CHOPIN, Frédéric, Polish composer (1810–49). A prelude and a polonaise played at Mme de Saint-Euverte's; Mme de Cambremer's delight in his "long, sinuous" phrases: I 361, 365 (cf. 849). Once played in Mme de Villeparisis's father's château: 761. Despised by Mme de Cambremer-Legrandin, and worshipped by her mother-in-law: II 842–6, 851, 977, 1008. Charlus missed hearing him play: 1042.

CLAPISSON, Louis, French composer (1808–66): I 328.

CLAUDEL, Paul, French poet and diplomat (1868–1955): I 470, 824; II 338.

CLAUSEWITZ, General Karl von, German military theorist (1780–1831): III 819.

CLEMENCEAU, Georges, French statesman (1841–1929): II 254, 307; praised by Swann: 605; his Dreyfusism unknown to the younger generation: III 1001.

CLÉMENTINE, Princesse, daughter of Louis-Philippe, mother of

Ferdinand of Bulgaria by her marriage to the Duke of Saxe-Coburg-Gotha: 11 250.

CLERMONT-TONNERRE, Duchesse Émilie de. Author of a book on country food: 11 523, 1043.

COMBES, Emile, French politician (1835–1921) who introduced anti-clerical laws when Prime Minister between 1902 and 1905: 111 819.

CONDÉ, Louis II, Prince de (known as "the Great") (1621–86): 11 590, 989. Charlus and Brichot on his alleged homosexuality: 111 306–7.

CONSTANTINE, King of Greece 1913–22, known familiarly as "Tino": 111 750, 795, 813, 875.

CONTI, Louis-Armand de Bourbon, Prince de, nephew of the Great Condé (1661–1685). His marriage to a bastard daughter of Louis XIV (Mlle de Blois) cited in connection with the marriage of Mlle d'Oloron and the young Cambremer: 111 682.

CONTI, François-Louis de Bourbon, Prince de, brother of the above (1664–1709). Echoes of Saint-Simon's portrait of him in Charlus's treatment of his menservants: 11 574. An invert?: 111 307. Saint-Simon praises his "marvellous intelligence", and in particular his knowledge of genealogy: 1006–7.

COPPÉE, François, French poet (1842–1908): 11 524.

COQUELIN, Constant, French actor (1841–1909) 1 80. Seen in the Bois de Boulogne: 454. His mulatto friend: 577. M. Bloch senior's irony at his expense: 833. Plays beginners' roles in gala performances: 11 1120. His view of Molière's Le Misanthrope: 111 1030.

CORNEILLE, Pierre, French dramatist (1606–84). Quotation from Mort de Pompée: 1 29. Quotation from Polyeucte, attributed by Bloch to Voltaire: 940. Françoise uses the word ennui in the Cornelian sense: 11 14. Political dissertations in his tragedies: 199. His "intermittent, restrained" romanticism: 570.

CORNÉLY, Jean-Joseph, French journalist (1845–1907). Although a monarchist, campaigned for the revision of the Dreyfus trial: 11 605.

COROT, Jean-Baptiste-Camille, French painter (1796–1875). Swann owns one of his paintings: 1 23, 27.

COUTURE, Thomas, French painter (1815–79). Allusion to his picture *Les Romains de la Décadence*: III 289.

COYSEVOX, Antoine, French sculptor (1640–1720): II 202.

CRÉBILLON *fils*, licentious novelist (1707–77): II 283.

DAGNAN-BOUVERET, academic French painter (1852–1929) admired by Norpois: II 229.

DANTE (Dante Alighieri), Italian poet (1265–1321). Strainings and contortions of water-lilies in the Vivonne reminiscent of the "peculiar torments" of the damned in the *Inferno*: I 184–5. The Verdurins and their "little clan" the "nethermost circle of Dante" (Swann): 313. Reading-room of the Grand Hotel alternately the *Paradiso* and the *Inferno*: 714; II 207; III 825.

DARIUS, King of Persia: I 545, 830; II 195; III 40.

DARU, Pierre Bruno, Quartermaster-General of Napoleon's Grand Army and later Academician (1767–1829): I 763.

DARWIN, Charles, British scientist (1809–82): II 369, 537, 653; III 806.

DAUDET, Alphonse, French writer (1840–97) Mention of *Tartarin de Tarascon*: III 195.

DAUDET, Léon, French journalist and novelist, son of the above (1867–1942): I 470; III 301, 844. (See the dedication to *The Guermantes Way*.)

DAUDET, Mme Léon. *See* Pampille.

DAVID, Jacques-Louis, French painter (1748–1825): III 929, 1079.

DAVIOUD, Gabriel (1823–81), architect of the Trocadéro: III 164.

DEBUSSY, Claude, French composer (1862–1918). Mme de Cambremer's enthusiasm for *Pelléas*: II 840–45 (cf. 851, 976, 986). Debussy and Wagner: 843–4. On the "wrong" side in the Dreyfus Case: 915. Morel plays Meyerbeer for Debussy: 986. M. de Chevregny finds *Pelléas* trivial: 1122. The street-criers' cadences remind M of *Pelléas*: III 112–13.

DECAMPS, Alexandre-Gabriel, French orientalist painter (1803–60). Bloch as exotic-looking as a Jew in a Decamps painting: II 194. War-time Paris reminds Charlus of the Orient of Decamps: III 837.

DECAZES, Duc, minister and favourite of Louis XVIII. Mme de Villeparisis's grandfather reluctant to invite him to a ball: II 196.

DEFFAND, Mme du (1697–1780). Famous for her *salon*: I 640.

DEGAS, Edgar, French painter (1834–1917). Mme de Cambremer's enthusiasm for him: II 840. His admiration for Poussin: 841. Nissim Bernard's type of "dancer" still lacks a Degas: 873–4.

DELACROIX, Eugène, French painter (1798–1863). War-time Paris reminds Charlus of his oriental scenes: III 837. Loathed by Mme de Guermantes: 1080.

DELAROCHE, Paul, French painter (1797–1856). Reference by M. de Guermantes to his *Princes in the Tower*: II 519.

DELAUNAY, Comédie-Française actor (1826–1903): I 80; III 784.

DELCASSÉ, Théophile, French statesman, architect of the *entente cordiale* (1852–1923): III 368.

DELTOUR, Nicolas-Felix, Inspector-General of Secondary Education, author of *Principles of Style and Compositio*: (1822–1904). Recommended by Andrée as an authority to quote in exams: I 976.

DERBY, Lord (Edward Henry Smith Stanley), British statesman (1826–93). Cited on the Irish question: II 182–3.

DÉROULÈDE, Paul, ultra-nationalist French politician and poet (1846–1914): III 823.

DESCARTES, René, French philosopher (1596–1650): III 353 (cf. I 796).

DESCHANEL, Paul, French statesman (1855–1922): I 470; II 219, 772; III 790.

DESHOULIÈRES, Mme, French poetess (1638–94): II 510.

DESJARDINS, Paul, French critic and philosopher (1859–1940). Quoted by Legrandin: I 130.

DETAILLE, Edouard, painter of military scenes (1848–1912): II 446, 658–9.

DETHOMAS, Maxime, French painter (1867–1929). His "superb studies" of Venice: III 640.

DIAGHILEV, Serge (1872–1929). Impresario of the Russian Ballet: II 770, 942.

DIANE DE POITIERS, favourite of Henri II: II 633.

DIANTI, Laura, Italian Renaissance beauty, second wife of Alfonso d'Este, Duke of Ferrara. Albertine's hair compared to hers during the game of "ferret" (Proust was evidently thinking of Titian's "Young Woman at her Toilet" in the Louvre, for

which Laura was then thought to have been the sitter): I
982.

DIEULAFOY, Professor Georges, French physician (1839–1911).
Called in to attend M's grandmother on her death-bed: II 349,
354–5.

DIEULAFOY, Mme Jeanne, French archaeologist (1851–1916): I
830.

DOSTOIEVSKY, Feodor, Russian novelist (1821–81). "Abomin-
ated" by Bergotte: I 598. The Dostoievsky side of Mme de
Sévigné: 703 (cf. III 385). His novels "devoured" by Albertine:
III 327. His "new kind of beauty": 384–7. Charlus and
Dostoievsky: 801–2. Rasputin's murder a Dostoievsky incident
in real life: 802. His way of telling a story: 1031.

DOUCET, Dress designer. Approved of by Elstir: I 961; and by
Mme de Guermantes: III 36, 57.

DOUDAN, Ximénès, French writer,. secretary to the Duc de
Broglie (1800–72): I 781; II 284.

DOYLE, Sir Arthur Conan, British writer (1859–1930). "It's pure
Sherlock Holmes": III 465.

DREYFUS, Alfred. See under Dreyfus Case in Index of Themes.

DRIANT, Colonel, right-wing politician and military commentator (under the pseudonym Capitaine Danrit) during the Dreyfus
Case: II 254.

DRUMONT, Edouard, anti-semitic politician and journalist
(1844–1917): II 299; III 35.

DU CAMP, Maxime, French man of letters (1822–94): I 470.

DUGUAY-TROUIN, French sailor (1673–1736). His statue in
Balbec: I 714; II 800.

DUMAS fils, Alexandre, French novelist and playwright (1802–
70). Reference to his play Les Danicheff: I 235; and to Francillon:
279–81. Admired by Mme de Guermantes: II 514 (cf. III 1065).

DUMONT D'URVILLE, French navigator (1790–1842): I 374.

DUPANLOUP, Mgr, French prelate, orator and polemicist
(1802–78): II 198, 746; III 969.

EDWARD VII, King of England (1841–1910). Mme de Guer-
mantes gives a reception for him and his wife: II 446, 469.
Reviled by Prince Von, defended by Mme de Guermantes: 548.
At Guermantes: III 600.
(See Prince of Wales.)

ELEANOR OF AQUITAINE, wife of Henry II Plantagenet, King of England (1122–1204): I 982.

ELIOT, George, English novelist (1819–80). Disliked by Bergotte: I 598. Andrée translates one of her novels: 1006. Her name crops up in M's dreams: III 118.

ELISABETH, Madame, sister of Louis XVI: II 583.

ELIZABETH, Empress of Austria, daughter of Maximilian-Joseph, Duke of Bavaria, sister of Sophie, Duchesse d'Alençon and Maria, Queen of Naples: II 193. Allusion to her death (in a riding accident) in 1898: 530. Referred to in connection with the Queen of Naples' visit to the Verdurin musical *soirée*: III 248, 313.

EMERSON, Ralph Waldo, American philosopher (1803–82). Subject of conversation at lunch with Rachel: II 287.

ENESCO, Georges, Rumanian violinist (1881–1955): III 289.

ENGALLI, Speranza, Italian opera singer: II 991.

ESTE, Isabella d': II 545.

ESTERHAZY, Major, one of the principal actors in the Dreyfus Case: II 105, 246, 249–50.

EUGÈNE, Prince, Austrian general (1663–1736). An invert?: III 307.

EUGÉNIE, Empress, wife of Napoleon III (1826–1920): II 731.

EULENBURG, Prince, friend and adviser of the Kaiser William II. Reference to a homosexual scandal in which he was involved: II 979.

FABRE, J-H, French entomologist (1823–1915): I 134; II 372 (allusion).

FAGON, Louis XIV's doctor: III 1055.

FALKENHAUSEN, General von (1844–1936): II 111.

FALLIÈRES, Armand, President of the Republic 1906–13: II 328.

FANTIN-LATOUR, Théodore, French painter (1836–1904). His flower paintings compared by Norpois to those of Mme de Villeparisis: II 283–4. Elstir his superior: III 733.

FAURÉ, Gabriel, French composer (1845–1924). Charlus and Morel play his piano and violin sonata: II 985–6 (cf. III 270). His melody *Le Secret*: III 553.

FAVART, Charles-Simon, French dramatist (1710–92). His comedy *La Chercheuse d'Esprit* discussed at the Verdurins': II 965–8.

FEBVRE, Frédéric, Comédie-Française actor (1835–1916): I 80; II 129.

FÉNELON, François de Salignac de la Mothe-, French writer and prelate (1651–1715). Brichot on his "curious" definition of intelligence: I 284; 814. Mme Poussin pronounces his name Fénélon: II 799.

FÉNELON, Comte Bertrand de. M's "dearest friend": II 799.

FERRY, Jules, French statesman (1832–93): I 1012.

FEYDEAU, Georges, French playwright (1862–1921). Allusion to *La Dame de chez Maxim* (*"ce n'est pas mon père"*): I 826; II 16. Allusion to *L'Hôtel du libre échange*: III 782.

FLAUBERT, Gustave, French novelist (1821–80) I 583. "Bourgeois through and through", according to Mme de Guermantes: II 487. His letters superior to his books, according to Mme d'Arpajon, who forgets his name: 508. Phrases of Flaubert in Montesquieu: 844. Morel and *L'Education sentimentale*: III 159. It was not affection for the bourgeoisie that made him choose the themes of *Madame Bovary* and *L'Education sentimentale*: 918.

FLORIAN, Jean-Pierre Claris de (1755–94). Author of one of the two fables which M. de Cambremer knows: II 946, 957.

FOCH, Marshal (1851–1929), Generalissimo of the Allied armies in 1918: III 775.

FOIX, Catherine de, Queen of Navarre (1470–1517): II 430–31.

FONTANES, Louis, Marquis de, French writer and politician, friend of Chateaubriand (1757–1821): I 763; II 1066.

FORTUNY, Venetian dress designer. Elstir speaks of him to M and Albertine: I 960. Mme de Guermantes wears his dresses: III 26, 36 (cf. 375–6). Albertine covets them; how they evoke the Venice of Carpaccio and Titian: 375–7. M orders six Fortuny gowns for Albertine: 401, 406. Albertine's Fortuny dressing-gown and two coats: 412. Reawakens M's nostalgia for Venice: 419. M sees the original of one of Albertine's Fortuny coats in a Carpaccio in the Accademia: 662.

FOUCHÉ, Joseph (1759–1820), Minister of Police under Napoleon and Louis XVIII: II 538.

FOULD, Achille, French politician (1844–1924), Minister of Finance under Napoleon III: II 132.

FRAGONARD, French painter (1732–1806): III 94.

GÉRÔME, Jean-Léon, French painter and sculptor (1824–1904): I 547.

GHIRLANDAIO, Florentine painter (1449–98): Swann identifies M. de Palancy's nose in one of his pictures: I 243.

GIOLITTI, Giovanni, Italian statesman (1842–1928). His name invoked by Norpois in conversation with Prince Foggi in Venice: III 650–51. Norpois calls Caillaux "the Giolitti of France": 808.

GIORGIONE, Italian painter (c. 1478–1510): I 425–6; II 442. Mme Putbus's maid "wildly Giorgionesque": 721, 780; III 390.

GIOTTO, Italian painter (c. 1266–1337). The Vices and Virtues in the Arena Chapel in Padua; Swann gives M photographs of them; the pregnant housemaid resembles the figure of "Charity": I 87–9, 131–3. M. de Palancy and his monocle remind Swann of the figure of "Injustice": 357. M identifies Florence with the genius of Giotto: 423. The procession of the "little band" recalls Giotto: 865. Albertine playing diabolo resembles his "Idolatry": 947. The allegorical figures appear in M's sleep: II 148. M and his mother visit the Arena Chapel: III 662–3.

GLEYRE, Charles, Swiss painter (1806–74): I 160.

GLUCK, Christoph Willibald von, German composer (1714–87): II 488, 1146. Quotation from his *Armide* attributed to Rameau: III 113.

GOETHE, Johann Wolfgang von, German poet (1749–1832): II 264; III 619, 804, 947.

GOGOL, Nikolai, Russian writer (1809–52): III 385.

GONCOURT, the brothers Edmond (1822–96) and Jules (1830–70), novelists, critics and diarists. M reads a volume of their unpublished Journal: III 728; pastiche of a passage therefrom: 728–36; M's reflections on it: 737–41; 804, 886, 918.

GONDI, Paul de. *See* Retz, Cardinal de.

GORRINGE, General. Commander of the Relief Force that failed to rescue Kut-el-Amara in 1916: III 1031.

GOT, French actor (1822–1901): I 80.

GOYA, Francisco de, Spanish painter (1746–1828): I 354.

GOZZOLI, Benozzo, Florentine painter (1420–97). M's father in his night-clothes resembles Abraham in a Gozzoli picture: I 39. Prominent members of the Medici family depicted in *The Procession of the Magi*: 576; III 63.

GRANDMOUGIN, Charles, French playwright and librettist (1850–1930): II 469.

GRANIER, Jeanne, French actress (1852–1939): II 513.

GRECO, El, Spanish painter (c. 1541–1614). Admired by M's father: I 753–4. Charlus resembles a Grand Inquisitor by El Greco: III 206. Paris during an air-raid compared to *The Burial of Count Orgaz*: 782.

GREGORY THE GREAT, Pope. Paris street-criers echo Gregorian chant: III 123, 133.

GRÉVILLE, Henry (Alice Fleury), French romantic novelist (1842–1902): I 641.

GRÉVY, Jules, President of the Republic 1879–87: I 235–7; III 683.

GRIBELIN, Registrar in the *Bureau des Renseignements*; testified against Dreyfus: II 247–8.

GRIGNAN, Mme de, daughter of Mme de Sévigné (1646–1705): I 818; III 9.

GUILBERT, Yvette, music-hall singer (1868–1944): II 1123.

GUILLAUMIN, Art Nouveau furniture-maker: I 813.

GUISE, Henri, Duc de (1550–88): I 591, 717; III 674.

GUIZOT, François, French statesman and historian (1787–1874): II 297.

GUTENBERG, Johannes, 15th-century inventor of printing by movable type: II 137; III 755.

GUYS, Constantin, French graphic artist (1802–92): I 453.

HAAS, Charles. Friend of Proust. Wears the same hat as Swann: II 601. Identified with Swann: III 199.

HADRIAN, Roman emperor: II 1032.

HAHN, Reynaldo, French composer, friend of Proust (1875–1947). Allusion to Pierre Loti's *L'Ile du Rêve*, for which Hahn wrote the music: III 793.

HALÉVY, Fromental, French composer (1799–1862). M's grandfather hums passages from his opera *La Juive*: I 98; "Rachel when from the Lord": 621; another quotation from *La Juive*: II 874.

HALÉVY, Ludovic (nephew of the above), novelist, playwright and librettist, collaborator of Meilhac (1834–1908). Admired by Mme de Guermantes: I 364; II 213, 513. Quotation from *La Belle Hélène*: III 685.

HALS, Frans, Dutch painter (c. 1580–1666). Allusion to one of his

masterpieces, *The Women Regents of the Haarlem Almshouse*: I
278. Discussed at the Guermantes dinner-party: II 543–6, 564,
569.

HANDEL, George Frederick, German composer (1685–1759):
III 215.

HANSKA, Comtesse. Balzac's "l'Etrangère", whom he married in
1850: II 1086.

HARCOURT, Alphonse-Henri-Charles de Lorraine-Elbeuf,
Prince d' (1648–79). His familiarity with his lackeys deplored by
Saint-Simon: III 860.

HARDY, Thomas, English novelist and poet (1840–1928). The
"stonemason's geometry" in his novels (cf. Vinteuil's "key-
phrases"): III 382–3.

HARUN AL-RASHID, Caliph of Baghdad 786–809: III 837.

HAUSSONVILLE, Louis-Bernard, Comte d' (1770–1840). Denies
knowing Necker, father of Mme de Staël; subsequent connection
of his family with Mme de Staël through the Broglies: III 1014
(cf. II 593; III 749).

HÉBERT, Ernest, academic French painter (1817–1908) admired
by Norpois: II 229.

HEGEL, Georg Wilhelm Friedrich, German philosopher (1770–
1831): III 774.

HELLEU, Paul, French painter and engraver (1859–1927) (said to
have been one of the models for Elstir): II 970.

HELVÉTIUS, Claude-Adrien, one of the *philosophes* of the
French Enlightenment (1715–71): II 238.

HENRI IV, King of France 1589–1610: II 35, 522; III 675.
Allusion to his father, Antoine de Bourbon: II 564.

HENRI V. *See* Chambord, Comte de.

HENRY VIII, King of England 1509–47. Allusion to his encounter
with François I on the Field of Cloth of Gold: II 485 (cf. I 433).

HENRY, Colonel, one of the principal actors in the Dreyfus Case,
whose suicide on 31 August 1898 was its most dramatic episode:
II 241, 248–9, 734; III 803.

HÉRÉDIA, José-Maria de, French poet (1842–1905): I 803.

HERVEY DE SAINT-DENYS, Marquis d', French sinologist and
man of letters (1823–92): II 744.

HERVIEU, Paul, French dramatist (1857–1915). An outspoken
Dreyfusist: III 236.

HINDENBURG, Field-Marshal von, Chief of the German General Staff 1916–18: III 783–4, 1029.

HIRSCH, Baron, German Jewish banker and philanthropist (1831–96): II 693.

HOGARTH, William, English painter and engraver (1697–1764). Albertine's English "Miss" resembles a portrait of Judge Jeffreys by Hogarth: I 887.

HOHENFELSEN, Countess, morganatic wife of the Russian Grand Duke Paul: III 883.

HOMER, Greek epic poet: II 198, 264, 339, 433, 518. Bloch's archaic Greek names for Homer's gods, borrowed from Leconte de Lisle: 865 (cf. I 97, 801–3, 826). References to the *Odyssey*: III 986, 993.

HOOCH, Pieter de, Dutch painter (1630–81). Vinteuil's "little phrase" recalls effects in his interiors: I 238.

HORACE, Roman poet. Reasons for the pleasure of reading his odes: I 813. His sycophancy to Maecenas, according to Brichot: II 984–5. Brichot recites to himself a Horatian ode: III 335.

HOYOS, Count, Austrian Ambassador in Paris: II 507; III 282.

HUGO, Victor, French poet, novelist and dramatist (1802–85): I 85, 470, 573. Disparaged by Mme de Villeparisis; M quotes to her a line from *Booz endormi*: 763, 775–7, 781. His dramatic works compared unfavourably to Racine's by Charlus; Saint-Loup finds this "a bit thick": 819. The Comtesse de Noailles' verse compared to his: II 104–5. Quotation from *Ultima verba* (*Les Châtiments*): 460. Discussed at the Guermantes dinner-table: 510–16. Mme d'Arpajon's opinion of him; reference to *Lorsque l'enfant paraît. . .* : 510 (cf. 674). Mme de Guermantes's opinion of him; quotes lines from *Contemplations* and *Feuilles d'automne*: 512; quotes *Booz endormi*: 550 (cf. 214, 514, 570). The earlier and the later Hugo; the former supplies "thoughts" (*pensées*) instead of food for thought: 570–71. M re-reads him; Françoise's footman has purloined his copy of *Feuilles d'automne*: 571. Charlus quotes *Booz endormi*: 583. Allusion to *Tristesse d'Olympio*: 1084, 1087. Charlus quotes from *Les Chants du Crépuscule*: 1178. *La Légende des Siècles* an example of the retrospective unity imposed on their works by great writers of the 19th century: III 157 (cf. 265). Reference to

Hernani (Doña Sol): 289. Surrounds himself with disciples in his old age: 292. The moon in his work; M recites *Booz endormi* to Albertine: 414. A line from *Contemplations* ("Et que tout cela fasse un astre dans les cieux!") inaccurately quoted: 737. Rachel to recite some of his poems at the Princesse de Guermantes's *matinée*: 1041. Mme de Guermantes quotes a line from *Contemplations*: 1058. Allusion to a line from *Tristesse d'Olympio* ("fils mysterieux"): 1086. A line from *À Villequier* quoted: 1095. Quotation from *Le Tombeau de Théophile Gautier* ("la porte funéraire"): 1098.

HULST, Monseigneur d', founder and Rector of the Institut Catholique de Paris (1841–96): III 334.

HUXELLES, Nicolas du Blé, Marquis d', Maréchal de France (1652–1730). Charlus impersonates him, after the portrait of him in Saint-Simon's *Memoirs*: II 1000. Charlus quotes the Saint-Simon portrait in the context of his dissertation on 17th-century inverts: III 307–8.

HUXLEY, Aldous, English writer (1894–1964). Mentioned parenthetically in connection with T. H. Huxley (*see below*): II 661.

HUXLEY, Thomas Henry, English scientist (1825–95). Anecdote concerning one of his patients: II 661.

HUYSUM, Jan van, Dutch flower painter (1682–1749): II 219.

IBSEN, Henrik, Norwegian dramatist (1828–1906). Disliked by Bergotte: I 598. Subject of conversation at lunch with Rachel: II 287. Presents the manuscripts of three of his plays to Mme Timoléon d'Amoncourt, who offers two of them to Mme de Guermantes: 691.

INDY, Vincent d', French composer (1851–1931): II 915, 959.

INGRES, Dominique, French painter (1780–1867). Shrinking of the "unbridgeable gulf" between him and Manet: II 436 (cf. 542: Mme de Guermantes's view). M. de Guermantes cites *La Source* as against Elstir: 519. His orientalism: III 837. Vicissitudes of Mme de Guermantes's attitude to his work: 1079–80.

IRVING, Sir Henry, English actor (1838–1905). Françoise's "stage effects" compared to his: II 373.

ISVOLSKI, Alexander Pavlovich, Russian statesman (1856–1919), Ambassador in Paris 1910–17: II 691.

JACQUET, Gustave-Jean, French painter (1846–1909). His portrait of Mme de Surgis-le-Duc: II 720, 733, 1178.

JAMMES, Francis, French poet (1868–1938). His name appears in M's dream: 11 789.

JEAN SANS PEUR. Assassin of Duc Louis d'Orléans in 1407: 11 1143.

JOFFRE, General, Chief of French General Staff 1911–14: 111 772, 775, 839.

JOHN OF AUSTRIA, Don, natural son of the emperor Charles V, defeated the Turks at the Battle of Lepanto (1571): 11 545.

JOINVILLE, Prince de, son of Louis-Philippe (1818–1900): 11 193, 250, 394.

JOMINI, Henri, Baron. Swiss general and military theorist (1779–1869): 111 819.

JOUBERT, Joseph, French moralist (1754–1824). Recommended to Mme de Villeparisis by Legrandin: 11 206; 571.

JUDET, Ernest, anti-Dreyfusist journalist: 11 256.

JURIEN DE LA GRAVIÈRE, French admiral (1812–92). Mme de Varambon thinks he is related to M: 11 516–17, 568.

JUSSIEU, Bernard de, French botanist (1699–1777): 11 171.

KAISER. *See* William II.

KALIDASA, Hindu poet of the 1st century BC: 1 832.

KANT, Immanuel, German philosopher (1724–1804). The "ordered and unalterable" design of Gilberte's tea-parties recalls his necessary universe: 1 545. Mme de Guermantes's unconventional behaviour recalls his theories on freedom and necessity: 11 495. Saint-Loup and Kant: 521–2. Brichot's view of him ("Pomeranian mysticism"): 111 284.

KESSLER, Count Harry, choreographer of *The Legend of Joseph* (1914): 111 662.

KITCHENER, Lord, British general (1850–1916). Allusion to his homosexuality: 111 1110 (Note 20).

KOCK, Paul de, French novelist (1794–1871). Comparisons between him and Dostoievsky dismissed by M: 111 385.

LA BALUE, Cardinal Jean (1421–91), Minister of Louis XI, by whom he was imprisoned for 10 years: 1 717.

LABICHE, Eugène, French playwright (1814–88). Swann, in his tirade against the Verdurins, suggests that the "little clan" are like characters in a Labiche comedy: 1 312. Saint-Loup's intellectually snobbish attitude to his father suggests the possible attitude of a son of Labiche to his: 788. Names that might have come out of

Labiche: II 698. Drinks no longer to be found except in his plays: 1108. M. d'Argencourt in old age like a character from a Regnard farce rewritten by Labiche: III 962.

LABORI, Maître Fernand, counsel for Dreyfus and Zola. His oratorical style: II 394. Frequents Mme Verdurin's *salon* during her Dreyfusard period: 774 (cf. 914; III 238–9).

LA BRUYÈRE, Jean de, French writer and novelist, author of *Les Caractères* (1645–96). Quotation from *Du coeur*: I 671–2; 814. Quotation by Charlus from *Du coeur*: 819. Françoise uses the verb *plaindre* in the same sense as La Bruyère: II 21. Loose quotation from *De la mode*: III 204. Quotation from *Du coeur*: 930.

LACHELIER, Jules, French philosopher (1832–1918): II 954.

LACLOS, Choderlos de, French writer, author of *Les Liaisons dangereuses* (1741–1803). The "ultra-respectable" author of the "most appallingly perverse" book: III 386 (cf. 918).

LA FAYETTE, Mme de, French writer, author of *La Princesse de Clèves* (1634–92): I 972; letter from Mme de Sévigné about her death: II 311, 646; III 735.

LAFENESTRE, Georges, French poet and critic (1837–1919): II 545.

LA FONTAINE, Jean de, French poet (1621–95). Allusion by Charlus to *The Two Friends* and *The Two Pigeons*: I 818. Reference to *The Miller and his Son*: II 558–9. M. de Cambremer knows only one of his fables: 946; this is *The Man and the Snake*: 956; but he also seems to know *The Camel and the Floating Sticks*: 996 (cf. III 236). Quoted by Brichot: III 335. Rachel recites his *Two Pigeons*: 1053–4.

LAMARTINE, Alphonse de, French poet and statesman (1790–1869). Recited poems in Mme de Villeparisis's father's château: I 761. A subject for the literary ladies of the aristocracy: II 202. Occasionally quoted by Mme de Guermantes: 214. Sneered at by Bloch: 251, 865.

LAMBALLE, Princesse de, friend of Marie-Antoinette, victim of the September massacres (1792): II 583.

LANDRU, famous French murderer: III 204.

LANNES, Marshal, general in the Napoleonic armies (1769–1809): II 113.

LA PÉROUSE, French navigator (1741–88): I 374.

LA ROCHEFOUCAULD, François VI, Duc de, Prince de Marcillac, author of the *Maxims* (1613–80). Legrandin finds a resemblance to him in Mme de Villeparisis: II 205–6. Brichot refers to him as "that Boulangist de Marcillac": 905. An apocryphal maxim quoted by Charlus: III 308.

LA ROCHEFOUCAULD, François VII, Duc de, Master of the Royal Hounds, son of the above. Saint-Simon appalled to find him hobnobbing with his lackeys: III 860.

LA TOUR, Quentin de, French portraitist (1704–88). Albertine resembles one of his pastels: III 356. His works destroyed by the revolutionaries: 918.

LAVOISIER, Antoine, French scientist (1743–94). His name invoked by Swann apropos of Vinteuil's creative genius: I 382.

LAWRENCE, Sir Thomas, English painter (1769–1830). Referred to in the Goncourt pastiche: III 732.

LAWRENCE O'TOOLE, Saint, Archbishop and patron of Dublin (c. 1127–1180). Referred to in one of Brichot's etymological dissertations: II 920.

LE BATTEUX, Abbé, French grammarian (1713–80): III 229.

LEBOURG, Art Nouveau furniture-maker: I 813.

LEBRUN, Pierre-Antoine, French poet (1785–1873): I 763; II 284; III 1014.

LECONTE DE LISLE, French poet (1818–94). Revered by Bloch ("my beloved master, old Leconte"): I 97 (cf. 803, 824, 964). Quoted on the sea: 761, 964. His authentic Greek spelling, copied by Bloch: II 865. The moon in his poetry: III 414. (Passages inspired by his translation of Hesiod: I 758; and by his *Orphic Hymns*: II 869.)

LEGOUVÉ, Ernest, Permanent Secretary of the *Académie Française* (1807–1903): II 470.

LEIBNIZ Gottfried Wilhelm, German philosopher (1646–1716): II 271. The *salons* of the Faubourg Saint-Germain likened to his monads: 497. Not modern enough for Mme de Cambremer: 954.

LELOIR, Maurice, 19th-century *Salon* painter. Mme Cottard compares him to Machard (q.v.): I 408.

LEMAIRE, Gaston, French composer (1854–1928): II 469.

LEMAÎTRE, Frédérick, French actor (1800–1876). Françoise's "stage effects" compared to his: II 373.

LENIN, Russian revolutionary and statesman (1870–1924): III 817.

LE NÔTRE, André, French garden designer (1613–1700). Charlus speaks of a house with a park laid out by Le Nôtre which has been destroyed by the Israels: I 820–21.

LEO X, Pope (1513–21): III 299.

LEONARDO DA VINCI (1452–1519). His *Last Supper*: I 43, 181. Quoted on painting (*cosa mentale*): 539. Gilberte's plaits a work of art more precious than a sheet of flowers drawn by Leonardo: 542. Dark glaze of shadows among rocks as beautiful as Leonardo's: 987. Albertine's face hook-nosed as in one of his caricatures: III 74.

LEROI-BEAULIEU, Anatole, economist and member of the *Académie des Sciences morales et politiques* (1842–1912). Advises M's father to stand for election to the *Institut*: II 153. Presses M's father's candidacy with Norpois: 231. His "stern Assyrian profile": 232. Norpois seeks his support on behalf of Prince Von: 271.

LE SIDANER, French painter (1862–1939). Favourite artist of the Cambremer's lawyer friend from Paris: II 834, 839–40, 850.

LESPINASSE, Mlle de (1732–76). Famous for her *salon*, which rivalled that of her former patron Mme du Deffand (q.v.): I 640.

LE VERRIER, Urbain, French astronomer (1811–77): III 301.

LISZT, Franz, Hungarian composer (1811–86). His "St Francis preaching to the Birds" played at Mme de Saint-Euverte's: I 357; Oriane has come up from Guermantes specially to hear it: 370. Once played at Mme de Villeparisis's father's château: 761. Mme de Villeparisis and "Alix" both claim acquaintance with him: II 204.

LLOYD GEORGE, David, British statesman (1863–1944): III 807.

LOMÉNIE, Louis de, French man of letters, frequenter of Mme Récamier's *salon* (1815–78): I 511, 781.

LONGUEVILLE, Duchesse de, sister of the Great Condé: II 564, 590.

LOTI, Pierre, French novelist (1850–1923): II 219. Mention of *Pêcheur d'Islande*: III 194–5. Allusion to his *L'Ile du Rêve*: 793.

LOUBET, Emile, President of the Republic during the revision of the Dreyfus Case: II 723; III 238, 1009.

LOUIS VI, the Fat, King of France (1081–1137): I 779; II 543, 1125.

LOUIS IX (St Louis), King of France (1215–70): I 65–6, 164; II 549, 1143.

LOUIS XI, King of France (1423–83): II 597, 600.

LOUIS XIII, King of France (1601–43): II 462, 572, 590, 1143; III 234.

LOUIS XIV, King of France (1638–1715). Aunt Léonie's routine resembles the "mechanics" of life at his court: I 128–9. Allusion to Racine's fall from grace: 606. Incidental allusions: 619, 825; II 298, 433, 440. The Duc de Guermantes's rules of social behaviour compared to those of Louis XIV; anecdotes from Saint-Simon: 452–3. Further allusions: 545, 551, 561, 590, 593, 670, 682, 801. Charlus's views on him; compared to the Kaiser: 979–80. Charlus's great-great-grandmother at the Court of Versailles: 984 (cf. 1125; III 1013). Further incidental allusions: III 306, 375, 682. His ignorance of genealogy, according to Saint-Simon: 1006.

LOUIS XV, King of France (1715–74): II 545, 556, 707; III 507, 565, 571, 730.

LOUIS XVI, King of France (1754–93): II 94, 1143.

LOUIS XVII, uncrowned King of France (1785–?1795): III 1057.

LOUIS XVIII, King of France (1755–1824): II 196. Shows his faculty for forgetting the past by appointing Fouché (q.v.): 538.

LOUIS THE GERMAN, Son of Louis I ("the Pious") and grandson of Charlemagne (804–76): I 65; II 265.

LOUIS-PHILIPPE, King of France (1773–1850): I 22, 112. His architectural "excretions": 319. His conversational talent: 763. The "pinchbeck age" of Louis-Philippe: II 545. Genealogical connections: 557–8, 707. The Citizen King: III 296.

LOUIS BONAPARTE, Prince, nephew of the Princesse Mathilde. Officer in the Russian Imperial Guard: I 585.

LOUIS, Baron, Minister of Finance under Louis XVIII and Louis-Philippe (1755–1837). Quoted by Norpois: I 498 (cf. III 807).

LOZÉ, French diplomat, Ambassador in Vienna 1893–7: III 646.

LUCINGE, Mme de, illegitimate daughter of the Duc de Berry: II 556 (cf. III 673).

LUINI, Bernardino, Milanese painter (c. 1475–c. 1533). Swann once resembled one of the three kings in his *Adoration of the Magi*: I 616. Swann compares a woman to a Luini portrait: III 390.

LULLY, Jean-Baptiste, Franco-Italian composer (1632–87). His "shrewd avarice and great pomp", according to Saint-Simon: I 337.

LUTHER, Martin, German religious reformer (1483–1546): II 265.

MACHARD, Jules-Louis, French painter (1839–1900). Mme Cottard speaks to Swann of one of his portraits which "the whole of Paris is rushing to see": I 407–8.

MACK, General, Austrian commander against Napoleon. His defeat at Ulm: II 115.

MACMAHON, Marshal (1808–93), President of the Republic 1873–79. Mme de Villeparisis related to him: I 22 (cf. 737).

MADAME. *See* Orléans, Charlotte-Elizabeth of Bavaria, Duchesse d'.

MAECENAS, patron of Virgil and Horace. Cited by Brichot; Charlus describes him as "the Verdurin of antiquity": II 984–5, 987.

MAES, Nicolaes, Dutch painter (1632–93). A painting attributed to him by the Mauritshuis in reality a Vermeer, in Swann's view [subsequently confirmed by the experts]: I 384.

MAETERLINCK, Maurice, Belgian poet and playwright (1862–1949). His *Les Sept Princesses* discussed at Mme de Villeparisis's and ridiculed by Mme de Guermantes: II 235–6. Mme de Guermantes and M. d'Argencourt discuss him: 257. Mme de Guermantes comes to admire him, in deference to fashion: III 27 (cf. 1066). The "vague sadness" of Maeterlinck; quotations from *Pelléas*: 113.

MAHOMET II, Sultan of Turkey 1451–81. Bloch resembles his portrait by Gentile Bellini: I 105. Stabbed his wife to death: 386.

MAILLOL, Aristide, French sculptor (1861–1944): III 775.

MAINTENON, Mme de (1635–1719), mistress, confidante and finally morganatic wife of Louis XIV: I 337, 759.

MALHERBE, François de, French poet (1555–1628): II 662.

MALLARMÉ, Stéphane, French poet (1842–98). "Alarm and exhaustion" induced in M's grandmother by his later verse: II 511. Sneered at by Brichot: 988. Mocked by Meilhac: III 27.

Poems of his to be engraved on Albertine's yacht and Rolls-Royce: 464.

MANET, Edouard, French painter (1832–83). Elstir's portrait of Odette contemporary with Manet's portraits: I 922. His *Olympia* once regarded as a "horror" by society people, but now accepted: II 436. Elstir once modelled himself on him: 519. Mme de Guermantes's view of his *Olympia* — "just like an Ingres": 542. Admired by Mme de Cambremer, though she prefers Monet: 840.

MANGIN, General Charles (1866–1925). A genius, according to Saint-Loup at Doncières: II 112. Cited by Saint-Loup again during the Great War: III 784.

MANSARD, Jules Hardouin, French architect (1646–1708): II 445.

MANTEGNA, Andrea, Italian painter (c.1430–1506). A Saint-Euverte footman resembles a soldier in one of his paintings: I 353. The roof of the Gare Saint-Lazare recalls one of his menacing skies: 694. Isabella d'Este and Mantegna: II 545. The Trocadéro reminds Albertine of the background of his *St Sebastian*: III 165. Vinteuil's septet conjures up "some scarlet-clad Mantegna archangel sounding a trumpet": 262. The Marquis de Beausergent in old age resembles a portrait study by Mantegna: 981.

MARDRUS, Dr Joseph-Charles-Victor, translator of the unexpurgated *Arabian Nights*, published 1898–1904: II 865.

MARGUERITE D'AUTRICHE, daughter of the Emperor Maximilian and wife of Philibert le Beau of Savoy (1480–1530). Her tomb at Brou: I 323.

MARIE-AMÉLIE, Queen, wife of Louis-Philippe. Once said to Mme de Villeparisis, "You are just like a daughter to me": II 192. Her portrait: 193, 394, 558. M's grandmother shocked by her behaviour: III 675.

MARIE-ANTOINETTE, Queen of France (1755–93): I 820–21. Charlus has her hats: II 583; III 812.

MARIVAUX, Pierre de Chamberlain de, French playwright and novelist (1688–1763): II 271. Characters known by their titles alone: 911.

MARY STUART, Queen of Scotland (1542–87): I 820.

MASCAGNI, Pietro, Italian composer (1863–1945). Reference to *Cavalleria Rusticana*, admired by Albertine: I 943, 946.

MASPÉRO, Gaston, French Egyptologist (1846–1916): I 515; III 333.

MASSÉ, Victor, French composer (1822–84). Odette's delight at the prospect of his operetta *La Reine Topaze*: I 268. The Verdurins take her to his *Une Nuit de Cléopâtre*; Swann's diatribe against him: 315–17.

MASSÉNA, Marshal, Napoleonic general (1758–1817): II 132.

MASSENET, Jules, French composer (1842–1912). Compared with Debussy: II 844. Albertine sings his *Poème d'amour*: III 3. Quotations from *Manon*: 460.

MATERNA, Mme, Austrian singer (1847–1918): I 27.

MATHILDE, Princesse, daughter of Jérome Bonaparte (1820–1904). Entertained by the Princesse des Laumes: I 358, 362. M meets her in the Bois de Boulogne with the Swanns: 583–6. Not at all royal in her ways: 753. Her relations with the Faubourg Saint-Germain: II 486–7. Mme de Guermantes invites her with the Duc d'Aumale: 538.

MAUBANT, French actor (1821–1902): I 27. Seen by M emerging from the Théâtre-Français: 80.

MAULÉVRIER, Marquis de, French Ambassador in Madrid 1720–23. Swann quotes Saint-Simon's description of him: I 28.

MAUREL, Victor, French opera-singer (1848–1923): II 587.

MAURRAS, Charles, right-wing writer and publicist (1868–1952): I 470. His novel *Aimée de Coigny*: III 824. Reference to his newspaper *L'Action Française*: 844.

MAYOL, Félix, music hall singer (1876–1941). Morel sings his *Viens Poupoule*: II 1100. Discussed by Charlus and the bus conductor: 1183.

MEILHAC, Henri, French playwright and librettist (1831–97), collaborator of Ludovic Halévy (q.v.). Admired by Mme de Guermantes: I 364 (cf. II 213, 513–14; III 1062). Imagined dialogue between the Princesse de Guermantes and her guests in her box at the Opéra suggests a scene from *Le Mari de la Débutante*: II 38–9. His Cleopatra: 917. Mallarmé mocked by him: III 27. Quotation from *La Belle Hélène*: 685.

MÉLINE, Jules, French statesman (1838–1925). Prime Minister during the Dreyfus Case; friend of M's father: II 154.

MEMLING, Jan, Flemish painter (c. 1433–94). Allusion to his St Ursula reliquary in Bruges: II 557.

MENANDER, Greek poet and dramatist: I 832.

MENDELSSOHN, Felix, German composer (1809–47). Charlus refers to him as "the virtuoso of Berlin": II 1043; III 649.

MENDÈS, Catulle, French poet (1841–1909). Referred to familiarly by Bloch's sister: I 830.

MENIER, Gaston, Chocolate manufacturer. Allusion (by Bloch) to his powerful and luxurious yacht: I 802.

MERCIER, General, Minister of War at the outset of the Dreyfus Case: II 495.

MÉRIMÉE, Prosper, French writer (1803–70). His style and influence: I 364 (cf. II 38, 213, 513–14). Admired by Mme de Villeparisis: 763. Mme de Guermantes has his type of mind: III 213 (cf. I 364; II 592); her favourite writer, together with Meilhac and Halévy: 513–14. He and Baudelaire despise one another: 592 (cf. III 27). His travels in Spain: III 333.

MERLET, Gustave, French literary academic (1829–91): I 976.

MÉTRA, Olivier, French composer and conductor (1830–89). His *Valse des Roses* one of Odette's favourite pieces: I 258, 263, 269.

METTERNICH, Princess Pauline von (1836–1921), wife of Metternich's son Richard, for several years Austrian Ambassador in Paris. Introduces Bergotte to Norpois in Vienna: I 512–13. A passionate Wagnerian: II 587; III 276.

MEULEN, van der, Flemish painter (1634–94): II 399.

MEURICE, Paul, writer and friend of Victor Hugo: III 292.

MEYER, Arthur, French journalist, ultra-Nationalist and anti-Dreyfusard (1844–1924): III 784, 884.

MEYERBEER, Giacomo, Franco-German composer (1791–1864). Morel plays him instead of Debussy: II 986.

MICHELANGELO Buonarotti, Italian painter, sculptor, architect and poet (1475–1564). Globes of mistletoe like the sun and moon in his "Creation": I 459. Françoise "the Michelangelo of our kitchen"; her search for the best cuts of meat compared to his care in choosing marble for the monument to Julius II: 480, 494. Albertine's face in bed at Balbec, as M approaches to kiss it, seems to rotate like a Michelangelo figure: 996. Vinteuil's creative fury compared to Michelangelo's in the Sistine Chapel: III 256. Brichot acquits him of homosexuality: 299. "Grimacing immobility" of a portrait study: 981.

MICHELET, Jules, French historian (1798–1874). Charlus quotes him on the Guermantes clan: II 296. Reference to his aesthetic approach to natural history: 650. Personifies the 19th century; his greatest beauties in his prefaces: III 157.

MIGNARD, Pierre, French portrait painter (1612–95). His portrait of Charlus's uncles: II 583. The Duc de Guermantes's "Mignard": 602–4.

MILL, John Stuart, British philosopher and economist (1806–73): II 954.

MILLET, Jean-François, French painter (1814–75): II 955.

MISTINGUETT, popular singer and dancer (1875–1956). Mme de Guermantes hesitates to make overtures to her, though finding her "adorable": III 1043.

MOLIÈRE, French dramatist (1622–73): I 30. Norpois avoids his word *cocu*: 503 (as does Cottard: II 996). Meeting between M's grandmother and Mme de Villeparisis compared to a scene in Molière: 746. Reference to *Le Misanthrope* — exam question on Alceste and Philinte: 949–50. Quoted by M's grandmother: II 322–3. Conversation between Charlus and the Duke of Sidonia recalls a Molière comedy: 663. Allusion to *Le Médecin malgré lui*: 665. Charlus as Scapin: 722. The only writer's name known to Céleste Albaret: 876. Reference to *Le Malade imaginaire*: 921. Reference to *L'Avare*: 951. Allusion to *La Comtesse d' Escarbagnas*: 1043. Charlus's imitation swordsmanship reminiscent of Molière: 1105. An invert, according to Charlus: III 306. Differing views of *Le Misanthrope*: 1030.

MOLTKE, General von, Prussian Chief of Staff during the Franco-Prussian war: III 766.

MONALDESCHI, Jean de, Italian nobleman assassinated at Fontainebleau in 1657 at the instigation of Queen Christina of Sweden: II 693.

MONET, Claude, French painter (1840–1926). Admired by Mme de Cambremer: II 838–40. Mentioned: III 311, 794.

MONSEIGNEUR, son of Louis XIV (1661–1711): II 452.

MONSIEUR (Philippe, Duc d'Orléans), brother of Louis XIV (1640–1701). Anecdotes from Saint-Simon: II 453, 682, 984, 1125. Called "Monsieur" because he was such an "old woman" (Charlus): 1144. His homosexuality: III 306–8.

MONTALAMBERT, Charles, Comte de, French politician and

publicist (1810–70). Frequented Mme de Villeparisis's *salon*: 11 198.

MONTESPAN, Mme de, mistress of Louis XIV: 11 801.

MONTESQUIEU, Charles de Secondat, Baron de, French writer and political philosopher (1689–1755). Anticipates Flaubert: 11 844. Brichot refers to him as "Monsieur le Président Secondat de Montesquieu": 905.

MONTMORENCY, Duchesse de, *née* des Ursins (1601–66). Mme de Villeparisis has inherited a portrait of her: 11 193, 203–4, 207, 228.

MORAND, Paul, French writer (1888–1976). Allusion to his novel *Tendres Stocks*: 111 821.

MOREAU, Gustave, French painter (1826–98). The idea of a "kept woman" suggests to Swann some fantasy by Moreau: 1 292. Allusion to his portrayal of Jupiter: 754. Some "stunning pictures" by him at Guermantes, according to Saint-Loup: 810. Mme de Guermantes talks about his *Death and the Young Man*: 11 540–41.

MORGHEN, Raphael, Italian engraver (1758–1833). His engraving of Leonardo's *Last Supper*: 1 43.

MOTTEVILLE, Mme de, memorialist (c. 1621–1689): 11 563.

MOUNET-SULLY, French tragedian (1841–1916): 11 1105; 111 208. His approach to Molière's *Le Misanthrope*: 1030.

MOUSSORGSKY, Modest, Russian composer (1839–81). The street criers' cadences remind M of *Boris Godunov*: 111 112.

MOZART, Wolfgang Amadeus (1756–91). Reference to his clarinet quintet: 1 363. "Mischievous unexpectedness" with which the piano takes over in his concertos: 491.

MURAT, Princesse, Queen of Naples: 1 828; 11 538; 111 276. (To be distinguished from Maria-Sophia-Amelia, wife of Francis II, last king of the two Sicilies — *see* Naples, Queen of.)

MUSSET, Alfred de, French poet and dramatist (1810–57). M's grandmother's choice of Musset's poems as a present for her grandson disapproved of by his father: 1 42. Despised by Bloch, apart from one "absolutely meaningless line": 97. Arrives "dead drunk" to dine with the Princesse Mathilde: 584. Mme de Villeparisis's poor opinion of him: 776. The Musset admired by the likes of Bloch: 824. A line of his attributed by Oriane to Emile Augier: 11 235. Critical opinions of him: 488–9. Mme d'Arpajon quotes a line from his *La Nuit d'Octobre* thinking it to be by Hugo: 514–15. Quoted in Joseph Périgot's letter: 588–9. His notion of "Hope in God": III 599. Quotation by Charlus from *La Nuit d'Octobre*: 611 (cf. 244 and 949, 951). Rachel to recite *Le Souvenir* at the Princesse de Guermantes's *matinée*: 1033.

NANTES, Mlle de, daughter of Louis XIV and Mme de Montespan; married the grandson of the Great Condé: III 682.

NAPLES, Queen of. Maria-Sophia-Amelia, daughter of Maximilian-Joseph, Duke of Bavaria. Her reaction to her sister's death discussed at the Guermantes' dinner-table: II 530–31. Her graciousness to Mme Verdurin: III 248–9; forgets her fan: 275–7, 284, 304, 313, 317; returns to fetch her fan, and takes Charlus under her protection: 324–7. Accused of espionage by Mme Verdurin during the war: 789.

NAPOLEON Bonaparte, (1769–1821): I 583–4. His strategy and tactics discussed by Saint-Loup at Doncières: II 110–17. The Prince de Borodino's possible descent from him and points of resemblance with him: 129–33. His place in Balzac: 558. Napoleonic titles: 586, 615. Discussion of whether he chewed tobacco or not, in the Goncourt pastiche: III 736. His strategy and tactics discussed by Saint-Loup in 1914: 782–3. Compared by Charlus to the Kaiser: 824.

NAPOLEON III (1808–73). Appears in Swann's dream: I 411–13. Mentioned: 471, 583. Captain de Borodino's relationship and resemblance to him: II 129–33. The Duc de Guermantes objects to his handing out of titles: 615. Features in Norpois's article on the eve of the Franco-Prussian war: III 652–4.

NATTIER, Jean-Marc, French portrait-painter (1658–1766). Jacquet's portrait of Mme de Surgis compared to his "Duchesse de Châteauroux": II 733; III 601.

NÉGRIER, General de (1839–1913). Discussed at Doncières: II 128–9 (cf. III 775).

NEMOURS, Duc de, son of Louis-Philippe (1814–96). Mme de Villeparisis tells an anecdote about him: I 778–9.

NERO, Roman emperor. Quoted by Brichot: II 926. Cited by M's mother as being probably "highly-strung": III 103.

NERVAL, Gérard de, French poet (1808–55). Illustrated editions of his books remind M of a "personal share" in the Water

Company: I 490. His *Sylvie*, "one of the masterpieces of French literature", figures a sensation of the same order as the taste of the madeleine: III 959.

NICHOLAS II, Tsar (1868–1918). Visits Paris: I 584. Françoise ashamed of France's treatment of him: II 342. Charlus speaks of him: III 813, 825–6.

NIETZSCHE, Friedrich Wilhelm, German philosopher (1844–1900): I 467. Admired by Saint-Loup: 787. His attitude to friendship and his relationship to Wagner: II 409 (cf. III 156). Quoted in Saint-Loup's letters to M during the war: III 777. Charlus ridicules Cottard's denigration of him: 804.

NIJINSKY, Vaslav, Russian ballet dancer (1890–1950): II 770.

NOAILLES, Anna de, French poetess (1876–1933). Alluded to as "an Eastern princess" said to write poetry "quite as fine as Hugo's or Vigny's": II 104–5. A "poet of genius": III 741.

NOAILLES, Duc de, friend of Sainte-Beuve: III 581.

NOAILLES, Duchesse de, *née* Champlâtreux, mother-in-law of Anna de Noailles. Sainte-Beuve's poem about her as a little girl: III 741.

OFFENBACH, Jacques, Franco-German composer (1891–80): I 788. Quotation from his *Les Brigands*: II 875. Quotation from *La Belle Hélène*: III 685.

OHNET, Georges, French novelist and playwright. References to his *Maître des Forges* and *Serge Panine*: I 280.

OLLIVIER, Emile, French statesman (1825–1913): II 244.

ORLÉANS, Louis d'. Assassinated by Jean sans Peur in 1407: II 1143.

ORLÉANS, Duc d', the Regent (1674–1723): II 1144. Married one of Louis XIV's bastards, Mlle de Blois, daughter of Mme de Montespan: III 682.

ORLÉANS, Duc d', eldest son of Louis-Philippe (1810–42): II 394, 557.

ORLÉANS, Philippe, Duc d', son of the Comte de Paris and grandson of the above (1869–1926): I 559, 836.

ORLÉANS, Charlotte-Elisabeth of Bavaria, Duchesse d', "the Princess Palatine" (1652–1722). Wife of Monsieur, and known as "Madame". Her correspondence: I 583; III 563 (cf. 670; III 308). Her masculine ways: 670. The "Wife of an Auntie": III 308.

ORLÉANS, Duchesse d', mother of Louis-Philippe. Betrayed by Mme de Genlis: III 386.

ORLÉANS, Prince Henri d', eldest son of the Duc de Chartres (1867–1901). Publicly embraces Esterhazy after the Zola trial: II 249–50.

OSSIAN, legendary Scottish bard impersonated by James Macpherson. A "mediocre mystifier": II 433.

OVID, Roman poet: I 810. "That worthy hack" (Brichot): II 1086. Quoted by Cottard: 1108.

PADEREWSKI, Ignace, Polish pianist and prime minister (1860–1941). Dechambre compared to him: II 926, 931.

PAILLERON, Edouard, French playwright (1834–99). Allusion to Oriane's "Pailleronism": II 514.

PALATINE, Princess. *See* Orléans, Charlotte-Elisabeth of Bavaria, Duchesse d'.

PALÉOLOGUE, Maurice, French diplomat, Ambassador in St Petersburg during the 1914–18 war. Veiled allusion: II 670. "Notoriously inadequate" in Serbia, according to Norpois: III 646. Pestered with telegrams from the Duchesse de Guermantes after the Russian Revolution: 833.

PALESTRINA, Italian composer (1525–94): II 990; III 133, 1080.

PALISSY, Bernard, French ceramic artist and scientist (c. 1510–90). Platter of seafood at Doncières resembles one of his ceramic dishes: II 118.

PAMPILLE (Mme Léon Daudet); published cooking recipes in *L'Action Française*. Her "delightful" books referred to by Mme de Guermantes: II 521. Her "incomparable recipe" (M. Verdurin): 931. "That true poet": III 29.

PAQUIN, dress designer. Approved of — "sometimes" — by Elstir: I 961. Mme de Guermantes recommends him: III 36.

PARIS, Comte de, eldest grandson of Louis-Philippe (1838–94). Swann "a particular friend" of his: I 16, 27, 441. Referred to as Philippe VII: 442. Favourably impressed by Odette, according to Norpois: 508–9, 521, 559, 561.

PARNY, Evariste-Désiré de, French poet (1753–1814): II 468.

PASCAL, Blaise, French philosopher and scientist (1623–62): I 28; II 17. Quoted by Saint-Loup: 101. Charlus and the Duc de Guermantes recall their tutor's lessons on him: 743–4. "We can make discoveries no less precious than in Pascal's *Pensées* in an advertisement for soap": III 554. Gulf between M and Gilberte as imaginary as Pascal's: 714. Quoted by Brichot (*le moi est haïssable*): 819.

PASQUIER (*le chancelier*), French statesman (1767–1862): I 22, 763. Friend of Mme de Boigne: III 581.

PATY DE CLAM, Colonel du. One of the principal actors in the Dreyfus Case. Norpois's views on him: II 248–9, 252, 255. Quotes lines from an adversary, the Dreyfusard poet Pierre Quillard, at the Zola trial: III 777. His "machinations and misrepresentations": 803.

PAU. General (1848–1932): II 129. Quoted by Charlus on the declaration of war in 1914: "I have been waiting forty years for this day. It is the most glorious day of my life": III 824–5.

PAUL, Saint. The "unforgivable sin": I 73.

PÉLADAN, Sâr, French writer and occultist (1858–1918): II 236.

PÉRIER, Jean-Alexis, French singer, creator of the role of Pelléas: II 1122.

PERRONEAU, Jean-Baptiste, French painter (1715–83). Admired by Elstir: II 435.

PÉTAIN, General (1856–1951): III 775.

PETRONIUS, Roman writer: III 285.

PHIDIAS, classical Greek sculptor. The Duc de Guermantes likened to the statue of Olympian Zeus said to have been cast in gold: II 294. Inscribed the name of the athlete he loved on the ring of his Olympian Zeus: III 334. Anglo-Saxon soldiers "like living statues by Phidias" to Charlus: 801.

PHILIBERT LE BEAU (1480–1504), Duke of Savoy. His initials intertwined with those of Margaret of Austria in the church of Brou: I 322–3.

PHILIPPE VI de Valois, King of France (1293–1350): II 452.

PHILIPPE LE HARDI, King of France (1245–85): II 543.

PHILIPPE-ÉGALITÉ, Duc d'Orléans (1747–93): II 608.

PICCINI, Niccoló, Neapolitan composer (1728–1800). His *Iphigenia* compared to Gluck's: II 488.

PICQUART, Georges-Marie, Colonel, later General and Minister of War (1854–1914). One of the principal actors in the Dreyfus Case: II 108. Discussed by Norpois and Bloch: 241, 247–8. Minister of War: 307 (cf. III 824). Bloch's appeal on his behalf:

738; 740. Frequents Mme Verdurin's *salon*: 774 (cf. 914; III 238); III 824.

PINDAR, Greek poet: II 198.

PIRANESI, Giambattista, Italian architect and engraver (1720–78): I 71.

PISANELLO, Antonio, Italian painter and medallist (c. 1380–1456). Patterns of foam in Balbec bay etched with the delicacy of a Pisanello: I 860. His flower drawings compared unfavourably with Mme de Villeparisis's by Legrandin: II 219. Queen Victoria's profile on English pennies might have been drawn by him: III 744.

PIUS IX, Pope (1792–1878). Françoise buys a photograph of him: I 525, 737.

PLANTÉ, Francis, French pianist (1839–1934): I 205; II 926.

PLATO, Greek philosopher: I 313. Françoise distorts Mme de Villeparisis's words as Plato distorts Socrates': 750. Françoise's mistakes due, like the fables in which Plato believed, to a false conception of the world and to preconceived ideas: II 372. Plato and homosexuality: III 204 (cf. 219, 835; II 985). Allusion to the *Symposium*: 284. Brichot in Charlus's company feels like Plato with Aspasia: 335. Analogous ideas may differ according to whether they have been expounded by Xenophon or Plato: 769.

PLAUTUS, Roman comedy writer: I 832.

PLINY the Younger, Roman writer: II 462.

PLOTINUS, 3rd-century philosopher: II 1017.

POE, Edgar Allan, American writer (1809–49): I 781.

POINCARÉ, Henri, French mathematician (1854–1912): II 115.

POINCARÉ, Raymond, President of the Republic 1913–20: III 772, 826.

POLIGNAC, Prince Edmond de. Rents the Prince of X.'s castle for the Bayreuth festival: II 557. Figures in Tissot's picture of the Rue Royale club: III 199.

POMPADOUR, Mme de (1721–64), mistress of Louis XV: II 591; III 565.

PONSARD, François, French poet and dramatist (1814–67). Allusion to his comedy *Le Lion amoureux*: II 488.

POREL, Director of the Odéon 1884–91: II 963, 966.

PORPHYRY, neo-Platonist philosopher: II 1017.

POTAIN, Dr, French physician (1825–1901). Cottard compared

to him: I 205 (cf. II 910). Despairs of Vinteuil's life: 233–4.

POURTALÈS, Comtesse Edmond de, Second Empire beauty and hostess. The Prince de Borodino dines with her: II 133. Her ignorance of the Dreyfus Case: 416. "Mélanie Pourtalès arranged things far better" (Oriane): 697.

POUSSIN, Nicolas, French painter (1594–1665). Gilberte's name, floating through the air, compared to a little cloud in a Poussin landscape: I 428. To destroy a park by Le Nôtre as bad as slashing a Poussin painting: 821. Discussed by M. and Mme de Cambremer; "an old hack" in her view, but Degas's admiration for him gives her pause: II 839–41. Anticipated Turner: 844.

PRADON, Nicolas, French poet and playwright, rival of Racine (1632–98): II 488.

PRASLIN, Duchesse de (Choiseul), daughter of General Sebastiani, murdered by her husband in 1847. Friend of Mme de Villeparisis's mother: I 779; II 557.

PRAXITELES, classical Greek sculptor: III 204.

PROUDHON, Pierre-Joseph, French philosopher (1809–65). Admired by Saint-Loup: I 787. M's grandmother gives Saint-Loup a collection of autograph letters by him: 925 (cf. II 71).

PUCCINI, Giacomo, Italian composer (1858–1924): III 215.

PUGET, Loisa, French poetess (1810–89): II 707.

QUILLARD, Pierre, French poet, Hellenist and journalist (1864–1912). Violent Dreyfusard; his encounter at the Zola trial with Colonel du Paty de Clam, who quotes from his symbolist play La Fille aux mains coupées: III 777.

RABELAIS, François, French writer (c. 1494–1553). Quoted by Norpois: II 254. Quoted by Brichot: 1085, who prefers him to Balzac: 1086.

RACINE, Jean, French dramatist (1639–99). Bloch quotes a famous line from Phèdre, which has "the supreme merit of meaning absolutely nothing": I 97. Bergotte's essay on him: 107. Quotation from Athalie: 117. Indirect quotation from Phèdre: 158. Gilberte gives M Bergotte's monograph: 437. M reads a passage on the old myths from which Racine drew his inspiration: 444. Quotation from Phèdre: 475, 477. Phrases from Bergotte: 478. Berma in Phèdre: 479–86. M discusses Phèdre with Bergotte: 603–5. Racine and Louis XIV: 606. Quotation from *Esther*: 739. Charlus on Racine: 819. Allusion to a line from *Athalie*: 858. Gisèle's essay, "Letter from Sophocles to Racine": 972–6 (cf. II 366; III 387). Berma in *Phèdre* again: II 46–8. Quotation from *Esther*: 392. Quotation from *Andromaque*: 460. M. de Vaugoubert's behaviour at the Princesse de Guermantes's recalls passages from *Esther*: 689–90. Pages at the Grand Hotel suggest the chorus from *Athalie*: 802 (cf. 1019). Nissim Bernard's young waiter likened to an Israelite in *Athalie*: 872–3. *Esther* quoted by Charlus: 1019. Quotation from *Esther*; Albertine compares M to Assuerus: III 10 (cf. 402). "Albertine-Esther": 94. Another scene from *Esther*: 115. Charlus's transition from violence to Christian meekness compared to the change of tone between *Andromaque* and *Esther*: 328. More quotations from *Esther*: 419. M sees the declaration scene in *Phèdre* as a sort of prophecy of the amorous episodes in his own life: 467–9. Quotation from *Phèdre*: 659. Phèdre as a Jansenist: 949. Berma identified with Phèdre: 1050.

RAMBUTEAU, Claude-Philibert Berthelot, Baron de, French politician and administrator, *préfet* of the Seine in 1833; introduced public urinals with individual compartments: III 188, 772.

RAMEAU, Jean-Philippe, French composer (1683–1764). Quotation from Gluck's *Armide* attributed to him: III 113. Albertine plays him on the pianola: 388.

RAPHAEL, Italian painter (1483–1520): I 812; III 158. Silhouettes of trees in Paris reminiscent of those in the backgrounds to his paintings: 757. Goncourt elevates Watteau above him: 804.

RASPAIL, François, French politician and scientist (1794–1878). Françoise buys a photograph of him: I 525, 737.

RASPUTIN, Gregory (c. 1871–1917). His murder a Dostoievsky incident in real life: III 802.

RAUDNITZ. Dress-designer. Mme Cottard swears by him: I 644.

RAVEL, Maurice, French composer (1875–1937): III 1080.

RÉCAMIER, Mme: II 431. Her *salon* at l'Abbaye-aux-Bois: 906, 1085; III 743, 1079.

REDFERN. Dress-designer: I 644.

REDON, Odilon. French painter (1840–1916). His "subtlety of expression" (Elstir): I 900.

REGENT, The. *See* Orléans, Duc d'.

REGNARD, Jean-François, French playwright (1655–1709): III 962.

REGNIER, Mathurin, French satirist poet (1573–1613). Quoted by the barrister at Balbec: I 755.

REICHENBERG, Suzanne, French actress (1853–1924), for thirty years the principal *ingénue* at the Comédie-Française. The Duc de Guermantes persuades her to recite for Edward VII: II 446. Mme Molé's attempt to emulate both the Duchesse and the Princesse de Guermantes like someone trying to be at once Reichenberg and Sarah Bernhardt: III 235.

REINACH, Joseph, French writer and politician (1856–1921). Dreyfusard activist: II 249, 255. His achievement in the Dreyfus Case "the most astonishing victory for rational politics the world has ever seen": 306–7. Frequents Mme Verdurin's *salon*: 774 (cf. 914). Mentioned: III 236, 951, 1009.

REJANE, French actress (1856–1920): II 513; III 1048.

REMBRANDT, Dutch painter (1606–69). Odette's "Rembrandt hat": I 262–3. His *Night Watch* "the supreme masterpiece" in Mme Verdurin's view: 278. The Swann dining-room as dark as "an Asiatic temple painted by Rembrandt": 545. Interior of the Grand Hotel seen from the lift reminiscent of a Rembrandt: 858. A little curio shop in Doncières at night like a composition by Rembrandt: II 95. Charlus's two Rembrandts: 584. The "gentle gravity" of certain of his portraits: 704. His Jewish scenes admired by Charlus: 1143. His portraits of women compared to Dostoievsky: III 384. The fantastic world of the *Night Watch*: 386. Unique rays that still reach us from the world of Rembrandt: 932. The "terrible ravaged face" of the aged Rembrandt: 943.

RENAN, Ernest, French historian (1823–92): I 545; III 266, 333.

RENOIR, Auguste, French painter (1841–1919). It took a great deal of time for him to be hailed as a great artist: II 338. His painting of the publisher Charpentier at home: III 742, 794.

RETZ, Paul de Gondi, Cardinal de (1613–79). "That *struggle for lifer* de Gondi" (Brichot): II 905.

RIBOT, Alexandre, French statesman (1842–1923): I 470; II 446.

RIGAUD, Hyacinthe, French portrait-painter (1659–1743): II 602.

RIMBAUD, Arthur, French poet (1854–91): I 781; III 619.

RIMSKY-KORSAKOV, Nicolai, Russian composer (1844–1908). Reference to *Sheherazade*; 11 238.

RISLER, Edouard, French pianist (1873–1929): 11 926.

RISTORI, Mme, Italian tragic actress (1821–1906). Recites *chez* "Alix": 11 202, 207.

RIZZO, Antonio, Italian architect and sculptor (1430–98). Swann's coachman Rémi resembles his bust of the Doge Loredan: 1 243, 250.

ROBERT, Hubert, French painter (1733–1808). M's grandmother gives him a photograph of the "fountains of Saint-Cloud" after Hubert Robert: 1 43. His art simulated by moonlight on Combray gardens: 124. The Hubert Robert fountain in the Prince de Guermantes's garden: 11 680–81; Mme d'Arpajon inundated by it: 681–2; Charlus's opinion of it: 683.

RODIN, Auguste, French sculptor (1840–1917): 111 775.

ROETTIERS, Joseph, 18th-century jeweller: 111 375.

ROLLAND, Romain, French writer and pacifist (1866–1944). Quoted by Saint-Loup in his letters to M during the war: 111 777.

RONSARD, Pierre de, French poet (1524–85): 11 933. Line from one of his *Sonnets pour Hélène*: 1185; 111 446

ROQUES, General, Minister of War in 1916: 111 953.

ROSTAND, Edmond, French poet and playwright (1868–1918), author of *Cyrano de Bergerac* and *L'Aiglon*: 11 219, 1105.

ROTHSCHILDS, The. Sir Rufus Israels' family compared to them: 1 558. The Prince de Guermantes allows a wing of his château to be burnt down rather than ask the help of his Rothschild neighbours: 11 604. The Duchesse de Guermantes entertains them: 111 32. Baron de Rothschild: 1 826. Baronne Alphonse de Rothschild: 11 304; Bloch's *gaffe* when introduced to her by Mme de Villeparisis: 525; constantly *chez* Oriane: 693; a rose named after her: 1039; at the La Trémoïlles'': 111 34. Edmond de Rothschild: 11 443.

ROUHER, Eugène, Minister of Napoleon 111 (1814–84): 11 132.

ROUJON, Henry, French Academician (1853–1914), author of a book (*Au milieu des hommes*) which Mme Verdurin offers to Charlus: 11 1079.

ROUSSEAU, Jean-Baptiste, French poet (1671–1741): 11 251.

ROUSSEAU, Jean-Jacques, French-Swiss writer and philosopher

(1712–78). M's father disapproves of his being given a volume of Rousseau as a birthday present: I 42.

ROUSSEAU, Théodore, French painter (1812–67): III 290.

ROUVIER, Maurice, French politician (1842–1911), Prime Minister during the Moroccan crisis between France and Germany in 1905: III 588.

RUBENS, Peter Paul, Flemish painter (1577–1640). Swann's Rubens: I 581. M. Bloch's bogus Rubens: 833. Made goddesses out of women he knew: 1013.

RUBINSTEIN, Anton, Russian pianist (1829–94): I 205. M's grandmother has a weakness for his discords and wrong notes: 789.

RUSKIN, John, English writer and artist (1819–1900). Quotations (unattributed) from *Stones of Venice*: I 425–6. Quoted by M's mother: 698. "A tedious old proser", according to Bloch, who calls him Lord John Ruskin: 794–5. M's work on Ruskin: III 660. Jupien's allusion to M's translation of *Sesame and Lilies*: 862.

SABRAN, Mme de. One of the mistresses of the Regent: II 557.

SAGAN, Prince de. Greets Odette in the Bois: I 689. His dashing style: I 522. His hats: 601. His last appearance in society: 746. References to the Princesse de Sagan: II 205, I 212, 250–52. Friend of Swann: III 1006.

SAINT-LÉGER LÉGER, Alexis, French poet and diplomat, better known under his pseudonym Saint-John Perse (1887–1919). "Is it poetry, or just riddles?" asks Céleste: II 878.

SAINT-MÉGRIN. Favourite or "mignon" of Henri III: III 812.

SAINT-SAENS, Camille, French composer (1835–1921). Allusion to his *Samson et Dalila* ("Israel, break thy chains"): I 98.

SAINT-SIMON, Duc de, author of the *Memoirs* (1675–1755). Quoted by Swann on Maulévrier: I 27–8. The "mechanics" of life at Versailles: 128 (cf. 337). One of Swann's favourite authors: 337. Françoise's class attitudes compared to Saint-Simon's: 531. His portrait of Villars quoted to illustrate the unforeseeableness of the language of great writers; 593. Cited in illustration of the superiority of creation to observation: 825. Françoise uses his language: II 66. Mme de Villeparisis has a portrait of him: 304. The Duc de Guermantes's punctilious courtesy as a host reminiscent of an ancestor of his described by Saint-Simon;

quoted on the ethos of Louis XIV's court and its similarity to the behaviour of the Duc de Guermantes: 452–3. "Admirable but fearsome": 476. Quoted by Charlus on the validity of a Guermantes title: 980. Charlus's Saint-Simonian tableaux-vivants; the Maréchal d'Huxelles: 1000. The caste system of Combray as rigid as Saint-Simon's: 1060. Mme de Guermantes's style of reminiscence recalls Saint-Simon: III 29. His euphemism for homosexuality: 212. "That old pest" (Brichot): 306. Quoted on the Maréchal d'Huxelles: 307–8 (cf. II 1000). Albertine enjoys talking about him to M: 540, 567. His portrait of the Marquis d'Allemans: 600–01. Quoted on the subject of noblemen who (like Charlus) associate with their inferiors: 860–61. Quoted on Louis XIV's ignorance of genealogy: 1006. M's book "the *Memoirs* of Saint-Simon of another age": 1101–2.

SAINT-VALLIER (father of Diane de Poitiers): III 812.

SAINTE-BEUVE, Charles-Augustin, French writer (1804–69). Quoted by Norpois on Alfred de Vigny: I 512. Admired by Mme de Villeparisis: 764. Approved by Andrée: 976. In describing the subtle distinctions between *salons* unwittingly betrays the vacuity of *salon* life: II 431. Preferred alternatively as critic and poet: 488. Depravity of taste shown in his prose style: 1123. Charlus's scandal-mongering "enough to supply all the appendixes of the *Causeries du Lundi*" (Brichot): III 334. The original flaw in the type of literature represented by his *Lundis*: 581. Allusion to his poem *La Fontaine de Boileau*: 741; 743. The grimacing smile that accompanies and disfigures his "spoken phrases": 934.

SAINTINE, Xavier, French novelist (1798–1865): I 160.

SALVANDY, Comte de, French writer and politician (1795–1856): I 763; II 284.

SAMARY, Jeanne, French actress (1857–90): I 80; II 968.

SAND, George, French novelist (1804–76). M's grandmother gives him the four pastoral novels: I 42 (cf. III 6). His mother reads *François le Champi* to him: 44–5. Saniette's story about the duke who didn't know that George Sand was a woman: 285. Attractive compromise between the provincial and the literary in *La Petite Fadette*: III 28. The marriage of Mlle d'Oloron and the young Cambremer "a marriage from the last chapter of a George Sand novel": 673. On opening *François le Champi* in the Prince de

Guermantes's library, M finds his whole childhood restored to him: 918–23, 1102.

SAPPHO, Greek poetess. M compares Albertine to her: 11 829–30.

SARCEY, Francisque, French drama critic (1827–99): 11 921.

SARDOU, Victorien, French playwright (1831–1908). All the notabilities of Paris "walk on" in one of his plays: 1 576, 832. Queens in his plays: 11 442.

SARRAIL, GENERAL. COMMANDER OF THE SALONIKA EXPEDITIONARY FORCE IN 1916: 111 953.

SAUSSIER, General. His role in the Dreyfus Case: 11 105.

SAVONAROLA, Girolamo, Italian preacher (1452–98). Mme Blatin the image of his portrait by Fra Bartolommeo: 1 576.

SAXE, Maréchal de, French general (1696–1750): 11 446.

SCARLATTI, Domenico, Italian composer (1685–1757). Mme de Cambremer requests Morel to play a "divine" Scarlatti piece: 11 987.

SCARRON, Paul, French poet and playwright (1610–60). Husband of Mme de Maintenon (q.v.): 1 606.

SCHILLER, Johann Friedrich von, German poet and dramatist (1759–1805): 11 511. Allusion to his comedy *Uncle and Nephew*: 721; 111 817, 865.

SCHLEGEL, Wilhelm von, German naturalist (1867–1845). Taught Mme de Villeparisis botany in her childhood: 11 284.

SCHLIEFFEN, Field Marshal von, Chief of the German General Staff 1891–1905. Saint-Loup refers to his famous "plan"; 11 111–12.

SCHLUMBERGER, Gustave, French historian (1844–1929): 11 219.

SCHOPENHAUER, Artur, German philosopher (1788–1860). Mme de Cambremer's knowledge of him: 111 761, 1041.

SCHUBERT, Franz, Austrian composer (1792–1828). M celebrates the renunciation of his love for Mme de Guermantes by singing Schubert's *Farewell*: 11 385.

SCHUMANN, Robert, German composer (1810–56). M hears him being played from his hotel room: 11 817. Fauré's Schumannesque sonata: 986. "Hushed serenity" of *Kinderszenen*: 111 255. Sudden dénouements of some of his ballads: 510. Mentioned in Saint-Loup's letters to M during the war: 777. Last words which

M hears on Saint-Loup's lips the opening lines of a Schumann song: 877.

SCOTT, Sir Walter, Scottish writer (1771–1832). References to Rob Roy and Diana Vernon: 11 647.

SCRIBE, Eugène, French playwright and librettist (1791–1861). Wrote the librettos of *Les Diamants de la Couronne*: 1 79; 11 466, 509–10; *Le Domino noir*: 1 79; *La Juive*: 1 621; 11 874; *Fra Diavolo*: 11 509; *Le Chalet*: 11 509; *Robert le Diable*: 11 986.

SERT, Jose Maria, Catalan painter (1876–1945). Designer for the *Ballets russes*; 111 376; *The Legend of Joseph*: 662.

SÉVIGNÉ, Mme de, author of the famous *Letters* (1626–96). "Sévigné would not have put it better!": 1 21 (cf. 11 341). A "worthy old snob" (Brichot): 285. M's grandmother's "beloved Sévigné"; her plan to follow her itinerary to Normandy: 695, 698. Quoted by M's mother: 699–700. M's grandmother gives him a volume of the *Letters* to read in the train to Balbec: 701. Reflections on her style; her Dostoievsky side: 702–3 (cf. 111 385). Quoted by M's grandmother on the food in the Grand Hotel: 746, 749. Criticised by Mme de Villeparisis: 749. Defended by Charlus against Mme de Villeparisis: 818–19. Françoise's Sévigné vocabulary; 11 18. Quoted on Mme de La Fayette's death: 311. Quoted by M's grandmother apropos of the "Marquise" in the Champs-Elysées: 322. Charlus has a rare edition of the *Letters* bound for M: 585. M's grandmother's devotion to Sévigné inherited by her daughter, who reads and quotes her constantly in letters to M: 797–8 (*see also* 814,, 835, 865, 958, 1051; 111 9, 136–7, 370). The name Sévigné draws a grimace from Mme de Cambremer-Legrandin: 852. M's mother scorns "hackneyed Sévigné: 111 672 (cf. 1 702).

SHAKESPEARE, William (1564–1616). Allusion to *A Midsummer Night's Dream* apropos of asparagus: 1 131. Effects of reading Shakespeare: 614. Transvestism in his comedies: 11 644. Allusion to *Romeo and Juliet* apropos of Charlus and Jupien: 651. *Hamlet* quoted by Saint-Loup: 1055. Reference to *Hamlet*: 1069. Lear-like majesty of Charlus in old age: 111 891, 962. The face of an old Shylock detectable in Bloch at close quarters: 1012.

SILVESTRE, Armand, French writer (1837–1901). Quoted by Charlus to Morel: 111 611.

SIMIANE, Pauline de, granddaughter of Mme de Sévigné (1674–1737). Quotations from her letters: I 702–3; II 462.

SOCRATES, Greek philosopher. His words distorted by Plato: I 750. Inverts take pleasure in recalling that he was one of them: II 639 (cf. 986). Quoted by Cottard: 1085–6. His jokes about young men: III 204. Jupien on Socrates: 861.

SODOMA (Giovanni Bazzi), Italian painter (c. 1477–1549): III 219.

SOPHOCLES, Greek dramatist. Gisèle's essay — "Letter from Sophocles to Racine"; I 972–6 (cf. II 366). Reference to Oedipus: III 892.

SPARTACUS, Roman slave leader: I 369.

SPINOZA, Baruch, Dutch, philosopher (1632–77). Admired by Charlus: II 1143.

SPITTELER, Karl, Swiss novelist (1845–1924). Brichot praises his anti-militarism: III 803.

STAËL, Mme de, French woman of letters (1766–1817). The Haussonville family descended from her, through her daughter and granddaughter: III 1014.

STAMATI, Franco-Greek pianist (1811–70). Charlus took lessons from him: II 1042.

STENDHAL (Henri Beyle), French novelist (1783–1842). "Stendhalian sweetness" of the name Parma: I 421 (cf. II 442–3). Mme de Villeparisis recalls her father's personal reminiscences of him: 763–4. Discussed with Saint-Loup at Doncières; Bloch "can't stand" him; Norpois compared to Mosca: II 106–7. Mme de Guermantes's invitation to dine with the Princesse de Parme evokes for M Fabrice and Count Mosca: 390. Far from being a Sanseverina, the Princess turns out to be excessively unStendhalian: 443. Reference to la Sanseverina: 1038. Symbols in his work discussed by M with Albertine: III 383 (cf. 556). Allusion to the preface of La Chartreuse de Parme: 561.

STEVENSON, Robert Louis, British writer (1850–94). "A very great writer", according to Swann, quoted in the Goncourt pastiche: III 736.

STRAUSS, Richard, German composer (1864–1949). "Vulgar motifs" of Salome: II 465–6. A "great composer": III 238. Allusion to The Legend of Joseph: 662.

STRAVINSKY, Igor, Russian composer (1882–1972). "Flowering

of the Russian Ballet reveals his genius: II 770. A "great composer": III 238.

SUGER, Abbé de Saint-Denis, minister and counsellor of Louis VI and Louis VII (1081–1151): I 275.

SULLY PRUDHOMME, French poet (1839–1907). His *Ici-bas tous les lilas meurent* the only poem Céleste and her sister know: II 878, 1163. His *Aux Tuileries* recited by Charlus to Morel: III 611.

SYLVA, Carmen, pen-name of Elisabeth, Queen of Rumania (1843–1916): II 207.

SYVETON, Gabriel, Nationalist Deputy who died in mysterious circumstances in 1904: III 825.

TACITUS, Roman historian. Françoise would have written like him: II 373.

TAGLIAFICO, Franco-Italian singer and composer (1821–1900). One of Odette's favourite musicians; his *Pauvre Fou* to be played at her funeral: I 258.

TAINE, Hippolyte, French critic, philosopher and historian (1828–93). The Princesse Mathilde offended by an article of his on Napoleon: I 583. He and Charlus agree about Balzac: II 1087. His name floats through M's dreams: III 118.

TALLEMANT DES RÉAUX (1619–92). Author of *Les Historiettes*. Anecdote about the Chevalier de Rohan: II 554.

TALLEYRAND, Charles-Maurice, French statesman (1754–1838): II 132. Dr du Boulbon quotes his phrase *"bien portant imaginaire"*: 317. Quoted by Brichot: 905, who refers to him as "Charles-Maurice, Abbé de Périgord": 912.

TALLIEN, Mme, wife of the revolutionary Jean-Lambert Tallien and leader of fashion under the Directory (1773–1835). Her "fine and flowing hair": II 557. War-time Paris compared to the Directory; Tallien styles in dress: III 743, Mme Verdurin and Mme Bontemps "old and ugly" versions of Mme Tallien: 747.

TALMA, François-Joseph, French actor (1763–1826): III 744.

THIBAUD, Jacques, French violinist (1880–1953). Compared to Morel: III 47, 289.

THIERRY, Augustin, French historian (1795–1856). M reads him in the garden at Combray: II 865.

THIERS, Adolphe, French statesman and historian (1797–1877): II 198, 213; III 654.

alludes to the *Surrender of Breda* in the Prado: 11 577. The Duc
de Guermantes's putative Velazquez: 600, 602. Albertine's hair
done up like a Velazquez Infanta's: 111 379.

VENDÔME, Louis-Joseph, Duc de. Great-grandson of Henri IV
and Gabrielle d'Estrées and one of Louis XIV's generals
(1654–1712). An invert?: 111 306–7.

VENIZELOS, Greek statesman, Prime Minister during World
War I: 111 813.

VERLAINE, Paul, French poet (1844–96): 1 781. Anathematised
by Brichot: 11 988. Mme de Guermantes offers M a Verlaine
recital by Rachel: 111 1081.

VERMANDOIS, Comte de, son of Louis XIV and Mlle de la
Vallière (1667–83). An invert?: 111 306.

VERMEER, Jan, Dutch painter (1623–75). Swann's essay on him: 1
215–16, 262–3, 325, 384, 505, 575 (cf. 11 733). The Duc de
Guermantes uncertain of having seen the *View of Delft* in The
Hague: 11 544. Swann's favourite painter; Charlus compares
Jacquet to him: 733. "Do you know the Vermeers?" asks Mme de
Cambremer; Albertine thinks they are living people: 843.
Bergotte gets up from his sick-bed to go and look at the *View of
Delft*; the little patch of yellow wall: 111 185–6. His pictures
fragments of an identical world: 384. Unique radiance that still
reaches us from his world: 932.

VERNE, Jules, French writer (1828–1905): 11 1058.

VERONESE, Paul, Venetian painter (1528–88). Roof of the Gare
Saint-Lazare recalls one of his skies, "of an almost Parisian
modernity": 1 694. Albertine's profile less beautiful than those of
Veronese's women: 917. His paintings of Venetian revels:
959–60 (cf. 11 673). Fruit and wine "as luscious as a beautiful
Veronese" (Ski): 971. Mentioned: 111 205, 640.

VIBERT, Jehan-Georges, French painter (1840–1902). M de
Guermantes prefers him to Elstir: 11 520 (cf. 545).

VIGNY, Alfred de, French poet (1797–1863). Swann recalls a
passage from his *Journal d'un Poète*: 1 399. Norpois's opinion of
him: 512. Quoted by M to Mme de Villeparisis: 775; her low
opinion of him: 776 (cf. 11 196). Anna de Noailles compared to
him: 11 104–5. Quotations from *La Colère de Samson*: 638. M
quotes two lines from *La Maison du Berger* to Albertine: 894.
Quotations from *Eloa* applied to Princess Sherbatoff: 907.

"Manly reticence" — an echo of *Servitude et Grandeur militaires*: III 767.

VILLARS, Duc de, Maréchal de France (1653–1734). His portrait by Saint-Simon: I 593. An invert?: III 307.

VILLIERS DE L'ISLE-ADAM, French Symbolist writer (1840–89). Referred to familiarly by Bloch's sister: I 830.

VIOLLET-LE-DUC, Eugène, French architect and writer (1814–79). Allusion to his restorations apropos of Combray: I 181. Denounced by Swann: 319, Restorations by pupils of his often give "the most potent sensation of the Middle Ages": II 911.

VIRGIL, Roman poet. Allusion to Book IV of the *Georgics*: I 19. Anecdotes from Virgil in the porch of Saint-André-des-Champs: 164. In Dante's *Inferno*: 185. "Virgil's Leucothea" (a Proustian error — the "white goddess" is not mentioned in Virgil): 1011. Cited by Brichot: II 962, 984–5. Charlus and Virgilian shepherds: 985; III 204 (cf. 333).

VOISENON, Abbé de, licentious novelist, friend of Voltaire (1708–75): II 283,

VOLTAIRE (François-Marie Arouet), French writer and philosopher (1694–1778). Bloch attributes to him ("Master Arouet") two lines from Corneille's *Polyeucte* I 940. Andrée quotes him on Racine: 975. Allusion to *Zaïre*: II 40. Brichot at las Raspelière sees himself as the equivalent of "M. de Voltaire" *chez* Mme du Châtelet: 906. Further allusion by Brichot: 1086.

WAGNER, Richard, German composer (1813–83). "Solemn sweetness" of a joyful celebration characteristic of *Lohengrin*: I 194 (cf. II 6). Odette's projected visit to Bayreuth: 328. Vinteuil's "little phrase" compared to a theme in *Tristan*: 381. Saint-Loup deplores his father's indifference to Wagner: 788. Plaintive whine of a closing door reminds M of the overture to *Tannhäuser*: II 406. Nietzsche and Wagner: 409 (cf. III 156). Mme de Guermantes's glib views on Wagner: 487, 489, 509; he sends the Duke to sleep: 509. His later manner compared to Victor Hugo's: 570. Allusion to the March in *Tannhäuser*: 673. The sound of the telephone compared to the shepherd's pipe in *Tristan*: 757. Odette a "Wagnerian": 775. Mme de Cambremer compares *Pelléas* and *Parsifal*: 842. Reflections on Debussy and Wagner: 843–4. Mme Verdurin and Wagner: 914, 936, 959. The Princesse de Guermantes a passionate Wagnerian: 1180. Vinteuil's sonata and *Tristan*; M's reflections on Wagner's themes, the mystery of creativity, the retrospective unity of the *Ring*, etc.: III 155–9 (cf. 166, 495). Early and late Wagner compared: 265 (cf. 699). Princess von Metternich's reaction to the hissing of Wagner: 276. Allusion to Beckmesser by Charlus: 278. Wagnerian leitmotifs: 451. Saint-Loup's reference to the wood-bird in "that sublime *Siegfried*": 777. "The music of the air-raid sirens like the Ride of the Walkyries" (Saint-Loup): 781 (cf. 802: "the only German music to have been heard since the war").

WATTEAU, Antoine, French painter (1684–1721). Swann's memories of Odette's smiles recall sheets of sketches by Watteau: I 262. Odette's "Watteau *peignoir*": 663. Dancer in the theatre with cheeks chalked in red "like a page from a Watteau album": II 180. Elstir a Watteau *à vapeur* (Saniette's pun): 970. Goncourt elevates him above Raphael: III 804. His works destroyed by the revolutionaries: 918.

WEDGWOOD, Josiah, Staffordshire potter (1730–93): II 537.

WELLS, H. G., English writer (1866–1946). Allusion to *The Invisible Man*: II 197.

WHISTLER, James McNeill, American painter (1834–1903): Carrière portrait of Mme de Guermantes "as fine as Whistler" (Saint-Loup): 810. Balbec seascape reminiscent of a Whistler "Harmony in Grey and Pink": 863. Elstir's portrait of Odette compared to a Whistler: 922. Balbec Bay the "gulf of opal painted by Whistler" (Elstir): II 23. Quoted by Charlus: 585. Charlus's evening coat a "Harmony in Black and White": 677. Charlus cites him as an arbiter of taste: III 304. Skyline in Carpaccio's *Patriarch of Grado* reminiscent of Whistler: 661. M. Verdurin has written a book about him, according to the Goncourts: 728 (cf. 794).

WIDAL, Fernand, French physician (1862–1929): II 308.

WIDOR, Charles, French composer and organist (1845–1937): II 446.

WILDE, Oscar, Irish writer (1854–1900). Allusion to his downfall in the dissertation on the plight of inverts: II 638.

WILLIAM II, the Kaiser, Norpois's views on him: I 500. Charlus hints that he is an invert: II 300 (cf. 979 and III 814). Saint-Loup on his intentions over Morocco: 428. Discussed at the dinner-table by Prince Von and Oriane; dislikes Elstir's

INDEX OF PLACES

personalities of Balbec identified by Albertine: 943. Farms in the neighbourhood; picnics on the cliffs: 965–6. End of the season at Balbec; M's memories of his stay: 1013–18. Balbec bay the "gulf of opal painted by Whistler": 11 23. M's desire for Albertine confused with his desire for Balbec: 363–5, 366–7. M's second visit: 778–1169. The manager of the Grand Hotel and his malapropisms: 778–83, 790–92. Life at the hotel; the lift-boy, the pages; a Racinian stage-set: 800–02 (cf. 872–3). Views of the sea: 811–12. The little train and its nicknames: 812. Girls on the beach: 867–9. A scandal at the Grand Hotel: 871. Nissim Bernard and the fledgling waiter: 871–4. Etymology of the name Balbec: 968–9. Roads near Balbec and their associations for M: 1045–6. Corrupting effect of the country round Balbec — "this too social valley": 1148–9. The two pictures of Balbec; Albertine's sleep evokes nights of full moon on the bay: 111 62–5. Albertine's trip to Balbec with the chauffeur: 132 (cf. 339–40). Bathing establishment at the Grand Hotel: 501–2. M's retrospective musings about the Albertine of Balbec and her possible Gomorrhan activities: 510–32 *passim*. Aimé's report on his investigative mission to Balbec: 525–7. "My Hell was the whole region of Balbec": 528–9. The Grand Hotel a stage-set for the different dramas of M's life: 552–3. M visits Balbec with the Saint-Loups: 697–8. M's memories of Balbec and the sea revived by a starched napkin: 901–3, 906–8. (*See also* Rooms *in* Index of Themes)

BAYEUX. One of the stops on the 1.22 train: 1 418–19. What its name evokes: 422. A stained glass window in its cathedral decorated with the arms of the Arrachepels: 11 837.

BAYREUTH. Odette's proposed trip: 1 327–9. The Prince of X . . . lets his castle during the festival: 11 557. Visitors to Bayreuth: 776, 844.

BÉARN. Correct way of pronouncing: 111 27.

BEAUMONT (f). Hill near Balbec with a view of the sea through woods: 11 1037–8 (cf. 1 760–61).

BEAUVAIS. Mme Verdurin's Beauvais tapestry settee: 1 226. Its cathedral: 319, 708; 11 8. Captain de Borodino posted there: 133. Mme de Villeparisis's Beauvais chairs: 193, 211, 280. Charlus's Beauvais chairs: 583. A Beauvais armchair illustrating the Rape of Europa: 768.

BENODET. One of the stops on the 1.22 train: I 419. What its name evokes: 422.

BERLIN. The Wilhelmstrasse: I 497. The Spree: II 253. Prince Von's wife a leading light in the most exclusive set in Berlin: 265. Unter den Linden (Norpois): III 653; Unter den Linden (Charlus): 835.

BOIS DE BOULOGNE, Paris. Verdurin dinner-parties in the Bois: I 287, 293–5, 310–11. Odette's encounter with a woman on the Island in the Bois: 397–8. The Swanns live near it: 447, 450. What it represents for M; Mme Swann's walks and drives there; the Allée des Acacias: 452–6. The Bois in autumn; the Allée des Acacias; "the Elysian Garden of Woman": 456–62. Associated with Swann's memory of Vinteuil's "little phrase": 574. M. Bloch drives through it in a hired victoria: 829. M invites Mme de Stermaria to dine with him on the Island in the Bois; visits it with Albertine: II 398–404. "Improper things" happen there at night: 537. M. de Charlus wants to admire the moonlight in the Bois: 584 (cf. 624). M goes for a walk there with Albertine and contemplates the girls: III 166–73. M walks there alone one Sunday in autumn; its charm and melancholy; "aflower" with girls: 570–73.

BONNÉTABLE, in the Perche region. Norpois went shooting there with Prince Foggi: III 647.

BOURGES. The cathedral: I 708; its soaring steeple in a Book of Hours: III 597.

BRABANT. Its "old-gold, sonorous" name: I 10. The lords of Guermantes were Counts of Brabant: 112, 187, 190–92, 810 (cf. II 539, 612, 614). Charlus claims to be Duke of Brabant: 974, 984.

BRITTANY. Evoked by Legrandin: I 142 (cf. 901). Towns of Brittany served by the 1.22 train: 419, 422. The Stermarias, an ancient Breton family: 730, 735; M imagines a life of poetry and romance in Brittany with Mlle de Stermaria: 740–41. The Island in the Bois evokes for M the "marine and misty" atmosphere of Mlle de Stermaria's Breton island: II 400–01, 413. Mme de Guermantes's Breton anecdotes: III 29. The Breton postal system: 132.

BROU. Tombs of Philibert le Beau and Marguerite d'Autriche in its church: I 322–3.

BRUGES. Visited by Rachel every year on All Souls' Day: II 125–7

BUTTES-CHAUMONT, public park in Paris. Andrée proposes to take Albertine there since she has never been before: III 11; M advises against: 12. Mme Bontemps reveals that Albertine used to go there constantly: 396. M is painfully reminded of this: 553–4. Andrée admits to having frequently made love to Albertine in the Buttes-Chaumont: 622 (cf. 560).

CARQUETHUIT (f), a small port near Balbec. Subject of an Elstir picture: I 894–6, 901. Reminiscent of Florida, according to Elstir: 913.

CARQUEVILLE (f). Mediaeval village with an ivy-covered church which M visits with Mme de Villeparisis: I 761, 768–70.

CHAMPS-ELYSÉES, Paris. "Melancholy neighbourhood" where Gilberte lives: I 156. Françoise takes M for daily walks there: 416, 427. M's first meeting with Gilberte there: 428–9. The importance it assumes in his life; games with Gilberte: 429–43, 524–32. The little pavilion and the "Marquise": 530–31 (cf. II 319–22). Its bad reputation as regards children's health: 533, 538. M sees Gilberte walking along the Avenue des Champs-Elysées with a young man: 671 (cf. III 712–14). Dr du Boulbon advises M's grandmother to go there for her health: II 313. M takes his grandmother there; her stroke: 319–23. M's nostalgic memory of the streets in the neighbourhood of the Champs-Elysées: III 889–90.

CHANTEPIE, Forest of (f), near Balbec. M. de Cambremer shoots there; etymology of the name: II 952–5, 993. M and Albertine drive through it: 1027 (cf. III 491, 498).

CHANTILLY. Residence of the Duc d'Aumale, where M. de Guermantes used to go and dine every week: II 608–9. The Poussins at Chantilly: 841.

CHARLUS (f). Little village in the heart of Burgundy: II 562. The Château de Charlus: 575.

CHARTRES. The cathedral: I 43, 57; the Queens of Chartres: 106; "a positive jewel in stone" (Norpois): 501. Comparison with Balbec church: 501; Notre-Dame de Chartres: II 7, 977; the windows of Chartres: III 165.

CHÂTEAUDUN, in the Eure-et-Loir department. The Curé's brother a tax-collector there: I 62. Mme Goupil has a dress made there: 109. Comtesse G— not even in "the second-best society of Châteaudun": 11 459. Etymology: 919.

CHÂTELLERAULT, in the Vienne department. Mme Bontemps has a villa near there, where Albertine takes refuge after leaving M: 111 443, 534.

CHATOU, near Versailles. The Verdurins organise an outing there to which Swann is not invited: 1 310–15.

CHAUMONT. Town on the upper Loire to which the duc de Broglie retired; reminds M of the Buttes-Chaumont: 111 553.

CHELSEA, London. Whistler "the Chelsea master": 1 863.

CHERRY ORCHARD (f). Farm-restaurant near Balbec where Nissim Bernard encounters the tomato-faced waiters: 11 883.

CHEVREUSE, Valley of. Albertine liked going there with Andrée: 111 558.

COMBRAY (f). M's memories of it: 1 9–204. The house, the little garden, the visitor's bell: 9–15. Evoked by the madeleine: 50–51. General description of the town: 52. "The daily but immemorial chronicles of Combray": 56–63. The church: 63–72. History of the parish: 111–15. The Square; walks round Combray; streets and villas: 123–4, 145. The two "ways": 146–7. The aesthetic standards of Combray: 152. The wind, "tutelary genius" of Combray: 158. The Combray of today and of yesterday; ruins of the castle: 181–3. The moral code of Combray: 467. Nothing less like the social "world" than the society of Combray: 615. Sociological theories of Combray: 792. The rites of Combray: 11 3. The name Guermantes evokes the air of Combray: 6–8. Combray evoked by Françoise: 12, 17–21. Sandstone steps of its houses: 79 (cf. 413). Sense of duty and code of manners Françoise has inherited from Combray: 332, 341–2. Referred to disdainfully by Françoise's daughter as "the back of beyond": 353 (cf. 149–50). M recalls arriving at Combray by night: 412–13. Mme de Guermantes's eyes and voice remind M of Combray countryside: 513. Rue de Saintrailles: 552. The Curé's magnum opus on the parish: 837, 917. The "Combray spirit" — the rule of caste: 1060 (cf. 111 654–5, 673); order and propriety: 111 7. Françoise's Combray "customary": 490. Venice compared to Combray: 111 637–40, 660. Combray's reaction to Gilberte's marriage: 693. M's disillusionment on revisiting the neighbourhood: 709–12, 716, 726. Occupied during the war: 773, 777–8;

the church destroyed: 822. A memory of Combray the point of departure for M's exploration of Time: 1103–7.

COMMANDERIE, La (f). House near Balbec rented by Bloch's father: II 1137; Charlus's anti-semitic observations on the subject: 1141.

COMPIÈGNE. The Verdurins take Odette there without Swann to watch the sunsets in the forest: I 318–19. The Marquis de Forestelle has a house in the neighbourhood: 320. Napoleon III's residence: III 653 (cf. I 585).

COULIVILLE (f). Village near Balbec. Sacrilegious subject represented on the capitals of its old church: II 1115. Morel takes Albertine to a brothel there: III 613.

COUTANCES. One of the stops on the 1.22 train: I 419. What its name evokes: 422.

COWES, Isle of Wight. Albertine wants to go there for the regatta: I 961.

CREUNIERS, Les (f). Rocks near Balbec, reminiscent of a cathedral: I 962. Andrée takes M there: 983, 986–7.

CROIX D'HEULAND, La (f). Farm-restaurant near Balbec: I 965; II 866.

DELFT. Home of Vermeer: I 215, 263. His *View of Delft*: II 544 (cf. III 185). Tulip-gardens in Delft: 594. The Master of Delft: 733.

DONCIÈRES (f). Garrison town not far from Balbec. Remembered by M: I 9. Saint-Loup on military service there: 782, 826, 845, 865, 926, 967. Description: II 67. M visits Saint-Loup there: 68–141. First impressions; the barracks, the Captain's house in the Place de la République: 71–3. First morning there; the view from Saint-Loup's room; mist, frost and hot chocolate: 78–9. The Hôtel de Flandre: 79–82. Walks through the town: 90–91, 93–4; Doncières by night: 95–7. The hotel where Saint-Loup and his friends dine, the Faisan Doré: 97–8 (cf. 1137); military comradeship: 102–19 *passim*. M's memories of "mornings at Doncières": 358–9, 405, and of evenings there (the inn, the panelled dining-room, the serving-girl): 411–12. M and Albertine meet Saint-Loup at Doncières station: 885, 887–9; meeting between Charlus and Morel, who is doing his military service there: 887–92 (cf. 913). Brichot gives the etymology of the name: 1137. Meetings at Doncières station; invitations from Saint-

Loup's friends; meeting with Bloch: 1137–40. Depoeticization of the name: 1147. Recollections of Doncières during the war: III 764–5, 774, 782, 830, 1029.

DOUVILLE or Doville (f). Station on the little local railway which is the stop for Féterne and la Raspelière: II 812, 897. Its etymology: 919. The village and its surroundings: 924–5; the toll-house: 927. Beauty spots round Douville: 1030; the "view of Douville": 1034. Painters from Paris spend their holidays there: 1068.

DRESDEN. Swann needs to go there for his study of Vermeer: I 384. Odette surrounded by Dresden pieces: 662. Mme de Guermantes "a statuette in Dresden china": II 9. The women at the Guermantes dinner party "like Dresden figures": 454. Dresden china plates: 673 (cf. III 731). The art gallery: 1120; III 57.

ECORRES, Les (f). Farm-restaurant near Balbec: I 965. Françoise's young footman born there: II 588. Remembered by M: III 488.

EGREVILLE or Epreville (f). Watering-place near Balbec where Mme Bontemps takes a villa: II 808. M sends the lift-boy there to fetch Albertine: 818, 822, 826. Etymology: 1026.

EGYPT. Odette's projected trip there with Forcheville one Whitsun: I 387. Norpois was Controller of the Egyptian Public Debt: 468. "Doubles" of the dead in ancient Egypt: II 32. Napoleon's Egyptian expedition: 539, 541–2.

FERNEY, Hermitage of. Residence of Voltaire: II 1086.

FÉTERNE (f). The Cambremer estate near Balbec. The notary goes there on Sundays: I 739. Hired cabs wait at the Grand Hotel for the Féterne guests: 758. Its marvellous gardens; its position overlooking the sea: II 792–5. Compared with la Raspelière: 838. The Dowager Mme de Cambremer talks of her little back garden and of her roses: 841. M invited there, but not the judge: 850–52. "Féterne is starvation corner" (Mme Verdurin): 1005. A dinner-party at Féterne: 1123–30.

FLORENCE. Poetry of the name; M conjures it up in his imagination ("a supernatural city"); abortive plan to visit it at Easter: I 419–27. Resurgence of M's desire to go there: 682. His memory of this desire makes it the paschal city: II 144, 150.

FLORIDA. Carquethuit reminds Elstir of certain aspects of Florida: I 913.

FONTAINEBLEAU. Albertine on the Fontainebleau golf club: 11 368. The forest of Fontainebleau: 554. Doncières has a spurious look of Fontainebleau: 1137. Water-grapes from Fontainebleau: 111 124.

FROHSDORF. Austrian residence of the Comte de Chambord, pretender to the French throne: 111 28.

GAETA, port in southern Italy. Its siege and capitulation in 1861 put an end to the Kingdom of the Two Sicilies: 111 249, 276, 327.

GOURVILLE (f). Village near Balbec: 11 1029; the plain of Gourville: 1044; the château of Gourville: 1124; etymology: 1136.

GRAINCOURT-SAINT-VAST (f). First station after Doncières on the little local railway; Cottard catches the train there: 11 895, 900. Cottard and Ski nearly miss the train there: 903, 953.

GRATTEVAST (f). On the little local railway, in the opposite direction from Féterne: 11 1026; M. de Crécy's sister has a house there: 1118.

GUERMANTES (f). Seat of the Guermantes family, not far from Combray. The ultimate goal of the "Guermantes way" — "a sort of abstract geographical term"; surrounded by river scenery (the Vivonne): 1 146–7, 180–83. M and his family never reach it on their walks: 187–8. M's longing to go there: 188, 194, 199–202. Permanent significance of the Guermantes way for him: 200–02. Swann reminded of Guermantes and its countryside on meeting the Princesse des Laumes: 370. Saint-Loup talks about the château: 810–11. M imagines the château: 11 7–9. Françoise talks about it: 18–19, 29. Mme de Guermantes stays on there late into the season: 53. "Shadowy, sun-splashed coolness" of the woods of Guermantes: 209. The Duchess's lunch-parties: 211–14. She and Charlus had played there together as children: 393. Carnations from Guermantes: 566. The Guermantes visitors' book: 570. Life there remembered by the Duke and his brother: 743. The Duchess tells an anecdote about a shooting party (the Marquis du Lau and the Prince of Wales): 111 29 (cf. 600). Gilberte reveals that it can be reached in a quarter of an hour from Combray: 710; the Guermantes way and the Méséglise way not irreconcilable: 711.

HAARLEM. The Frans Halses there discussed at the Guermantes dinner-party: 11 543–4. Tulip gardens in Haarlem: 594.

HARAMBOUVILLE (f). One of the stopping places on the little local railway. A farm labourer gets into the little clan's compartment and is ejected by Cottard: 11 904. Mme Verdurin plans an outing there: 1002. The Cambremers lunch with friends there: 1127. Its etymology (Herimbald's town): 1145–6.

HERMENONVILLE (f). M. de Chevregny's station: 11 1122. Etymology of the name (Herimund's town): 1135, 1137, 1145–7.

HAGUE, The. Swann needs to go there for his study of Vermeer; the Mauritshuis: 1 384. M has been there: 11 544. Its art gallery lends Vermeer's *View of Delft* for an exhibition in Paris: 111 185.

HOLLAND. Swann's fondness for it; Odette imagines it to be ugly: 1 270. M has once been there: 11 544. Albertine has been there: 843. Her excursions in the Dutch countryside: 111 392. M anxious to prevent her from returning: 421. (*See* Amsterdam; Delft; Haarlem; Hague, The.)

HUDIMESNIL (f), near Balbec. M's experience with the three trees near there: 1 770–73 (cf. 111 263).

INCARVILLE (f), near Balbec. Albertine "en pension" there with Rosemonde's family: 11 808, 812–13. M meets Cottard there and they go to the Casino: 822–3, where they see Albertine and Andrée dance together: 823–4. Albertine meets Mme Bontemps's friend with the "bad name" there: 882. M and Albertine drive through it: 1037. Brichot refers to Balbec as Incarville: 1088 (cf. 111 228). M. de Crécy's old castle perched above Incarville: 1121–2. Etymology of the name (the village of Wiscar): 1135. Its cliff: 1145. The Marquis de Montpeyroux and M. de Crécy visit the little train at Incarville station: 1146. The arcades of Incarville where Albertine would wait for M: 111 448. (Sometimes confused with Parville (q.v.).)

INFREVILLE (f), near Balbec. Albertine proposes to call on a lady there: 11 827–8. Later, she denies ever having been near the place: 111 104.

ITALY. Swann brings back photographs of old masters from his visits to Italy: 1 19. M's parents promise him a holiday in the north of Italy: 419. Dreams of Italy: 420. Evocations of Florence, Venice, Parma, etc: 420–27 (cf. 691; 11 150); "Precious lustre" of streets in old Italian towns: 11 146–7. Mme de Guermantes invites Swann to go with her to Italy: 615–17. Trip to Venice: 111

637–70. (*See* Florence; Milan; Orvieto; Padua; Parma; Pisa; Rome; Siena; Trieste; Venice.)

JARDIES, Les. Balzac's house on the outskirts of Paris: II 1086.

JOSSELIN. Residence of the Rohans in Brittany: III 29.

JOUY-LE-VICOMTE (f). Town near Combray where M's grandmother buys books for him: I 42. M. Pupin's daughter goes to boarding school there: 60. Its canals can be seen from the top of the steeple of Combray; its etymology: 114–15. Operations in the neighbourhood during the Great War: III 773.

LAGHET, Notre-Dame de. Place of pilgrimage in the Alpes-Maritimes; Odette has a medal from there: I 242, 394.

LAMBALLE. One of the stops on the 1.22 train: I 419. What its name evokes: 422.

LANNION. One of the stops on the 1.22 train: I 419. What its name evokes: 422.

LAON. Gilberte Swann often goes to spend a few days there: I 159. Its cathedral: II 7–8.

LAUMES, Les (f). Village in Burgundy. The Duc de Guermantes is Prince des Laumes: III 597.

LONDON. Visited by the Verdurins: I 552. Visited by Mme de Cambremer Legrandin; the British Museum: II 207. Prince Von has a house there: 265. Mme de Guermantes goes shopping there: III 36. (*See* Chelsea; Twickenham.)

MAINEVILLE (f). Last stop before Balbec on the little local railway: I 711. M and the little band hire a couple of two-seater "tubs" there: 988. Its cliffs visible from the Grand Hotel: 995. Its luxury brothel: II 813. Princess Sherbatoff catches the train there: 904, 911, 921. An unsuspecting newcomer takes the luxury brothel for a grand hotel: 1111–12. Morel's assignation with the Prince de Guermantes 1112–13. Experiences in the brothel of Charlus and Jupien: 1114–17. Albertine leaves the train there on fine evenings: 1147.

MANS, LE. The notary staying in the Grand Hotel comes from there: I 726. The "high society" of Le Mans: 734. Albertine buys a ring left in a hotel there: III 162.

MARCOUVILLE-L'ORGUEILLEUSE (f). On the little local railway: I 711. Just visible from Rivebelle: 756. M and Albertine visit its church; "I don't like it, it's restored" (Albertine): II 1046–7 (cf. III 165). Its etymology: 1135.

MARIE-ANTOINETTE (f). Farm-restaurant near Balbec adopted by the "little band": I 965; II 866; III 489.

MARIE-THÉRÈSE (f). Farm-restaurant near Balbec: I 965.

MARTINVILLE-LE-SEC (f), near Combray. One of the fiefs of Guermantes: I 183. The twin steeples of its church and the sketch they inspire M to write in Dr Percepied's carriage: 196–8. M reminded of them by the three trees near Hudimesnil: 770. The article on the steeples sent to *Le Figaro*: II 412 (cf. III 4–5, 579–84, 595–6). M reminded of the steeples in a carriage on the way to dine with Saint-Loup: 412, and in a carriage on the way to visit Charlus: 569. Symbolic importance of the impression produced by the steeples: III 263, 381, 899, 912.

MÉSÉGLISE-LA-VINEUSE (f), near Combray. One of the two "ways" for walks round Combray (also known as "Swann's way"): I 146. Méséglise "as inaccessible as the horizon" for M: 146. Itinerary of the Méséglise walks: 147–53, 158–60. Its climate somewhat wet: 163–4, 167. What M owes to the Méséglise way: 169. His desire for a peasant-girl bound up with his desire for Méséglise: 171 (cf. 705, 764; II 56, 96, 781). Permanent significance of the Méséglise way for M: 200–02. Swann yearns after his park near Méséglise: 294. Françoise sings its praises: II 20. Françoise's daughter reluctant to go back there ("the people are so stupid"): 149–50. The Prince des Laumes is Deputy for Méséglise: 491. Its dialect: 754. Legrandin becomes Comte de Méséglise: III 689. Staying with Gilberte at Tansonville — back to the Méséglise way: 709. Not irreconcilable with the Guermantes way: 711. Théodore now the chemist there: 712. The battle for Méséglise during the Great War: 778.

MEUDON, near Paris. The natural heights of Meudon: II 399. Presbytery of Meudon (reference to Rabelais): 1086.

MILAN. The Curé of Combray impressed by the number of steps in the cathedral: I 114. The Ambrosian Library: III 401. A church in Milan: 869.

MIROUGRAIN (f), near Combray. Aunt Léonie has a farm there: I 126. One of her tenant farmers buys it: III 689.

MONTE-CARLO. Admired by Odette: I 270. Féterne like a garden in Monte-Carlo: II 841. "Superb", according to the lift-boy at the Grand Hotel: 1058–9.

MONTFORT-L'AMAURY, near Paris. Mme de Guermantes

proposes to go and see the famous stained-glass windows of its
church on the day of Mme de Saint-Euverte's garden-party: 11
709–10.

MONTJOUVAIN (f), near Combray. M. Vinteuil's house there: 1
122–3, 160–61. M's walks in the vicinity: 169. Scene of sadism
witnessed there by M: 173–80 (cf. 11 630). The scene revived in
M's memory by Albertine's revelation about Mlle Vinteuil: 11
1152–68 (cf. 111 13, 71, 126, 267, 341, 620, 657).

MOROCCO. Saint-Loup posted there; writes to M: 11 360. He
talks about it to M ("Interesting place, Morocco"); hopes to get a
transfer: 428 (cf. 528, 531, 534–5).

NEW YORK. How Françoise pronounces it: 1 480–81.

NICE. Odette once lived there: 1 242, and enjoyed a sort of
amorous notoriety there: 340–42. Her mother said to have sold
her to a rich Englishman there: 399. Nissim Bernard dined there
with M. de Marsantes: 832 (cf. 11 286).

NORMANDY. 18th-century houses in a quaint Norman town: 1
70. Charm of the plains of Normandy: 108. Normandy skies
evoked by Legrandin: 142. "Celestial geography" of Lower
Normandy: 144. Its towns different in reality from what their
names suggest: 420. Its architecture and landscapes: 422.
Apple-trees in Normandy flower later than in the region of
Paris: 11 220. Albertine associated with Normandy: 111 104,
533, 552. (See also Balbec.)

NORWAY. Mme de Guermantes goes on a cruise in the
Norwegian fjords: 11 495–6.

ORLEANS. Its cathedral the ugliest in France, according to
Charlus: 11 633.

ORVIETO. The Creation of Woman in one of the sculptures of its
cathedral: 111 387.

PADUA. Giotto's Vices and Virtues in the Arena Chapel: 1 87–8,
131; Swann a fervent admirer of them: 357. Mantegna altarpiece
in the church of San Zeno and frescoes in the Eremitani chapel:
353. St Anthony of Padua: 549. Mentioned in a quotation from
Alfred de Musset: 824. The life of Fabrice del Dongo related to
Stendhal by a Canon of Padua: 111 561. Visited by M and his
mother: 663.

PARIS. Swann's house on the Quai d'Orléans: 1 17–18 (cf. 266).
The dome of Saint-Augustin seen across a jumble of roofs — a

Piranesi view of Paris: 71. "Melancholy neighbourhood" of the Champs-Elysées where Gilberte lives: 156. Swann scours the boulevards in search of Odette: 249–53. Odette walks in the Rue Abbattucci (now Rue de la Boétie): 262. Odette's idea of the smart places in Paris: 265–6. The frozen Seine from the Pont de la Concorde: 431. M's plan of Paris and obsession with the Swanns' neighbourhood: 447, 450–51. M's mother meets Swann in the Trois Quartiers: 449–50. Paris in autumn: 456. The Sainte-Chapelle "the pearl of them all" (Norpois): 501. Restaurants of Paris: 522–4. M's reactions to Parisian architecture; Gabriel's palaces compared unfavourably to the Trocadéro: 527. Paris "darker than today"; indoor and outdoor lighting; Parisian "winter-gardens": 637. Spring in Paris; Mme Swann's walks in the Avenue du Bois de Boulogne (now Avenue Foch): 682–90. The Gare Saint-Lazare: 694. Paris street names: 737. Rue d'Aboukir, in the Jewish quarter: 793. The Hôtel de Guermantes, a palace in the heart of Paris: 11 9–10. Streets of Paris aflower with unknown beauties: 56. Suburbs of Paris: 157, 159. Rachel and her professional friends — another Paris in the heart of Paris (Place Pigalle, Boulevard de Clichy): 165. Paris in the late afternoon: 210. The Europe district: 443. Poor quarters of Paris reminiscent of Venice; roof-top views: 594. Place de la Concorde on a summer evening: 657. A populous, nocturnal Paris brought miraculously close to M by the telephone: 757, 760. M. de Chevregny sees all the shows in Paris: 1122. Charlus's dissertation on the ecclesiastical background of Paris street names; the Judengasse: 1141–3. Andrée to take Albertine to the Buttes-Chaumont (q.v.): 111 11–13. Street cries of Paris: 111–15, 121–4, 132–5. Charm of the old aristocratic quarters lies in the fact that they are also plebeian: 112. M's drive through Paris with Albertine: 163–74; houses in the boulevards and avenues "a pink congelation of sunshine and cold": 163–4; girls in shop-doors, in the streets, in the Bois (q.v.): 164–72; Albertine on the Trocadéro (q.v.): 164–5; charm of the new districts: 165; full moon over Paris: 173. M meets Gisèle in Passy: 175. The "spoken newspaper" of Paris: 218. Albertine spends three days in Auteuil: 339–40. Paris by moonlight, seen from the Porte Maillot: 414. Long summer evenings in Paris: 491. Paris in war-time: 743–885 *passim*. Fashion and pleasure, in the absence of the arts; comparison with the Directory: 743–55. The black-out: 755–8. Zeppelin raids: 780–82. Nightfall over Paris; comparison with 1815: 785–6, 827–30. Paris as Pompeii: 834 (cf. 864); or as Harun al-Rashid's Baghdad: 837. Hotels and shops closed: 837–8. M walks through Paris in an air-raid: 863, 871. The catacombs of the Métro: 864. The Prince de Guermantes's new house in the Avenue du Bois: 888–9. The streets near the Champs-Elysées: 889–90. (*See* Abbaye-aux-Bois; Bois de Boulogne; Buttes-Chaumont; Champs-Elysées; Trocadéro.)

PARMA. Poetry of the name: I 421. Parma violets: 639, 685 (cf. II 443). Evoked for M on meeting the Princesse de Parme: II 442–3. The Duc de Guermantes spends a winter there: 497. The Princess's palace there: 817.

PARVILLE-LA-BINGARD (f). Station on the little local railway: II 887. View of Parville from la Raspelière: 1031. Etymology: 1037. M drops Albertine there after their outings: 1050, 1053. The cliffs of Parville: 1055, 1167. Albertine's revelation about her relationship with Mlle Vinteuil occurs as the train enters Parville station: 1151–3. (Sometimes confused with Incarville (q.v.).)

PIERREFONDS. The Verdurins take Odette to see the château: I 318–19. The Marquis de Forestelle has a house in the neighbourhood; Swann considers inviting himself to stay in order to intercept Odette at the château: 320–21.

PISA. One of the Italian towns that M imagines visiting: I 423–4 (cf. III 169).

POMPEII. "Arrested in an accustomed movement", as at the destruction of Pompeii: I 970. "Like a hearse on some Pompeian terracotta": II 328. War-time Paris compared to Pompeii: III 834, 864.

PONT-À-COULEUVRE (f). On the little local railway: I 711. The manager of the Grand Hotel meets M there: II 778, 782. M. de Cambremer has seen no snakes there: 956; Brichot gives its etymology: 956–7.

PONT-AVEN. One of the stops on the 1.22 train: I 419. What its name evokes: 422 (cf. 710, 936; III 542).

PONTORSON. One of the stops on the 1.22 train: I 419. What its name evokes: 422.

QUESTEMBERT. One of the stops on the 1.22 train: I 419. What its name evokes: 422.

QUETTEHOLME (f), near Balbec. Goal of some of M's excursions with Mme de Villeparisis; its rocks: I 758. M and Albertine drive through it on the way to the church of Saint-Jean-de-la-Haise: II 1026–9, 1044–6. Albertine sends M telegrams and postcards from there: 1053.

QUIMPERLÉ. One of the stops on the 1.22 train: I 419. What its name evokes: 422 (cf. 710, 936; III 542).

RASPELIÈRE, la (f). Cambremer house rented for the season by the Verdurins: I 466; II 779–80, 795. Its situation and view; etymology of the name: II 836–7. Compared to Féterne: 838, 841–2. Mme Verdurin's "Wednesdays" there: 885–6. M takes the train with the "little clan" to go and dine there: 894–5. The dinner-party: 929–1011. M's first impressions; the Verdurins' enthusiasm for the place: 935–6. The changes they have made and the Cambremers' reactions to them: 945, 948–9, 953–4, 976–7, 982. M calls there with Albertine; its garden and its "views"; excursions in the neighbourhood: 1030–36. Similarities between la Raspelière and Quai Conti: III 286–8.

RHEIMS. The cathedral: I 67. Mme Swann and her daughter go there: 148. "A positive jewel in stone" (Norpois): 501. The statues of Rheims: 794 (cf. 961). Biscuits of Rheims: II 475. Destruction of the cathedral: III 821–3, 869.

RIVEBELLE (f), near Balbec. The summer lasts longer there than at Balbec: I 727. Splendours of Rivebelle almost wholly invisible from Marcouville: 756. Dinners with Saint-Loup there: 861–86 *passim*. The restaurant and its garden; the waiters and the diners; M gets drunk: 865–73. The women in the restaurant: 875–7 (cf. II 405–6). M and Saint-Loup meet Elstir: 883–7. Seen across the bay: 1017 (cf. II 851). M remembers getting drunk there: II 174. Further memories of evenings at Rivebelle: 405–6, 410, 412–13 (cf. 1068). Its islands and indentations seen from the coach on the way to la Raspelière: 925. Denigrated by Mme Verdurin: 1002–3. Waiters from Rivebelle at the Grand Hotel: 1021–2. The "view of Rivebelle" at la Raspelière: 1032. M takes Albertine to lunch there; her interest in the waiter: 1048–9. M returns alone, and again drinks too much: 1049. Lesbian dinner-party there: III 84. Final evocation of Rivebelle: 903.

ROBINSON. Restaurant-cabaret in the suburbs of Paris: II 450.

ROME. Piranesi views of Rome: I 71. The Rome embassy (will

Vaugoubert get the post?): 497–9. Norpois was ambassador there: 606. M has never been there: 11 1120.

ROUEN. Bookstall at one of the doors of the cathedral: 111 112. British soldiers based there during the war; it has become "another town"; beauty of the emaciated saints of the cathedral: 835.

ROUMANIA. Status of the Jews there: 1 793 (cf. 11 194). Ronsard known there as a nobleman rather than a poet: 11 932–3.

ROUSSAINVILLE-LE-PIN (f), near Combray. Its castle keep visible from the little closet smelling of orris-root: 1 13. Françoise buys a turkey in Roussainville market: 76, where she goes every Saturday: 119 (cf. 128). Its etymology: 112. Roussainville woods: 163, 169–73. Its white gables carved in relief against the sky: 164. M has never been there: 166, though he longs to do so: 170, and yearns for a village girl: 171–2 (cf. 705). Gilberte used to play with little boys in the castle keep: 111 711–12, 715. Fought over during the war: 778.

RUSSIA. Status of the Jews there: 1 793. The pogroms: 11 108.

SAINT-ANDRÉ-DES-CHAMPS (f), near Combray. Its twin spires: 1 159. M and his family shelter under the porch; its Gothic sculptures and their living models: 164–6, 168 (cf. 899; 11 425). "An old church, monumental, rustic, and golden as a haystack": 201. The ethos of Saint-André-des-Champs, as illustrated by Françoise: 11 149, 381 (cf. 111 585); by Albertine: 381, 384 (cf. 111 616); by Andrée: 111 616; by Saint-Loup: 760; by the butler: 872; by Françoise's cousins, the Larivières: 876–7.

SAINT-CLOUD. Open-air restaurants there patronised by the Verdurins: 1 293–5. M's mother moves to a house there during his absence at Balbec: 697, 700. M goes there with Albertine: 11 404. He advises her to go there rather than to the Buttes-Chaumont: 111 13. Seen from the Bois de Boulogne: 172. Visited by the Duc and Duchesse de Guermantes: 591–2.

SAINT-FRICHOUX (f), near Balbec. M sends the lift-boy to find Albertine there: 11 818. Last station before Doncières: 887. Etymology: 963.

SAINT-JEAN-DE-LA-HAISE (f). Isolated church in the neighbourhood of Balbec, painted by Albertine: 11 1026–9. Buried in foliage: 1045. "All spires and crockets"; its stone angels: 1046.

SAINT-MARS-LE-VÊTU (f), near Balbec. Goal of some of M's

excursions with Mme de Villeparisis: I 758. Charlus and Morel have lunch in a restaurant there: II 1039. Albertine curious as to its etymology: 1047 (cf. III 529). Its piscine steeples: 1047. Remembered by M: III 489, 529, 552.

SAINT-MARS-LE-VIEUX (f). Station on the little local railway: I 711; II 921. M drives there: 1029, 1044.

SAINT-MARTIN-DU-CHÊNE (f). Charlus takes a house near there: II 963. Brichot gives the etymology of the name: 964. Charlus takes the train there: 1075.

SAINT-PIERRE-DES-IFS (f). One of the stations on the little local railway. Glorious girl with a cigarette gets into the train there: II 912. Charlus takes a house near there: 963; the name associated with him: I 1145.

SICILY. Charlus's ancestors Princes of Sicily: I 804. The Guermantes plan to go there: II 615. Prince Foggi has an estate there: III 651. (*See also* Agrigento.)

SIENA. "Seductive charms" of: I 620. Balbec "as beautiful as Siena" (Swann): 710. M has not yet been there: II 1120.

SOGNE, La (f), near Balbec. Albertine goes to the races there: I 937. M sends the lift-boy to find Albertine there: II 818. Stop on the little railway; Brichot gives the etymology of the name: 924. The Cambremers' station: 1009–10.

SPAIN. Norpois plans to take M's father there: I 500 (cf. 694, 753–4; II 187). Spain "all the rage" (Cottard): 537.

SUSA, capital of ancient Elam (now part of W. Iran) and residence of Darius and later Kings of Persia. Nissim Bernard like a figure from Susa restored by Mme Dieulafoy: I 830. Bloch's appearance likewise evokes reflections on monuments from Susa: II 194–5. The throne-room at Susa: 689.

TANGIER. Saint-Loup meets Mme de Stermaria there: II 360.

TANSONVILLE (f), the Swanns' place near Combray. M remembers his stay there with Mme de Saint-Loup (Gilberte): I 7 (cf. III 709 sq.). Description of Swann's park; the white fence; the lilacs, the ornamental pond and the water plants; the hawthorns: 147–53, 156–8, 166, 169. Swann yearns after it in the spring in Paris: 294. Remembered by Françoise: II 20. The Saint-Loups settle in there: III 692. M goes to stay: 694, 709–28; the house and park: 715–16. Tansonville during the war (Gilberte's letters): 773–4, 777–8.

TARN. Correct way of pronouncing: III 27.

THIBERZY (f), near Combray. M's cousins come over from Thiberzy for lunch on Sundays: I 70. Etymology: 113. Françoise goes there to fetch a midwife: 118.

TOURAINE. Mme Bontemps has a house there: III 364. M hopes that Albertine has gone there: 438. Saint-Loup sent down to find her: 443, 480–84. Albertine's death: 485–7. M sends Aimé there to investigate: 533; his report on Albertine and the laundry-girl: 534–6.

TOURS. *Rillettes* of Tours: II 475. Horror of the name for M: III 552.

TRIESTE. Albertine has spent "the happiest years of my life" there with Mlle Vinteuil's friend: II 1152. It becomes, for M, no longer "a delightful place" but "an accursed city": 1156–9.

TROCADÉRO, Paris. M finds more style in it than in Gabriel's palaces: I 527. The Trocadéro museum: 709. M persuades Albertine to go to a gala matinée there instead of calling on the Verdurins: III 102, 115. Léa due to appear there: 140–41. M sends Françoise to recall Albertine: 148–54. M and Albertine discuss its architecture: 164–5. The towers of the Trocadéro: 785.

TWICKENHAM, London. Residence of the exiled Comte de Paris. Swann invited there: I 19, 466 (cf. III 1010).

VENICE. Remembered by M: I 9. M's first idea of Venice gleaned from a reproduction of a Titian drawing with the lagoon in the background: 43–4. The "Staircase of the Giants" in the Doges' Palace: 353. Potency of the name: 420. Plan for a spring holiday there; the Venice of M's imagination: 423–7 (cf. 586, 682). The Frari Titian and the Carpaccios of San Giorgio degli Schiavoni: 475. Bloch's pronunciation of the name in English (Ruskin's *Stones of Venice*): 794–5. Mentioned in a quotation from Musset: 824. The Venice of Carpaccio and Veronese evoked by Elstir: 959–60. M's dream of Venice: II 147–8. Blend of softness and brittleness of Venetian glass: 360. Perspectives in Venice: 378. Its poor quarters resemble those of Paris: 594. Mme de Cambremer-Legrandin detests the Grand Canal: 841. M's persistent longing for Venice: III 21, 104, 167–8, 174. Albertine's Fortuny gowns conjure up the Venice of the Doges: 375–6, and seem to be the "tempting phantoms" of the invisible Venice M has dreamed of for so long: 401, 406. Evocation of Venice in the spring: 419–21.

M visits Venice with his mother: 637–70; impressions of the city: 637–43; M's solitary excursions; Venetian women: 641–3, 663–7; its social life: 644; the baptistery of St Mark's: 660–61; Carpaccio: 661–2; *O sole mio*; the vision crumbles: 667–9. Mme Verdurin visits Venice during the war: 746. M's unsatisfactory "snapshots" of Venice: 897–8. The uneven paving-stones; resuscitation of his real memory of Venice: 899–900, 902–3, 905, 910.

VERSAILLES. Swann's liking for it; Odette finds it boring: I 270. M crosses the Bois de Boulogne on his way to Trianon: I 456; its chestnut-trees and lilacs: 459. Rachel takes a little house in the neighbourhood: II 123. The view from the terrace of the palace: 399. The Princesse de Guermantes's garden, with its Hubert Robert fountain, is "Versailles in Paris": 607, 680. Doncières has a spurious look of Versailles: 1137. Albertine visits Versailles with the chauffeur: III 127–32. M takes Albertine there: 412–13. Nude statues of goddesses among its groves and fountains: 538.

VICHY. Bloch thinks of taking a cure there: II 226. Mme Cottard declines to go there on the grounds that "it's too stuffy": 997. Albertine once knew a woman of ill repute there: 1134. Albertine on the subject of Vichy water: III 126.

VIEUXVICQ (f), near Combray. Relationship of its steeple to the twin steeples of Martinville: I 196–8.

VITRÉ. One of the stops on the 1.22 train: I 419. What its name evokes: 422.

VIVONNE (f). River near Combray. Its water-lilies recalled with the rest of Combray and its surroundings by the taste of the madeleine dipped in tea: I 51. The apse of Saint-Hilaire seen from its banks: 71. Its course visible from the top of the steeple: 114. Meeting with Legrandin on its banks: 141. Runs along the "Guermantes way"; description of its course: 182–6. Its unattainable source: 187. M's dreams of a life of pleasure by the Vivonne; its association with Guermantes: 199, 201 (cf. II 7, 12, 24). Seeing it again, M finds it "narrow and ugly": III 709–10; he discovers its source: 711.

VOISENON (f). The Prince de Guermantes's country seat: III 593.

INDEX OF THEMES

AEROPLANES. Freemasonry of aviation enthusiasts: II 415 (cf. III 100–01). M sees an aeroplane for the first time: 1062 (cf. III 159). M and Albertine visit aerodromes: III 100–01. "One of those 120 horse-power machines, brand-name Mystère": 159. An aeroplane high in the sky above Versailles — beauty of the sound of "that little insect throbbing up there": 413. Albertine's lie about a visit to an aerodrome with Andrée: 626. Flying angels in Giotto's Padua frescoes reminiscent of airmen looping the loop: 663. Aeroplanes at evening over war-time Paris: 755–6 (cf. 828). Beauty of war-planes at night discussed by M and Saint-Loup: 781. Air-raids: 828–30, 862–4.

ALCOHOL. M's doctor prescribes alcohol for his suffocations, to the distress of his grandmother, who sees him "dying a drunkard's death": I 534. M's drunken euphoria on the train to Balbec: 700–03. His sensations after drinking too much champagne and port at Rivebelle: 867–70. Charm that alcohol gives to the present moment; inebriation brings about for a while "a state of subjective idealism, pure phenomenalism": 873–4 (cf. III 1093). Alcoholic slumbers: 878–9. M gets drunk in Aimé's restaurant; different kinds of intoxication; he sees himself in a mirror: II 174–5. M drinks seven or eight glasses of port to overcome his diffidence with girls: 867–8. Effect of cider on Albertine: 1048. At Rivebelle again; M's solitary drinking; the pattern on the wall: 1049.

AMERICANS. Swann's liaison with an American: I 212. American lady and her daughter at Balbec: 1015. American lady whose only book is a copy of Parny's poems: II 468. American multi-millionairess married to a French prince: 556. American lady bursts into M's room at the Grand Hotel: 821. An American called Charles Crecy marries a niece of Mme de Guermantes: 1121. American Jewesses in their night-dresses in Paris hotels during air-raids: III 782. Charlus on the Americans during the war: 822. American hostesses: 889, 892. Bloch's American friend in the new context of Parisian society: 1005–10.

ANTI-SEMITISM. *See* Dreyfus Case; Jews.

APPLE-TREES. On the "Méséglise way" — their circular shadows on the sunlit ground: I 159. Seen from the road near Balbec: 760. M's night-long contemplation of a branch of apple blossom: 760 (cf. 906). Mme de Villeparisis's painting of apple blossom: II 219–20. "Dazzling spectacle" of apple-trees in spring: 808–9. Compared to hawthorns: 813 (cf. 1187).

AQUARIUM. M. de Palancy's monocle a "symbolical fragment of the glass wall of his aquarium": I 356–7 (cf. II 39). Berma in *Phèdre* like a branch of coral in an aquarium: 604. Dining-room in the Grand Hotel, Balbec "an immense and wonderful aquarium" at night: 732 (cf. III 531). Garden of the Rivebelle restaurant like "an aquarium of gigantic size lit by a supernatural light": 871. Subaqueous domain of the Princesse de Guermantes's box at the Opéra: II 33–9. The lover separated from the outside world as though he were in an aquarium: 292. Charlus lives like a fish in an aquarium, unaware of his own visibility: 1083.

ARABIAN NIGHTS. Swann's secret life as mysterious as Ali Baba's: I 19. Aunt Léonie's *Arabian Nights* plates: 19, 61, 76, 965. Jews at Balbec suggest illustrations to the *Arabian Nights*: 794. Quoted apropos of a Paris restaurant proprietor: II 422. Oriane de Guermantes pictured as someone more wonderful than Princess Badroul-Boudour: 464. M's mother gives him both French translations, Galland and Mardrus: 865–6. M obliged to show the ingenuity of a Sheherazade to keep Albertine amused: III 127. Mendacious but nonetheless charming tales: 142. M imagines himself a character in the *Arabian Nights*: 250 (cf. 901). Purlieus of Venice like a city in the *Arabian Nights*: 641, 665. Wartime Paris reminds M of the *Arabian Nights*: 837. M compares the scene in Jupien's brothel to one of the tales: 862. The name Basra recalls Bassorah and Sinbad the Sailor: 1031. M's book the *Thousand and One Nights* of another age?: 1101–2.

ART. *See* Literature; Music; Painting.

ASPARAGUS. Discussed by Aunt Léonie and Françoise: I 59. M enraptured by their iridescent colours: 131. The kitchen-maid allergic to their smell: 135. Elstir's *Bundle of Asparagus*: II 520. The Duc de Guermantes on green asparagus; E. de Clermont-Tonnerre quoted on the subject: 522–3.

BALLET. Bakst's decors for the Russian Ballet: I 1009 (cf. III 2). Dancer admired by Rachel: II 180–81. The impact of the Russian Ballet: 770 (cf. III 238). Charlus's influence on Morel as an artist compared to Diaghilev's: 942. Mme Verdurin "an aged Fairy Godmother" to the Russian dancers: III 238. Theatrical designs of Sert, Bakst and Benois: 376. Reference to the "dazzling" *Legend of Joseph* by Sert, Strauss and Kessler: 662.

BEAUTY. Element of novelty essential to beauty: I 705. "The complementary part that is added to a fragmentary and fugitive stranger by our imagination, over-stimulated by regret"; "a sequence of hypotheses which ugliness cuts short": 766. Youth in pursuit of beauty: 845. "Fluid, collective and mobile beauty" of the girls of the "little band"; "noble and calm models of human beauty": 848. Elstir's ideal of beauty: 909. Beauty is "ordered complexity": II 47. "True beauty is so individual, so novel always, that one does not recognise it as beauty": 260. "The mysterious differences from which beauty derives": III 119. Perverse notion that true beauty is represented by a railway carriage rather than Siena, Venice or Granada: 132. "The possibility of pleasure may be a beginning of beauty": 136. The identity of the woman we love is far more important than her beauty: 448.

BELIEF. Our beliefs are neither engendered nor destroyed by facts: I 162. A fetishistic attachment to things survives the disappearance of our belief in them: 460. The part played by belief in the image we form of a person: 916. Our beliefs of more importance to our happiness than the person we see, since it is through them that we can see the person: 1010. Only imagination and belief can "create an atmosphere": II 26. "Irreducible essence" which, when we are young, our beliefs confer on a woman's clothes: 401. Invisible and variable atmosphere created around us by our beliefs: III 145. "Invisible belief that sustains the edifice of our sensory world": 453. Belief engendered by desire: 522–3, 524–5, 622–3. Dubious belief which leaves room for the possibility of what we wish to be true: 599. A large part of what we believe "springs from an original mistake in our premises": 671.

BICYCLES. Albertine pushing a bicycle: I 850; "spinning through the showers": 954 (cf. III 498). The lift-boy on his bicycle: II

884. "Winged messengers of variegated hue" — hotel messengers on bicycles: III 133. "Fabulous coursers" — girls and their bicycles in the Bois de Boulogne: 167; "angel or peri, half-human, half-winged" — another girl cyclist: 170. Albertine at the pianola revives M's memories of her cycling at Balbec: 389, 391; "speeding through Balbec on her mythological wheels": 498.

BIRDS. M's bedroom in winter — building a nest like a sea-swallow: I 7–8. Pigeons in the Champs-Elysées — "the lilacs of the feathered kingdom": 439, 442. Birdsong in the forests near Balbec, to which M listens like Prometheus to the Oceanides: 774 (cf. II 1027). The "little band" at Balbec like "a flock of gulls": 846; "an assembly of birds before taking flight": 850 (cf. III 171). Cooing of pigeons: II 144 (cf. III 407–8). Blue-tits in the blossoming apple-trees near Balbec: 809. Gulls on the sea at Balbec — like water-lilies: 836, 839; admired by Albertine: 842–3, 857, 859–60. Unknown bird chanting matins in the Lydian mode: III 394–5. "Melancholy refrain" of the pigeons: 407–8.

BODY. The body's memory more enduring than the mind's: I 6–7 (cf. III 716). We localise in a person's body all the potentialities of his or her life: II 31. Touching prescience of women for what will give pleasure to the male body: 170. Illness makes us aware of that unknown being, our body: 308. Albertine's naked body: III 74 (cf. 538). The body's "terrible capacity for registering things"; 431. "Possession of a body . . . the great danger to the mind": 1092.

BRITISH. See English.

BROTHELS. Odette's dealings with procuresses: I 401–2. Swann's visits to brothels; the girl with the blue eyes: 405–6. Bloch takes M to a house of assignation; "Rachel when from the Lord": 619–22. Uninterestingness of women met in brothels: II 160–61, 376 (cf. III 138, 169). Saint-Loup's enthusiasm for brothels; Mme Putbus's maid and Mlle d'Orgeville: 719. Luxury brothel at Maineville: 813; mistaken for a grand hotel: II 111–12; the Prince de Guermantes's assignation with Morel, and the experiences of Charlus and Jupien with Mlle Noémie: II 112–17. Women of the "closed houses": III 138, 169. M and two laundry-girls in a house of assignation: 561. Morel, Albertine and a fisher-girl in a brothel at Couliville: 613. Social gossip in the Maineville brothel: 678. Jupien's brothel in war-time Paris: 837–66. The Métro in war-time like a Pompeian brothel: 864.

CLASS. "Hindu" view of society at Combray — a rigid caste system: I 16–17 (cf. II 1060). For M's grandmother, distinction of manners independent of social position: 21. M's great-aunt disapproves of Swann for associating with people outside his "proper station": 22. For Aunt Céline, "one man is as good as the next": 28. Françoise's "class" pessimism: 538. Social mobility of Swann: 554. Intermediate class between the Faubourg Saint-Germain and the world of the merely rich: 687–8. Mutual misunderstanding between the aristocracy and the middle classes: 756. Distinctions in middle-class life even more stupid than in "society": 828. Physiognomical variety of the French middle class: 903. Similarities between people of the same generation more evident than those between people of the same class: II 707. M makes no class distinctions: 1059, but his mother is imbued with the "Combray spirit" in the matter of caste: 1060. "Every social class has its own pathology": III 9. "The classes of the intellect take no account of birth": 754.

DEATH. Swann *père*'s behaviour on the death of his wife: I 15–16. The Celtic belief in metempsychosis: 47. The "seamy side", as opposed to the abstract idea, of death: 88. Françoise's reaction to Aunt Léonie's death: 167. Love and death and the mystery of human personality: 336. Our unconscious resistance to the oblivion death will bring: 720–23. Resurrection of the soul after death perhaps a phenomenon of memory (q.v.): II 86. Unpredictability of the hour of death; the sick person's first acquaintance with the Stranger that has taken up residence in him: 324–7 (cf. III 1096). M's grandmother's death: 357. Signs of death on Swann's face: 715. "The dead exist only in us": 786. "The dead annex the living"; true and false sense in which we may say that death is not in vain: 796–7. Our indifference towards the dead: 798. Diversity of the forms of death: 896 (cf. III 197). Mme Verdurin's reaction to the deaths of the "faithful": 925–6, 930–31 (cf. III 240–41). "Each alteration of the brain is a partial death"; the phenomena of memory and life after death: 1017–18. Imminence of death makes us appreciate life: III 77 (cf. 493). Bergotte's death; "Dead forever? Who can say?": 180–86. Swann's death; "there are almost as many different deaths as there are people": 197–200. Presentiments of death: 406, 408, 411. In good health we imagine we are not afraid of death: 430. Albertine's death: 485. "The idea that one will die is more painful than dying, but less painful than the idea that another person is dead": 519. Our fear of the dead as judges: 521 (cf. 632). M's hopes of being reunited with Albertine in death: 522. Our inability to picture the reality of death: 530. Death little different from absence; a person may go on living after death as a sort of cutting grafted on to the heart of another: 534. "It is not because other people are dead that our affection for them fades; it is because we ourselves are dying": 608. "Nobody really believes in a future life": 632. "Death merely acts in the same way as absence": 658. Death cures us of the desire for immortality: 660. The abyss of death between us and the women we no longer love: 713. Saint-Loup's death: 877. Death subject to certain laws; accidental death may be predetermined: 881. Charlus's roll-call of the dead: 894. Beatific visions of Combray and Venice make death a matter of indifference to M: 900, 904 (cf. 1094). Death as a deliverance: 947. Old age is like death, in that some face them both with indifference, not because they have more courage than others but because they have less imagination: 970. Ubiquity and familiarity of death: 1025. "Every death is for others a simplification of life": 1027. Berma's dialogue with death: 1048–9. The last and least enviable forms of survival after death: 1064. M's renewed fear of death not for himself but for his book: 1094–6. The idea of death takes up permanent residence within him: 1100. Men's works will die as well as men: 1101.

DOCTORS. *See* Medicine.

DREAMS. M's dreams of a woman: I 4–5. Swann's dream of leaving Odette: 385. Swann's dream of Odette and Forcheville: 411–15. M's dream about Gilberte: 677–8. M's dreams after dining at Rivebelle: 878. Beauty of the dream-world; nightmares and their fantastic picture-books: II 83–6. Saint-Loup's dream of Rachel's infidelity: 123–4. M's dream of Venice: 147–8. M's dreams of his dead grandmother; he speaks of her to his father; dream language: 787–9, 806–7, 810. Pleasures experienced in dreams: 1015. A dream may have the clarity of consciousness: 1018. The stuff of dreams: III 117–18; inventiveness in dreams:

topper: 601. The Duchess's red satin dress, ostrich feather and tulle scarf: 606, and her black shoes: 619. Her Tiepolo evening cloak: 686, 745. Sartorial elegance of the Balbec lift-boy: 818–19. The dowager Mme de Cambremer's get-up: 834. Albertine's motoring toque and veil: 1028, 1046–7, (cf. III 53). Albertine's clothes, inspired by Elstir; her grey outfit with plaid sleeves: 1089. Charlus on dress; the Princesse de Cadignan: 1089–90. The Princesse de Guermantes's eccentricity of dress; her Gainsborough hat: 1179. Albertine's delight in the accessories of costume: III 24–5, 57. Mme de Guermantes's elegance; "the best-dressed woman in Paris"; her Fortuny gowns: 25–6. M discusses clothes with her: 30, 35–6, 57–8. Different attitudes towards clothes of rich and poor women: 57–8. Albertine's black satin dress: 97. The dairymaid's sweater: 140. Charlus's interest in women's clothes, and his views on Albertine's: 220–23. Albertine and Fortuny; reminders of Venice: 375–8, 401, 406, 412, 419 (cf. 662). Paris fashions in war-time: 743–4. Young Mme de Saint-Euverte's Empire dress: 1078.

DREYFUS CASE. Its effect on Society: I 556–7 (cf. II 194, 704–5, III 236–7). Aimé persuaded of Dreyfus's guilt: 864. Saint-Loup a Dreyfusard; the Case discussed at Doncières: II 104–8, 118. Mme Sazerat ("alone of her kind at Combray") a Dreyfusard: 154 (cf. 299). M and his father take opposite sides: 154. Rachel's view: 167. Mme de Villeparisis's aloofness: 194 (cf. 244, 256). Bloch and Norpois discuss the Case: 239–41, 247–56. Views of the Duc and Duchesse de Guermantes: 241–6; of Mme Swann: 260 (cf. 272); of Mme Verdurin ("a latent bourgeois anti-semitism" — but cf. 770–71): 260; of Mme de Marsantes: 260–61; of Prince Von: 264 (cf. 703); of Charlus: 297–300; of the two butlers: 306–7. Reinach's achievement; Dreyfusism and heredity; France divided from top to bottom: 306–7. Dreyfusists in a Paris restaurant: 415–16. Mme de Guermantes's ambivalence: 495 (cf. 533, III 35). Swann's Dreyfusism: 600–06 (cf. 715–16, 723–4, 738–9). Saniette a Dreyfusard: 605. The Duc de Guermantes deplores Swann's "treachery": 702–5. Saint-Loup changes his tune: 723–4, 738. The Prince de Guermantes and his wife converted to Dreyfusism: 731–40 (cf. 1179–80). The Duc de Guermantes converted (temporarily) to Dreyfusism by three Italian ladies: 766–7. Influence of the Case on the *salons* of Mme

Verdurin ("the active centre of Dreyfusism") and Mme Swann: 770–74 (cf. 914–15; III 236–9). Brichot's anti-Dreyfusism: 915 (cf. 605). M. de Cambremer's anti-Dreyfusism: 998–9 (cf. III 236). The Duc de Guermantes, the Jockey Club and the Dreyfus Case: III 32–35. Complex influence of the Case on Society: 236–9; continuing social anti-semitism: 586 sqq. The Dreyfus Case in retrospect (1916): 747–9; after the war: 1001.

DRINK. *See* Alcohol.

ENGLISH, ENGLISHMEN. "Our friends across the Channel" (Odette): I 84. English visitors to Combray: 114. Affectation of British stiffness in Odette's handwriting: 242. Odette as a child sold by her mother to a rich Englishman in Nice: 399. M's ignorance of English: 547, 586. Odette's Anglomania: 559, 567, 576, 588; speaks to Gilberte in English: 627; her English accent: 638. Bloch's mispronunciation of English: 794–5. English visitors "athirst for information" about Elstir: 884. "Positively British stiffness" of the Duchesse de Guermantes's get-up at the Opéra: II 50. "In France we give to everything that is more or less British the one name that it happens not to bear in England" (*smoking*): 499 (cf. I 530: *water-closets*). Prince Von on the ineptitude of the British army ("the English are so *schtubid*"): 547–8. The Duc de Châtellerault poses as an Englishman: 658, 660. English soldiers during the war — like Greek statues, "unimaginable marvels" (Charlus): III 801, 835; "our loyal allies", English fair play, "the brave tommies" (Odette): 815. The Duc de Guermantes's anglophilia: 808. Change in English attitude towards the Germans: 808–9. Bloch's English *chic*: 996.

FAUBOURG SAINT-GERMAIN. Swann's position in the aristocratic world of the Faubourg Saint-Germain: I 16, 208, 235. *Noli me tangere* of the Faubourg: 313. Psychology of the women of the Faubourg: 365. Odette's detachment from the Faubourg: 558–60 (cf. 687–8). The Faubourg Saint-Germain has no more to do with the mind of a Bergotte than "with the law of causality or the idea of God": 600. Its barriers: 687–8. Nine tenths of the men of the Faubourg appear to the middle classes as crapulous paupers: 756. Not lavish with tips: 759. Excess of politeness one of its professional "wrinkles": 778. The Guermantes's position in the Faubourg; M's romantic notions about it; "the well-trodden doormat of its shore": II 23–7. Its attitude to the

Imperial nobility: 130 (cf. 486). Jews in the Faubourg: 194. Mme
de Marsantes's edifying influence on it: 257–8. Nicknames in the
Faubourg: 448–9. Relations of the Princesse Mathilde with the
Faubourg: 486–7. Party ritual in the Faubourg; "the prime and
perfect quality of the social pabulum": 532–4. Its silliness,
aggravated by malice: 559. Its mysterious life: 564. Walking-
sticks common in a certain section of the Faubourg: 598. Odette
taken up by certain elements of the Faubourg: 771–6; also
Gilberte when she suddenly becomes rich through a legacy: 774
(cf. III 677, 686). Mme de Montmorency's old house in the
Faubourg: 777. Mme Verdurin and the Faubourg: 899–900 (cf.
III 236–7). Charlus's morals unknown to the Faubourg: 932.
How the Faubourg speaks to any bourgeois about other
bourgeois: III 592. During the war, Mme Verdurin and Mme
Bontemps firmly installed in the Faubourg: 749. Brichot's
success with the Faubourg: 817–20. Mme Verdurin becomes
Duchesse de Duras and then Princesse de Guermantes and
occupies a "lofty position" in the Faubourg: 998. Its decline —
"like some senile dowager now": 1000.

FLOWERS. Lime-blossom from the trees in the Avenue de la Gare
at Combray used for Aunt Léonie's infusions: I 51, 55. Mme
Loiseau's fuchsias: 67. Legrandin's evocation of spring flowers:
137. Lilacs at Tansonville: 147–8, 202. M falls in love with
hawthorn in Combray church: 121, 123 (cf. 983–4, II 1186–7).
Hawthorn blossom at Tansonville: 150–53. M bids farewell to
his hawthorns: 158. Flowers in Swann's park: 148–9, 153.
Poppies and cornflowers in the fields beyond Tansonville: 151.
Spring flowers by the Vivonne; "blue flame of a violet": 182.
Buttercups: 183. Water-lilies: 184–5. Odette gives Swann a
chrysanthemum picked from her garden: 239. Chrysanthemums
in Odette's house: 240; chrysanthemums, and cattleyas, her
favourite flowers; "a fleshy cluster of orchids": 241. The
cattleyas: 253–6; "do a cattleya" = "make love": 255–6, 297,
403, 405. Odette wears violets in her bosom: 262, 461; or in her
hair: 454. Gilberte and Odette like a white lilac beside a purple:
608. The "winter-garden"; Mme Swann's flowers; Parma
violets, chrysanthemums: 637–41 (cf. 461; III 164); guelder-
roses: 683. Cornflowers near Balbec: 764. Human kindness
blossoms like a solitary poppy: 796. Geranium cheeks of one of

the girls at Balbec (Rosemonde?): 847, 888, 1008. The "little band" like a bower of Pennsylvania roses: 856. Elstir's flower-piece: 906 (cf. 11 125). Albertine's cheeks like rose petals; M's "passionate longing for them such as one feels sometimes for a particular flower": 949 (see also 11 377). Hawthorn near Balbec: 983–4. Cherry-blossom, pear-blossom and lilac in Parisian suburbs: 11 157–60. Mme de Villeparisis's flower painting: 219–20; her knowledge of botany: 284. Albertine "a rose flowering by the sea": 364. Scarlet geraniums in the Bois: 400. Botanical discussion at the Guermantes': 535–7. The fertilisation of flowers; the orchid and the bee; an analogy with the conjunction of inverts: 623–5, 628–9, 650–56. Apple-blossom in sun and rain: 808–9. Hawthorn and apple-blossom: 813, 1186–7. Albertine's laugh, "pungent, sensual and revealing as the scent of geraniums": 823. The garden at la Raspelière: 948. Elstir's roses: 974. Albertine's hair like black violets: 111 11. The syringa incident: 48–9, 613–14, 625. Elstir's passion for violets: 135, 137. Honeysuckle and white geraniums in Vinteuil's sonata: 251; his music has "the perfumed silkiness of a geranium": 381–2.

FOOD. Stewed beef at Combray: 1 11. Coffee and pistachio ice: 36. Lunch at Combray; Françoise's culinary largesse: 76–7. Almond cake: 123. Françoise's preparations for dinner: 130–31. Asparagus: 131. Françoise's roast chicken: 131–2, 145. Swann's gingerbread: 436. Dinner for Norpois; Françoise's boeuf en gelée: 480, 493–4; pineapple and truffle salad: 495; Nesselrode pudding: 502. Chocolate cake for tea chez Gilberte: 545 (cf. 965). Lobster à l'Américaine: 579. "A blackish substance which I did not then know to be caviare": 591. Soles for lunch at Balbec: 724. Mme de Villeparisis orders croque-monsieurs and baked eggs: 751. Hotel dining-room at Doncières; Flemish profusion of victuals: 11 97–8; exquisite dishes presented like works of art: 118. Chicken financière at the Guermantes dinner party: 522. The Duke's leg of mutton with Béarnaise sauce: 611. Dinner at la Raspelière; bouillabaisse: 930; grilled lobsters (demoiselles de Caen): 931; strawberry mousse: 971. Tea at la Raspelière — "shortbread, Norman puff pastries, trifles, boat-shaped tartlets . . .": 1033. The street cries of Paris — winkles: 111 112; snails: 113; artichokes: 114; fish: 122–3; fruit and vegetables: 122–4.

Albertine's rhapsody on ice cream: 124–6. Display in a butcher's shop: 134. Mme de Villeparisis and Norpois dine in Venice — red mullet and risotto: 646 (cf. 1118). Dinner party at the Verdurins' described by the Goncourts: 731–2.

FRIENDSHIP. Among the bourgeoïsie, as opposed to the aristocracy, "always inseparable from respect": I 338. M's friendship with Saint-Loup; melancholy reflections on the subject: 790–92; his inability to find spiritual nourishment elsewhere than in himself makes him (in contrast with Saint-Loup) incapable of friendship: 837. Friendliness of a great artist superior to that of a nobleman: 886. Friendship an abdication of self and thus fatal to an artist; M prepared to sacrifice its pleasures to that of playing with the "little band" of girls: 968–9 (cf. II 409). The stuff of friendship: II 102–3. Mystery of instinctive, non-physical liking between men: 103. Our relations with friends "as eternally fluid as the sea itself": 278. Further reflections on friendship; its superficiality; "halfway between physical exhaustion and mental boredom"; yet even so deadly a brew can sometimes be precious and invigorating; from the realm of ideas M "thrown back upon friendship": 409–13. Virtues of friendship enshrined in Saint-Loup: 428–31. Friendship and love: III 363. Necessity of lying between two friends one of whom is unhappy in love: 449. Friendship and treachery: 635. Revival of old friendships: 694, 753. M's tarnished friendship with Saint-Loup: 706. Recollections of their friendship after Saint-Loup's death: 878. A great friendship does not amount to much in society: 883. A "simulacrum", an "agreeable folly": 909, which leads nowhere: 1036.

FURNITURE. Aunt Léonie's rooms at Combray; her prie-dieu and velvet armchairs with antimacassars: I 53–4. Mme Verdurin's high Swedish chair of waxed pinewood: 223; her Beauvais settee and chairs: 226. Furnishings of Odette's house in the Rue La Pérouse: 240–42. Odette's taste in furniture: 266–7 (cf. 544, 580, 662–3). The Iénas' Empire furniture: 368–9 (cf. II 537–42). "Henri II" staircase in Swann's house: 544. Furniture in the Swanns' drawing-room: 580–81, 662–3. Aunt Léonie's sofa, on which M makes love to one of his girl cousins, and which he later presents to the madam of a brothel: 622. Saint-Loup's Art

Nouveau furniture: 813 (cf. 11 572–3). Furniture of the hotel at Doncières: 11 80–82. Mme de Villeparisis's Beauvais tapestry settees and chairs: 193, 280. Mme de Guermantes on Empire furniture: 537–42. The Guermantes' Boulle and Saint-Loup's Bing furniture: 572–3. Charlus's Louis XIV *bergère* and Directory *chauffeuse*: 575–6; his Bagard panelling and Beauvais chairs: 583. Furniture at la Raspelière: 948–9, 953, 976–7. M's Barbédienne bronze: 111 174. Furniture from la Raspelière at Quai Conti: 286–7. (*See* Rooms.)

GAMES. Gilberte and her friends play battledore and shuttlecock in the Champs-Elysées: 1 428. Prisoner's base in the Champs-Elysées: 429. Golf at Balbec; Andrée's "record" round; Octave, "I'm a wash-out": 938–9. Albertine plays diabolo: 947, 992. "Ferret" (hunt-the-thimble) with the little band: 980–83. "Golf gives one a taste for solitary pleasures": 992. Cottard and Morel play écarté at la Raspelière: 11 990 sqq.

GERMAN, GERMANS. "Straightforward bluntness" of the Princesse Mathilde, inherited from her Württemberger mother, recalls the Germany of an older generation: 1 583–4. The name Faffenheim-Munsterburg-Weinigen expresses "the energy, the mannered simplicity, the heavy refinements of the Teutonic race": 11 264–5. "The vice of a German handclasp" (Prince Von's): 448. Charlus's "German habit" of fingering M's muscles: 942. M's mother's admiration for the German language despite her father's "loathing for that nation": 111 102–3. Gilberte impressed by the "perfect breeding" of the German officers billeted at Tansonville: 774. Charlus's pro-Germanism: 797–801; "that splendid sturdy fellow, the Boche soldier": 835–6. Saint-Loup's respect for the bravery of the Germans: 871, and for German culture: 877. M's reflections on his own attitude towards the Germans: 950–52.

HABIT. "That skilful but slow-moving arranger" who helps us to adapt to new quarters: 1 8–9 (cf. 721–2). Suffering caused by the interruption or cessation of habit: 9–11. The force of habit blunts one's sensitivity to a work of music: 571. Contradictory effects of habit: 692. "Our faculties lie dormant because they can rely upon habit": 706. The analgesic effect of habit: 721–2. Without habit, life would seem continually delightful: 766. We prefer to friends we have not seen for some time people who are the mirror of our habits: 777. Habit dispenses us from effort: II 81. Modification in our habits makes our perception of the world poetic: 83. Habit the hardiest of all plants of human growth: 123. The many secretaries employed by Habit: 765. A second nature that prevents us from knowing our first: 781. Effect of habit on M's view of the Grand Hotel: 791. Sleep and habit: 1014. "The regularity of a habit is usually in direct proportion to its absurdity": III 37. Habit prevents us from appreciating the value of life: 77–8. "In love, it is easier to relinquish a feeling than to give up a habit": 363. A new aspect of Habit — a "dread deity" that can be as cruel as death itself: 426. The "immense force of Habit" lacking in M's love for Gilberte and Mme de Guermantes: 436. Habit produces the illusion of necessity in love: 514. Laws of habit as applied to the idea of Albertine's infidelities: 546–7. "The heavy curtain of habit . . . which conceals from us almost the whole universe": 554. Force of habit infinitely outweighs the hypnotic power of a book: 569–70. Our habits in love survive even the memory of the loved one: 694. Our habits develop independently of our moral consciousness: 867. What is dangerous in love . . . is not the beloved, but habit: 1076.

HAWTHORN. *See* Flowers.

HEREDITY. Arbitrary laws of filial resemblance; Gilberte and her parents: I 608–9. Saint-Loup's hereditary virtues: 791–2. "We take from our family . . . the ideas by which we live as well as the malady from which we shall die": 953. Inheritance of mannerisms of speech, etc. (the "little band"); "the individual is steeped in something more general than himself": 970. Andrée's hair inherited from her mother: 1008. Heredity gives uncles the same faults as they censure in their nephews: II 717–18, 720–21. Hereditary resemblance of M's mother and grandmother; "the dead annex the living": 796–7, 1159, 1166. "The souls of the dead from whom we sprang . . . shower upon us their riches and their spells" — M comes to resemble all his relatives: III 73, 103–5, 360–61. Heredity and bad habits: 153. "We do not create ourselves of our own accord out of nothing"; hereditary accumulation of egoisms: 598. Atavistic wisdom of Mme de Marsantes: 696. Moral cells of which an individual is composed more durable than the individual himself: 972. Berma's daughter inherits her mother's defects: 1048. Hereditary need for spiritual nourishment in the Duchesse de Guermantes: 1057.

HISTORY. M's grandfather's interest in history: I 22, 26. Swann's curiosity about Odette's occupations comes from the same thirst for knowledge with which he had once studied history: 299. Charlus's aristocratic prejudices reinforced by his interest in history: 812–14. The Duc de Guermantes's politeness a survival from the historic past: II 432–3. Aristocratic names bring history to life: 556–64. The wisdom of families inspired by the Muse of History: III 692–3. History and Society: 1009–14.

HOMOSEXUALITY. *See* Inversion.

INTOXICATION. *See* Alcohol.

INVERSION. "What is sometimes, most ineptly, termed homosexuality": II 629. The race of inverts: 637–56; their predicament; "a race upon which a curse is laid"; an extensive freemasonry: 637–40; "improperly" called a vice: 640 (cf. 635: "we use the term for linguistic convenience"); types of invert — the gregarious, the solitaries, the zealots, the gynophiles, the affected, the guilt-ridden backsliders: 641–8; typical career of a solitary invert: 646–9; subvarieties of invert; those who care only for elderly gentlemen; the miracle of their conjunction: 650–52 (cf. 629); botanical analogy: 650–53; inversion can be traced back to a primeval hermaphroditism: 653. Numerous progeny of the exiles from Sodom: 655–6. M. and Mme de Vaugoubert: a case of reversal of roles: 666–71. Characteristic voice of the invert: 688. Discussion between Charlus and Vaugoubert: 689–90 (cf. III 39). A "diplomatic Sodom": 699–700. Bloch's sister and an actress cause a scandal: 871, 879. Nissim Bernard and the waiters: 871–4, 883–4. "Astral signs" by which the daughters of Gomorrah recognise one another (as do also "the nostalgic, the hypocritical, sometimes the courageous exiles of Sodom"): 880–81. Instinctive behaviour of inverts on entering a strange drawing-room: 937–8. "By dint of thinking tenderly of men one becomes a woman": 939. The cold shoulder of the invert on meeting his kind; rivalry among inverts; speed of mutual recognition: 949–52. Connection between inversion and aesthetic sensibility: 985–6 (cf. III 220). Giveaway signs — voice, gestures, manner of speech: 999–1000. Charm of unfamiliarity in the conversation of an invert: 1074–5. Gomorrah disseminated all over the world: 111 15. Gomorrah of today a jigsaw puzzle made up of unexpected pieces: 84. Distinction between conventional (classical) homosexuality and the "involuntary, neurotic" homosexuality of today: 204–6. Charlus's "camping": 209. Significance of the term "one of them" or "one of us": 212 (cf. 11 973). Jealousy among inverts; attitude towards relations with women: 214–16. Paternal feelings of inverts: 244. Furtive party conversation among inverts: 244–5. Charlus and Brichot discuss the statistics of "what the Germans call homosexuality"; historical examples, present-day trends: 299–312. Recognition between daughters of Gomorrah in a crowd; a typical Gomorrhan encounter: 358–9. "Physiological evolution" of Saint-Loup: 695–706, 717. Homosexuals make good husbands: 701, 723 (cf. 310). "The phenomenon, so ill-understood and so needlessly condemned, of sexual inversion": 948. Inverts as readers: 948–9.

(For references to homosexuality, male and female, related to specific individuals, see the Index of Characters under Albertine; Andrée; Argencourt; Bernard, Nissim; Bloch's sister(s) and cousin(s); Cambremer, Léonor; Charlus; Châtellerault; Foix; Gilberte; Guermantes, Prince de; Jupien; Léa; Legrandin; Lévy, Esther; Morel; Odette; Saint-Loup; Théodore; Vaugoubert; Vinteuil, Mlle).

JEALOUSY. Swann's jealousy: 1 297–351 passim, 384–415 passim. Inquiries of the jealous lover compared to the researches of the scholar: 298–9, 341. Jealousy compared to physical pain: 300. Jealousy as it were the shadow of love: 301. Jealousy composed of an infinity of different, ephemeral jealousies: 404. Swann's jealousy in retrospect; "that lamentable and contradictory excrescence of his love" revives for another woman: 563–6. A certain kind of sensual music the most merciless of hells for the jealous lover: 870. Saint-Loup's jealousy of Rachel: 11 122–4, 167–73, 181–7, 360–62. Jealousy cannot contain many more ingredients than other products of the imagination; it outlives love: 361–2. Jealousy among inverts: 645–6 (see also 111 214). Swann speaks of his jealousy to M: 728–9. Jealousy a resource that never fails: 828–9. "Jealousy belongs to that family of morbid doubts which are eliminated by the vigour of an affirmation far more surely than by its probability": 862. "Every impulse of jealousy is unique and bears the imprint of the person who has aroused it": 1156–7. Arbitrary localization of jealousy: 1158. M's jealousy: 111 13–23, 48–190 *passim*, 337–442 *passim*; retrospective jealousy: 425–568 *passim*. An intermittent and capricious disease: 22; quickly detected, and regarded, by the person who is its object, as justifying deception: 55, 85. Delayed-action jealousy: 81–2. Jealousy a form of tyranny: 86. "The demands of our jealousy and the blindness of our credulity are greater than the woman we love could ever suppose": 91. "Revolving searchlights" of jealousy; "a demon that cannot be exorcised": 98. Jealousy may perish for want of nourishment: 100. Jealousy like a historian without documents, "thrashing around in the void": 143. Jealousy is "blindfold"; like the torture of the Danaides or Ixion: 147–8. A social form of jealousy (Mme Verdurin): 280. Blind ignorance of the jealous lover: 303. Albertine on M's jealousy: 337–8. Jealousy lacks imagination: 442. For jealousy there can be neither past nor future, but invariably the present: 500. To the jealous man reality a "dizzy kaleidoscope": 529. Retrospective jealousy proceeds from the same optical error as the desire for posthumous fame: 530. In jealousy we choose our own sufferings: 556. Retrospective jealousy a physical disease: 659. "Jealousy is a good recruiting-sergeant": 955–6.

JEWS. M's grandfather distrusts M's Jewish friends (Bloch): I 98–9. Mme de Gallardon on Swann's Jewishness: 364–5. Swann illustrates all the successive stages in social behaviour through which the Jews have passed: 466. Jews in society: 556–7, 560. A brothel-keeper offers M a Jewess as a special treat (Rachel): 620–21. Bloch affects anti-semitism: 793 (cf. 799, 802; 11 255). Jewish colony at Balbec: 793–4. The Bloch family: 825–34. Albertine's anti-semitism: 941, 964 (cf. 11 369). *Mater Semita*: 11 182 (cf. 246). Jews in a French drawing-room; racial atavism: 194–5. The "Syndicate": 244 (cf. 723). Mme de Marsantes's anti-semitism: 261, 264 (cf. 167, 182). Charlus and the Blochs: 297–9. Mme Sazerat both Dreyfusist and anti-semitic: 299. Jewishness and Dreyfusism (Reinach and Bloch): 306–7. Reflections on Jews in a Paris restaurant: 424. Swann returns to "the spiritual fold of his fathers": 603. Jews compared with inverts: 638–9. M. de Guermantes on the Jews: 703. Swann's

Jewishness; "certain Jews in whom there remain in reserve . . . a boor and a prophet": 715–16; "that stout Jewish race": 730. Charlus's tirade against the Jews: 1141–4. Jews discussed by the Duc and Duchesse de Guermantes: III 34–5. Morel's anti-semitism, the effect of a loan from Nissim Bernard through Bloch: 47–8 (cf. II 1144). Anti-semitism in society; Gilberte changes her name from Swann to Forcheville: 586–7 (cf. 597–9). Strong family feeling among Jews; Bloch's devotion to his father's memory: 972.

(*See* Dreyfus Case.)

LANGUAGE. Hereditary transmission of speech characteristics: I 970–71. The two laws of language — "we express ourselves like others of our mental category and not of our caste"; the ephemeral vogue for certain modes of expression: II 242–3. The term "mentality": 243–4. Refined expressions used in a given period by people of the same intellectual range: 955, 960. Expressions peculiar to families: III 331. Involuntary, give-away expressions blurted out under the impact of sudden emotion: 851. Quality of language rather than aesthetic theory the criterion for judging intellectual and moral value of a work: 916.

Language of individual characters. Albertine's slangy speech: I 850, 943–5; her voice and vocabulary: 970–71; significant changes in her vocabulary: II 365–71; III 10.

Voices and speech mannerisms of the "little band": I 969–71.

Bergotte's mannerisms of speech and vocabulary: I 592–9.

Bloch's affected style of speech and mock-Homeric jargon: I 97, 800–01, 826, 832; II 251, 865, 1137.

Bréauté's voice and pronunciation: III 33–6.

Brichot's pedantic language: I 275–6; II 905, 912, 987–8, 1084–6.

Mme de Cambremer-Legrandin's pretentious vocabulary and pronunciation: II 208, 846–9, 954–60, 1010.

Colourful language of Céleste Albaret and her sister: 875–7; Céleste's "strange linguistic genius": III 10, 127.

Cottard's puns: I 217 sqq.

Mme Cottard's stately language: I 642, 648–54.

Françoise's malapropisms: I 168; her colourful idiom: 180; her language, "like the French language", thickly strewn with errors: II 18; speaks the language of Mme de Sévigné: 18, of La Bruyère: 21, of Saint-Simon: 66; her speech traditional and local, "governed by extremely ancient laws": 61 (cf. 753); her vocabulary contaminated by her daughter's slang: III 151, 771 (cf. II 149–50, 353, 754).

Verbal mannerisms of the Guermantes set: I 364, 367–73, 550, 562. The Duke's odd vocabulary: II 233, 242–6, 432; his bad French: 746, 985 (cf. III 33). Old-fashioned purity of the Duchess's language; her richly flavoured vocabulary; voice and accent that betray "a rudeness of the soil": II 513–14, 521–2, 592, III 26–30.

Jupien's cultured speech: II 15–16, 319.

Legrandin's flowery speech: I 73, 138–44.

The idiom of Norpois: I 470–71, 486–517 *passim*; II 231–71 *passim*; III 644–54.

Rachel's language, "the jargon of the coteries and studios": II 169–70.

Saint-Loup's mannerisms of speech; cultivates up-to-date expressions: I 806, 819–20; II 69, 528–9, 780.

Saniette's pedantic phraseology: III 226, 229.

Swann's verbal mannerisms: I 105–6, 370, 543, 550.

Mme de Villeparisis affects "the almost rustic speech of the old nobility": II 203.

LAUGHTER. Not a well-defined language: I 628. "Let us show all pity and tenderness to those who laugh": II 822. Verbal descriptions incomplete without the means to represent a laugh (Charlus): 974.

Laughter of individual characters. Albertine's laughter — "somehow indecent, like the cooing of doves or certain animal cries": I 981; M longs to hear it again: II 808; "pungent, sensual and revealing": 823; "deep and penetrating": 824; "provoking": 887; "that laugh in which she gave utterance as it were to the strange sound of her pleasure": 1154; "that laugh that I always found so disturbing": III 115, 125; "insolent" laughter on the beach at Balbec: 171; "blithe and tender" laugh on awakening: 394.

Bloch's braying laugh which echoes his father's: I 825.

M. de Cambremer's laugh and its possible meanings: II 956–7, 1011.

Charlus's "insolent and hysterical" laughter: 11 682; his tinkling laugh with its ancestral sonorities: 974.

Mme Cottard's "charming, girlish" laugh: 1 279.

Gilberte's laugh which seems to be tracing an invisible surface on another plane: 1 529, 628.

Insolent and coquettish laugh of the Princesse de Laumes: 1 363, 365.

Odette's little simpering laugh: 1 240.

"Merry angelus" of Ski's laugh: 111 291.

Mme Verdurin dislocates her jaw from laughing too much: 1 206; symbolical dumb-show as a substitute for laughter: 223–4 (cf. 11 987).

M. Verdurin's dumb-show of "shaking with laughter": 1 286.

LETTERS. Note from M to his mother at Combray: 1 30–31. Letters from Odette to Swann: 213, 242, 246. Swann's letter of feigned disappointment and simulated anger to Odette: 246. Odette's letter to Forcheville: 307–8. Anonymous letter to Swann about Odette's infidelities: 387–90. Express letter (*pneu*) from M to Gilberte: 437. Norpois's promptness in answering letters: 472. M's New Year letter to Gilberte: 524. M's self-justifying letter to Swann: 529–30. Gilberte's letter of invitation to M; her signature: 538–41; her writing-paper: 543. M's letters to Gilberte during the crisis of his love: 630–34, 660–61. The pain of hostile letters from the beloved: 675. Correspondence between M and Gilberte concerning the imaginary "misunderstanding" between them: 680–82. Saint-Loup's letter from Doncières: 928. Charlus's violent letter to Mme de Villeparisis: 11 277. Saint-Loup's vituperative letter to M: 318. The footman's letters, peppered with quotations from the poets: 332; example of these: 588–9. Saint-Loup writes to M from Morocco: 360. Note to M from Mme de Stermaria: 406. Letter to Charlus from the Princesse de Guermantes: 742 (cf. 1180–81). M's unemotional letter to Gilberte: 765. The charm of first letters from women: 868. Mme de Cambremer's letter inviting M to dinner; the rule of the three adjectives: 977–8 (cf. 1123). Charlus's letter to Aimé: 1023–5. Charlus's letter to Morel announcing his imaginary duel: 1099–1101. Charlus's letter from a club doorman: 111 38–9. M's mother writes to him, quoting Mme de Sévigné: 136–7. Albertine's note to M after leaving the

Trocadéro: 153–4. Letter from Léa to Morel intercepted by Charlus: 211–12. Albertine's farewell letter: 426–7. Letter which M receives from a niece of Mme de Guermantes: 457. Letter from Albertine after Saint-Loup's *démarche*; M's reply: 461–5. "How little there is of a person in a letter": 462. Albertine's second letter and M's reply: 477–8. M's letter to Andrée: 478. Albertine's posthumous letters: 486–7. Aimé's letter from Balbec; his grammatical eccentricities: 525–6. Aimé's letter from Touraine: 535–6. Letters congratulating M on his article in the *Figaro*: 602–4. Bourgeois conventionality in letters: 603–4. M receives a letter from his stockbroker: 654–5. Letters announcing marriages: 670–73. Letters from Gilberte at Tansonville during the war: 773–4, 777–8. Saint-Loup's letter from the front: 773–6. Charlus's posthumous letter: 832–3.

LIFTS. Lift in the Grand Hotel, Balbec; M's sensations on going up in it: I 715, 857. Professor E——'s lift and his mania for working it: II 327–8. Lift in M's flat; sentence of solitary confinement represented by the sound of its not stopping at his floor: 363 (cf. III 352).

LITERATURE. Reflections on reading; the art of the novelist: I 44–6, 90–93. Style and genius of Bergotte: 97, 101 7, 589–604 (cf. II 337–40); the nature of originality in literature: 591; relation between speech and writing: 592–7; "unforeseeable beauty" of the work of great writers: 593; style of the writer and character of the man: 599–600. A good book is something special and unforeseeable: 705. Mme de Villeparisis's literary judgments; her incomprehension of great writers: 763–4 (cf. II 189). Creation in a writer superior to observation: 825. Literature and fashionable society: II 189–93; literary talent the living product of a certain moral conformation that conflicts with purely social duties: 190. Vagaries of literary reputation; problems of appreciating new original writers; does art, after all, progress like science?: 337–9. Depravity of taste in literary criticism: 488–9. Profit which a writer can derive from the conversation of aristocrats: 569–73. The same people are interesting in a book and boring in life: 591. Practical men wrong to despise the pursuit of literature: 1069. Incompleteness a characteristic of the great works of the nineteenth century; their retrospective unity; the importance of prefaces: III 157. Sensual pleasure helpful to literary work: 181.

Literature and music — is literature, which analyses what we feel about life, less true than music, which recomposes it?: 381; unique identity underlying the works of a great writer; M's observations on Dostoievsky, Barbey d'Aurevilly, Hardy, Tolstoy, Baudelaire: 382–7. Certain novels bring us into temporary contact with the reality of life — "the almost hypnotic suggestion of a good book": 569–70. Discrepancy between the thoughts of author and reader; basic flaws in literary journalism: 580–83. Objections against literature raised by M's reading of the Goncourt Diaries: 737–43. Relation of literature to life: 801–2. Reflections on literary creativity: 914–59; falsity of realism in literature; absurdity of popular or patriotic literature: 915–21; "the function and the task of a writer are those of a translator": 926; aberrations of literary criticism: 928–30; "real books . . . the offspring not of daylight and casual talk but of darkness and silence": 934; in literary creation, imagination and sensibility are interchangeable: 937–8; writing is for the writer a wholesome and necessary function comparable to exercise, sweat and baths for a man of more physical nature: 939; "a book is a huge cemetery": 940; our passions inspire our books, and intervals of repose write them: 945; futility of trying to guess an author's models: 945–6; a writer's works "like artesian wells": 946; a work of literature a kind of optical instrument enabling the reader to see himself more clearly: 949.

The narrator and his work. M's first efforts to express himself in writing; the impact of Bergotte: I 103–4. His desire to translate his sensations and impressions: 169–70. His wish to be a writer; despair at his lack of talent and the "nullity" of his intellect; renounces literature forever: 188–90, 194–5. The steeples of Martinville inspire him to composition: 196–8. Norpois advocates a literary career for M: 474–5, but in such terms as to make him doubly determined to renounce the idea: 487–9; his "prose poem" fails to impress Norpois: 490–91 who sees in it the malign influence of Bergotte: 510–12 (cf. II 228). Bergotte restores his confidence: 613–14. Inability to settle down to work; writing and social life: 623–5, 866; M is distracted from work by the "unknown beauties" who throng the streets of Paris: II 56, and by his pursuit of Mme de Guermantes: 65. "If only I had been able to start writing!": 151. He sends an article to *Le Figaro*: 360,

412. "The invisible vocation of which this book is the history": 412. Trees near Balbec seem to warn him to set to work before it is too late: 1046. He scans *Le Figaro* in vain for his article: III 4–5, 114. Continued procrastination; changes in the weather an excuse for not working: 76–8. Musings on art and literature while listening to Wagner; is there in art a more profound reality than in life, or is great art merely the result of superior craftsmanship?: 155–9, 196. Vinteuil's septet restores his faith in art and in his vocation: 262–5 (cf. 381–2, 388). Appearance of his article in *Le Figaro* at last; a boost to his self-confidence as a writer; the pleasure of writing incompatible with social pleasures: 579–84. Renewed discouragement during a visit to Tansonville: 709, and after reading an unpublished passage from the Goncourt diaries which convinces him not only of his own lack of talent but of the vanity and falsehood of literature: 728, 737–43 (cf. 886–7, 897–8). Renunciation, for several long years, of his project for writing: 743. Salvation at last; the uneven paving-stones; M's doubts suddenly dissipated; involuntary memory the key: 898–902. Reflections on the work he has now decided to undertake: 903–60, 1087–1107; deciphering "the inner book of unknown symbols": 913; "this most wonderful of all days": 923; the work of art "the only means of rediscovering Lost Time"; the materials for his work stored up inside him: 935–6; "my whole life ... might and yet might not have been summed up under the title: A Vocation": 936; Albertine, by causing him to suffer, more valuable to him than a secretary to arrange his "paperies": 947 (cf. 1091); Swann the inspiration for his book: 953–4; his discovery of the destructive action of Time at the very moment of conceiving the ambition to intellectualise extra-temporal realities in a work of art: 971, 974; his duty to his work more important than that of being polite or even kind: 1035–6; the readers of his book will be the readers of their own selves: 1089; a church or a druid monument?: 1098; his indifference to criticism: 1098–9; the *Arabian Nights* or the *Memoirs* of Saint-Simon of another age?: 1101–2; the dimension of Time: 1103–7 (cf. 1087–92).

"In this book ... there is not a single incident which is not fictitious, not a single character who is a real person in disguise ... everything has been invented by me in accordance with the requirements of my theme": III 876.

LOVE. Prerequisite of love, that it should win us admission to an unknown life: I 108. Love may come into being without any foundation in desire: 214. Modes of production of love; "the insensate, agonising need to possess exclusively": 252. The illusion that love exists outside ourselves: 434–5. Love creates "a supplementary person": 505. "No peace of mind in love"; "a permanent strain of suffering": 625–6. Love "radiates towards the loved one", then returns to its starting-point, oneself: 655. "Not like war": 673. Effects of absence and the passage of time; sufferers from love's sickness are "their own physicians": 676–9. Effects of Habit: 692–3 (cf. III 363, 436, 1076). "Those who love and those who enjoy are not always the same": 695. Features of our first love attach themselves to those that follow: 890 (cf. 955; III 694–5, 946). "The most exclusive love for a person is always a love for something else": 891. The women we love are "a negative of our sensibility": 955. "Loving helps us to discern, to discriminate": 969. Silence is "a terrible strength in the hands of those who are loved": II 122. The illusion on which the pains of love are based: 162–3. Mme Leroi on love: "I make it often but I never talk about it": 199. "A charming law of nature", that we live in ignorance of those we love: 291–2. Memories are accompaniments to carnal desire: 374–5. "The moment preceding pleasure" restores to Albertine's features "the innocence of earliest childhood": 380. Self-deception and subjectivity of love: 384. Role of costume in love: 401. Intimacy creates social ties which outlast love: 402. "This terrible need of a person": 759. Role of pity in love: the human need to "repair the wrongs" we do to the loved one: 860–61. Love makes us "at once more distrustful and more credulous": 862. Those who love us and whom we do not love seem insufferable: 949. The "invisible forces" within the woman we love to which we address ourselves "as to obscure deities": 1164–5. "The possession of what we love is an even greater joy than love itself": III 44. Apostrophe to girls — to define them we need to cease to be sexually interested in them: 58–60. "O mighty attitudes of Man and Woman": 74. "Beneath any carnal attraction that goes at all deep, there is the permanent possibility of danger": 76. "Love is an incurable malady": 80. More than any others, "fugitive beings" inspire love: 86–8. The object of our love is "the extension of that being to all the points in space and time that it has occupied and will occupy": 95; the "revolving searchlights of jealousy": 98–9; love is "kept in existence only by painful anxiety", "we love only what we do not wholly possess": 101–2. Love is "reciprocal torture": 105. "To be harsh and deceitful to the person whom we love is so natural!": 106. All love "evolves rapidly towards a farewell": 360. "In love, it is easier to relinquish a feeling than to give up a habit": 363. "Love is space and time made perceptible to the heart": 392. The unknown element in Albertine "formed the core" of M's love: 438–9 (cf. 505–6). "There is not a woman in the world the possession of whom is as precious as that of the truths which she reveals to us by causing us to suffer": 506 (cf. 631–2, 933–4, 941–7). "One wants to be understood because one wants to be loved, and one wants to be loved because one loves": 506. Natural to love "a certain type of woman"; "unique, we suppose? She is legion": 512–16. "Death does not make any great difference": 534. "We fall in love for a smile, a look, a shoulder": 541. Love is "a striking example of how little reality means to us": 577. "A mistake to speak of a bad choice in love, since as soon as there is a choice it can only be a bad one": 624. Reasons for love remaining platonic: 847–8. Love is "a portion of our mind more durable than the various selves which successively die within us", a portion of the mind which gives the understanding of this love "to the universal spirit": 933–4. Value of love and grief to the writer; "ideas come to us as the successors to grief"; "had we not been happy . . . the unhappinesses that befall us would be without cruelty and therefore without fruit"; the painful dilemmas consequent on love "reveal to us, layer after layer, the material of which we are made": 941–7.

LYING. Odette's lies; fragment of truth that gives her away: I 303–4; signs of distress that accompany her lying: 306, 317, 323. Nissim Bernard's perpetual lying: 832. Andrée's lying; people who lie once will lie again: 947. Albertine's polymorphous lies prompted by a desire to please everybody: 1000–01. Unconscious mendacity: II 63. A complete lie more easily believed than a half-lie: 741. Albertine's lies; the Infreville story: 827–30 (cf. III 104); how she gives herself away when lying: 1133–4; how to decipher her lies; jealousy multiplies the tendency to lie in the person loved: III 55–6, 85; a liar by nature: 93; her contradictory lies; we fail to notice our mistress's first lies: 141–50; her aptitude for lying; her "charming skill in lying naturally": 176–8, 187–91. "Impenetrable solidarity" of the little band as liars: 177. A lie "the most necessary means of self-preservation": 168. Lovers' lies to a third person: 210–11. Value of lies and liars to literary men; "the perfect lie . . . is one of the few things in the world that can open windows for us on to what is new and unknown": 213. Disparity between the truth which a lying woman has travestied and the idea which the lover has formed of that truth: 339. Perseverance in falsehood of those who deceive us: 391. Lying formulas that turn out to have been prophetic truths: 470, 517–18. "Lying is essential to humanity"; we lie to protect our pleasure or our honour; "one lies all one's life long, even, especially, perhaps only, to those who love one": 623 (cf. 1113). Lying is a trait of character as well as a natural defence: 631–2. "One ruins oneself, makes oneself ill, kills oneself all for lies" — a lode from which one can extract a little truth: 948.

MARRIAGE. Swann's marriage: 1 465–6, 502–8, 559–66. "Ignominious marriages are the most estimable of all": 507. The "subservience of refinement to vulgarity" the rule in many marriages: 559. Marital schemes of the Prince de Foix and his friends: 11 419–20. Skin-deep Christianity of the Guermantes set invariably leads to "a colossally mercenary marriage": 424. Happy marriages arranged by inverts for their nieces: 721. Reflections on the marriage of Gilberte to Saint-Loup and of Jupien's niece to young Cambremer: 111 672–82; effects of these marriages: 682–93. An "unfortunate" marriage may be the only poetical action in a man's life: 696. Advantage for a young husband of having kept a mistress: 697–8. Homosexuals make good husbands: 701, 723–4.

MEDICINE. Mysterious flair of the diagnostician; "we realised that this imbecile (Cottard) was a great physician": 1 536–7. Bergotte's views on the sort of doctor needed by an artist: 614–15. M's grandmother's illness — rival prescriptions of Cottard and du Boulbon: 11 308–17; Professor E—'s diagnosis: 324–8 (cf. 664–6); Cottard has "something of the greatness of a general" when deciding on a course of treatment: 333; the specialist X—, nose expert: 335–6; Professor Dieulafoy: 354–5. Medicine is "a compendium of the successive and contradictory mistakes of medical practitioners": 308. "To believe in medicine would be the height of folly, if not to believe in it were not a greater folly still": 308–9. Doctors create illness by making patients believe they are ill (du Boulbon): 313. "A great part of what doctors know is taught them by the sick": 314. Du Boulbon on nervous disorders: 315–16. "Doctors, like stockbrokers, employ the first person singular": 423 (cf. 930). Innumerable mistakes of doctors; "medicine is not an exact science"; "Medicine has made some slight advance in knowledge since Molière's day, but none in its vocabulary": 665–6. Cottard and his rivals at Balbec: 824–5. Toxic actions "a perilous innovation in medicine": 824–5. Medicine "busies itself with changing the sense of verbs and pronouns": 930. Cottard on sleeping draughts and on the digestion: 993–4. Medicine has developed the art of prolonging illnesses, but cannot cure the illnesses it creates: III 180–81. Bergotte and his doctors: 183–4.

MEMORY. The body's memory more enduring than that of the mind: I 6–9 (cf. III 716). Voluntary memory preserves nothing of the past itself: 47. The madeleine; taste and smell alone bear "the vast structure of recollection": 48–51 (cf. III 899–900). The three strata of memory: 203. The "terrible recreative power" of memory: 400. A mistake to compare the images stored in one's memory with reality: 462. Role of memory in our gradual assimilation of a new piece of music: 570–71. Memory presents things to us in reverse: 622. Memory's conflicting photographs: 936, 951 (cf. 978; III 487). Process of recapturing a line of verse: II 34 (cf. 1016–17). Resurrection of the soul may be conceived as a phenomenon of memory: 86. Sleep and memory: 89–90 (cf. 1016–18; III 117–19). Influence of the atmosphere in stimulating memory: 144 (cf. III 17–18, 488–500). Process of recapturing a name; advantages of an imperfect memory: 674–6. Arbitrariness of the images selected by memory: 779. M's "complete and involuntary recollection" of his grandmother; "with the perturbations of memory are linked the intermittencies of the heart"; restoration of the self that experienced the resuscitated sensations: 783–4. Soporifics and memory: 1016–18. Poor memories of men and women of action: III 31. Resuscitation of memory after the amnesia of sleep; "the goddess Mnemotechnia": 117–19. Memory "a void from which at odd

Opalescent moonlight in a fountain at Doncières: 11 93–4. Charlus's desire to look at the "blue light of the moon" in the Bois with M: 584. Crescent moon at twilight over Paris: 657 (cf. 1052). Moon through the oaks at la Raspelière: 997, and over the valley: 1006. Full moon over Paris: 111 173. Albertine asleep by moonlight: 394. Moonrise over Paris; the moon in poetry: 414. Venetian *campo* by moonlight: 665. Effects of moonlight in war-time Paris: 757–8; "cruelly and mysteriously serene": 828; "like a soft and steady magnesium flare": 830; "narrow and curved like a sequin": 836.

MOTOR-CARS. M hires a motor-car for Albertine: 11 1028–9. Effect of the motor-car on our ideas of topography and perspective; difference between arrival by car and by train (cf. 1 693); the charm of motoring: 1036–8. A drive through Paris: 111 163–73. M's delight in the sound of motor-cars and the smell of petrol: 418–19. Albertine's Rolls-Royce, her favourite car: 427, 464.

MUSIC. Vinteuil's sonata; the ineffable character of a first musical impression; the "little phrase": 1 227–31. Insanity diagnosed in Vinteuil's sonata: 234. The "little phrase" becomes the "national anthem" of Swann's love for Odette: 238–9; its effect on Swann: 258–9, 288, 375, 378–83, 573–5. The music of the violin, "the sapient, quivering and enchanted box": 378. Great musicians reveal to us a new world in the depths of the soul: 380–81. "Inexorably determined" language of music: 382. Role of memory in our gradual assimilation of a new composition; originality of Vinteuil's sonata; "great works of art do not begin by giving us the best of themselves"; works such as Beethoven's late quartets create their own posterity: 570–73. M's attempts to grasp the truths expressed by music: 751. Intoxicating and sensual effect of music enhanced by that of alcohol: 869–70. A great pianist is "a window opening upon a great work of art": 11 43–4. People feel justified in enjoying vulgar music if they find it in the work of a good composer (such as Richard Strauss): 465–6. Conversation about music with Mme de Cambremer; Debussy and Wagner; reflections on theories, schools, fashions and tastes: 842–6. Music evoked by Paris street cries – *Boris, Pelléas*, Palestrina, Gregorian chant: 111 111–14, 123, 133. Rhythms of sleep compared to those of music; it is the lengthening or shortening of the interval that creates beauty: 117, 121. Music helps M to "descend into himself" and discover new things; it also enables us to know the essential quality of another person's sensations: 156. Vinteuil's septet: 250–67. Tone colour: 255–6. Unique, unmistakable voice of a great composer is proof of "the irreducibly individual existence of the soul": 258. "The transposition of creative profundity into terms of sound": 259. Music "the unique example of what might have been . . . the means of communication between souls": 260. Inferior compositions may prepare the way for later masterpieces: 265. Albertine at the pianola; M's pleasure in elucidating the structure of musical compositions; "a piece of music the less in the world, perhaps, but a truth the more": 378–9. Is music, which recomposes what we feel about life, truer than literature, which analyses it?: 381. Great music must correspond to some definite spiritual reality: 381–2; or is this an illusion?: 388. Visual images evoked by music: 388–9. Bird singing in the Lydian mode: 395. Melancholy refrain of pigeons compared to phrases in Vinteuil: 407–8. The "little phrase" and M's love for Albertine: 571–2.

(See also Bach; Beethoven; Chopin; Debussy; Schumann; Wagner under Index of Persons.)

NAMES. By pronouncing a name one secures a sort of power over it (Guermantes): I 138. The name "Gilberte" heard for the first time by M at Tansonville: 154; and later in the Champs-Elysées: 418. Poetry of place-names: 416–27. Imaginative difference between words and proper names: 421. Images evoked by names of Italian, Norman and Breton towns: 421–2, 710. Effect on M of Gilberte calling him by his Christian name for the first time: 437–8. "Names are whimsical draughtsmen": 590. Names of the cathedral towns: 708. Place-names on the way to Balbec; contrast between place-names with and without personal associations: 711–12. Pleasures of collecting old names: 804–5. The name Simonet: 859, 865; importance of the single "n": 904 (cf. II 382). "The names which designate things correspond invariably to an intellectual notion, alien to our true impressions"; Elstir recreates things by renaming them: 893. Affective content of names and how it decays; changing connotations of the name Guermantes: II 4–9. M incapable of integrating the name Guermantes into the living figure of the Duchess: 24. Poetic German landscape evoked by the name Faffenheim-

Munsterburg-Weinigen: 264–5. We hate our namesakes: 382. Nicknames in society: 448–9. Poetry of the name Isabella d'Este: 545. Names change their meaning for us more in a few years than words do in centuries: 522. The nobility are the etymologists of the language of names, but are oblivious of its poetry: 533. M's aesthetic pleasure in historic names: 563. The name Surgis-le-Duc stripped of its poetry: 732. Noble names of Normandy: 814. Depoeticisation of place-names in the region of Balbec: 1145–8. Bitter-sweet charm in the possessive use of a Christian name: 111 95. Albertine after her departure scarcely exists for M save under the form of her name, which he repeats to himself incessantly: 439. Place-names near Balbec become impregnated with baleful mystery: 529. Habit strips names of their charm and significance: 547. Venomous overtones of the name of Tours: 552. Succession to a name is a melancholy thing: 999. "A name: that very often is all that remains for us of a human being . . . even in his life-time": 1012.

OLD AGE. The "great renunciation" of old age as it prepares for death: 1 156. Disillusionment of old age; the futility of writing letters: 526. The day when one feels that love is too big an undertaking for the little strength one has left: 11 913. "Old age makes us incapable of doing but not, at first, of desiring": 111 650. Charlus in old age: 891–7. Metamorphoses due to old age seen at the Guermantes *matinée*: 960–94. We see our age in a mirror: 970. Old age is of all the realities of life "the one of which we preserve for longest a purely abstract conception": 973–4. The phenomenon of old age seems, in its different modes, to take into account certain social habits: 986. The Duc de Guermantes in old age: 1068–74. Norpois and Mme de Villeparisis in old age: 1116–19 (cf. 644–6).

PAINTING. Swann's penchant for finding likenesses to real people in the old masters: 1 243–4, 352–3, 576. Elstir at work: 893–912; metaphors in his works: 894; description of his *Carquethuit Harbour*: 894–8; painting and photography: 896–7. Reflections on portrait-painting: 920–22. Profundities of "still life": 929 (cf. 11 118). Race-courses and regattas as subjects for painting: 958–63. "The original painter proceeds on the lines of the oculist" — the visual world is created afresh: 11 338–9. M's reflections on painting while studying the Guermantes' Elstirs;

Elstir's relation to earlier painters; analysis of a waterside carnival; the painter's eye; the immortalisation of a moment: 434–8. Conversation about painting with Mme de Cambremer at Balbec: 831–41. The "little patch of yellow wall": 111 185. Aesthetic truth and documentary truth in portraits: 738–9. "The artist may paint anything in the world that he chooses"; the artist of genius may be inspired by commonplace models: 741–3.

(*See also* Botticelli; Carpaccio; Giotto; Greco; Hooch; Leonardo; Manet; Mantegna; Michelangelo; Monet; Poussin; Rembrandt; Renoir; Turner; Vermeer; Veronese; Watteau; Whistler *under* Index of Persons.)

PARTIES. Dinner-party at the Verdurins' at which Swann hears the Vinteuil sonata: 1 217–36. Dinner-party at the Verdurins' at which Forcheville is present: 273–88. Musical *soirée* at Mme de Saint-Euverte's: 351–84. Elstir's afternoon party to introduce Albertine: 929–35. Afternoon party at Mme de Villeparisis's: 11 193–294. Theatrical *soirée* at Mme de Villeparisis's for which M arrives too late: 384–96. Dinner-party at the Duchesse de Guermantes's: 432–568. Evening party at the Princesse de Guermantes's: 657–748. Dinner-party at la Raspelière: 929–1011. Musical *soirée* at the Verdurins' (Quai Conti): 111 226–332. Afternoon party at the Princesse de Guermantes's: 957–1088.

PHOTOGRAPHY. Swann studies photographs of Odette: 1 318; he prefers an old daguerreotype to more recent photographs: 664 (*see also* 111 202). M's photograph of Berma, which he studies in bed: 525, 527. Charlus on photography: "A photograph acquires something of the dignity which it ordinarily lacks when it ceases to be a reproduction of reality and shows us things that no longer exist": 821. Saint-Loup photographs M's grandmother: 843–4 (cf. 11 786, 803–7). An old photograph of the "little band": 881–2. Influence of photography on painting: 896–7. Saint-Loup's photograph of Mme de Guermantes seems to M like a "supplementary prolonged encounter" with her: 11 77–8. By "a cruel trick of chance", M sees his grandmother as a photograph: 141–3. Similar effects produced by photography and kissing: 378–9. Contrasting photographs of Odette, "the earlier a photograph the older a woman looks in it": 111 202.

Saint-Loup's stupefaction on seeing M's photograph of Albertine: 445–7.

POLITICS. Diplomacy and politics; the "governmental mind" (Norpois): I 469–70. M discovers to his surprise that, in politics, to repeat what everyone else is thinking is the mark not of an inferior but of a superior mind: 494–5. Mme de Villeparisis's "advanced" but anti-socialist opinions: 762. Saint-Loup's "socialistic spoutings": 787, 836. Elusiveness of truth in politics: II 248–9. Subtlety of politicians, a perversion of the science of "reading between the lines", accounts for the behaviour of the Guermantes circle and in particular the Duchess's paradoxical judgments; the Duke as politician: 490–93.

RAILWAYS. Arrival by train at Combray: I 52, 68, 124. The railway time-table "the most intoxicating romance in the lover's library": 319; time-tables minister to M's longing for aesthetic enjoyment: 424. The "fine, generous" 1.22 train to Normandy and Brittany: 418–19, 696. The "wizard's cell": 425. Reflections on rail travel; railway stations "marvellous but tragic" places; the Gare Saint-Lazare: 693–4 (cf. II 1038). Journey to Balbec: 701–8. Concomitants of long railway journeys: sunrise, hard-boiled eggs, illustrated papers, packs of cards, rivers: 704. Whistling of locomotives at Doncières: II 138. Difference between arrival by train and by motor-car: 1038 (cf. I 693). Return journey from Venice to Paris: III 670. Halt by a sunlit line of trees on M's train-journey back to Paris from the sanatorium: 885–6. M's memory of the hooting of the trains at night at Combray: 915.

The "little train". M's first journey on it; names of stations: I 711–12. Various colloquial names for it — "crawler" (Saint-Loup): 926, "tram", "rattletrap" (Albertine): 937. Service suspended in winter: 1014. Further nicknames: II 812. Break-down at Incarville: 822. Leisurely arrival at Balbec station: 885. M travels with Albertine to Doncières: 886–94. M travels with the "faithful" to Douville: 895–925, 1067–92. Stations on the little railway: 1111–12, 1118, 1122, 1132, 1137, 1144–9. Halts on the little railway a setting for social intercourse: 1146–9. M's last journey on the little train — Albertine's shattering revelation as it enters Parville station: 1150–53.

ROOMS. M remembers various bedrooms in which he has slept: I
6–9, 203–4. His bedroom at Combray: 10–11. The little room at
the top of the house smelling of orris-root: 13, 172. Aunt
Léonie's rooms; the charm of country rooms, reflecting "a whole
secret system of life": 53–6. Uncle Adolphe's sanctum: 78 (cf.
533). M's room in summer: 89–90. Rooms in Odette's house in
the Rue La Pérouse: 240–42. M's bedroom in the Grand Hotel,
Balbec: 416, 716–17, 722–5, 987–8, 1016–18. Waiting-room in
Swann's house: 567–8. Mme Swann's drawing-room: 580–82,
638–41, 682–3. Dining-room of the Grand Hotel: 724–6, 732,
929 (cf. II 760–61). M's grandmother's room in the Grand
Hotel: 757. Saint-Loup's room at Doncières: II 71–2. "Un-
breathable aroma" of every new bedroom: 79–80. Silent but alive
and friendly rooms in the hotel at Doncières: 80–87. Dining-
room at Doncières: 97–8. Mme de Villeparisis's drawing-room:
193. M's bedroom in Paris: 358–9, 405–6; III 1–3, 364–5, 378,
388–9, 417–18. Card-room at the Princesse de Guermantes's — a
"magician's cell": II 713–14. Drawing-room at la Raspelière: II
934–5 (cf. III 286–7). Verdurin drawing-rooms at Rue Montalivet and Quai Conti: III 201–2, 286–8. Room in Andrée's
grandmother's apartment: 398. M's bedroom at Tansonville:
715–16. Eulalie's room at Combray: 914–15.

SADISM. Scene of "sadism" at Montjouvain between Mlle
Vinteuil and her friend: I 175–80. Sadists of Mlle Vinteuil's sort
are "purely sentimental, naturally virtuous": 179. Real sadism —
"pure and voluptuous cruelty" — uncommon: II 177. The sadist
in Charlus — a medium: 1042. Irresistible sadism as a motive for
crime: III 204. Sado-masochistic scene in Jupien's brothel: 843,
and reflections thereon: 853–6.

SEA. The sea reflected in the glass of the book-cases in M's room at
Balbec: I 416. M's longing to witness a stormy sea: 416. The sea
seen from M's window at Balbec; variety of seascapes: 723–5,
757–8, 860–64 (see also II 791, 811–12). Sea glimpsed from high
ground through trees: 760–61 (cf. II 1045). The "little band"
inseparable from the sea: 891 (cf. II 364; III 61–3, 461). The sea
in Elstir's pictures: 894–8, 962–3. M's efforts to see the sea
through Elstir's eyes: 963–4. "Perpetual re-creation of the
primordial elements of nature which we contemplate when we
stand before the sea": 967. M's pleasure in returning to the sea: II

791, 807-8. The "rural" sea: 811-12. Sight and sound of the sea from a hill near Douville: 927-8. The sea from la Raspelière: 1031-2. "The plaintive ancestress of the earth": 1045. M and Albertine lie on the beach at night listening to the sea: 1053 (cf. III 65). Albertine asleep reminds M of the sea: III 63-5.

SELF. "Our social personality is a creation of the thoughts of other people": I 20. Mystery of personality: 336. Revival of an old self can make us experience feelings long dead: 691-2 (cf. II 784-5). "Fragmentary and continuous death" of our successive selves: 722. Oneself: a subject on which other people's views are never in accordance with one's own: 797-9 (cf. II 280-82). Uses of self-centredness: 827. Eclipse of one's old self at a social gathering: 931. Friendship an abdication of self: 968. M's "Self" which he rediscovers periodically when he arrives in a new place: II 80. Recovery of one's own self after sleep: 86-7. Ephemeral personalities of characters in a play make one doubt the reality of the self: 176. Contrast between one's own picture of one's self and that seen by others: 280-82. Our body "a vase enclosing our spiritual nature": 784. Our unfaithfulness to our former selves: 888. "Experience of oneself which is the only true experience": 952. "We lack the sense of our own visibility": 1083. M's several "selves", notably the philosopher and "the little barometric mannikin": III 4. "We detest what resembles ourselves": 103. We do not see our own bodies, which other people see, while the object of our thoughts is invisible to them: 179. Our ignorance of ourselves: 425-6 (cf. 485). The "innumerable and humble 'selves' that compose our personality": 437 (cf. 499: "a composite army", and 540). Self-plagiarism: 443. "Man is the creature who cannot escape from himself, who knows other people only in himself": 459. "Our ego is composed of the superimposition of our successive states": 555. Other people are "merely showcases for the very perishable collections of one's own mind": 568. "Spare selves" that are substituted for a self "that has been too seriously wounded": 607-9. Death of one's former self no more distressing than the continuous eclipse of the various incompatible selves that make up one's personality: 656-7. "Through art alone are we able to emerge from ourselves": 932 (cf. 155, 915).

SERVANTS. Françoise's tyranny over other servants: I 134-5. Servants must be actuated by different motives from ours: 389.

Servants observe and misinterpret the behaviour of their
employers as human beings do animals: 748. Lunch below stairs,
Françoise holds court: 11 11–23. Françoise less of a servant than
others: 61. "Monstrous abnormality" of the life led by servants:
61–2. Defects of his servants reveal to M his own shortcomings:
62. M's pity for servants: 805. Power of divination in servants:
853. Servants recognise their own kind, as do convicts and
animals: 1020. Servants only make clearer the limitations of their
caste the more they imagine they are penetrating ours: 111 770.
Clichés in the servants' hall as in social coteries: 880.

SLEEP. Depersonalisation due to sleep; the sleep of things;
disorientation in time and space: 1 3–9. Distortion in sleep of the
sleeper's real perceptions: 413–14. Sleep in a train: 703–4. Sleep
after evenings at Rivebelle; mysteries into which we are initiated
by deep sleep; a form of intoxication; a potent narcotic; the body
measures time in sleep: 877–80. Sleep at Doncières; poetic
landscape of sleep; the "secret garden" in which different kinds
of sleep grow "like unknown flowers"; "sleeping like a log": 11
82–7; "organic dislocations" produced by sleep after great
fatigue take us back to our earlier selves; "a charming fairy-tale":
89–90. Remains of waking thoughts subsist in sleep; diminutions
that characterise sleep reflected symbolically in dreams: 147–8.
The act of awakening is one of forgetting: 347. Insomnia helps us
to appreciate sleep: 676. The world of sleep; an "inward Lethe":
787. Mme Cottard falls asleep at la Raspelière; Cottard on
soporifics: 993–5. Sleep like a second dwelling, a different world
in which we lead another life; distortion of time during sleep;
sensual pleasure enjoyed in sleep a positive waste: 1013–16. Sleep
itself the most powerful soporific; Bergson on soporifics; sleep
and memory: 1016–18. Albertine's sleep: 111 63–9, 108–11,
366–7, 374, 394. Refreshing quality of heavy sleep; changing
rhythms of sleep; varieties of sleep; images of pity in sleep:
116–21. Insomnia and narcotics (Bergotte): 184. "That curiously
alive and creative sleep of the unconscious": 345. Sleep and the
memory of Albertine: 456, 497–8. After all these centuries we
still know very little about sleep: 736–7.

SMELL. Taste and smell alone bear "the vast structure of
recollection": 1 50–51.

    Evocative smells: Scent of the lilacs of Tansonville: 1 147, 202;

bitter-sweet almond fragrance of hawthorn blossom: 123, 150–51 (cf. 11 1186); musty smell of the little trellised pavilion in the Champs-Elysées recalls Uncle Adolphe's sanctum at Combray: 530, 533 (cf. 77); smell of a log fire and the paper of one of Bergotte's books linked in M's memory with the names of villages round Combray: 712; evocative power, for M, of a smell of leaves: 774–5; scent of twigs which Françoise throws on the fire revives memories of Combray and Doncières: 111 19; smell of petrol reawakens memories of motoring at Balbec: 418.

Isolated smells: Smell of vetiver in an unfamiliar room: 1 8, 717; smell of orris-root in the little closet: 13, 172; smell of varnish on the staircase at Combray: 30; smell of cooking from the Oiseau Flesché: 52; country smells concentrated in Aunt Léonie's rooms: 53–4; "glutinous, insipid, indigestible and fruity" smell of her bedspread: 54; odour of unbleached calico in the draper's shop: 69; balmy scent of the lime-trees on evening walks: 124; M's chamber-pot "a vase of aromatic perfume" after eating asparagus: 131; aroma of roast chicken the "proper perfume" of one of Françoise's virtues: 132; smell of asparagus gives the kitchen-maid asthma: 135; fragrance of Odette's chrysanthemums: 240; fragrance of acacias in the Bois: 452; Odette's scent, whose "fragrant exhalations" perfume the whole apartment: 542, 547; lemon fragrance of guelder-roses: 683; Odette's drawing-room permeated with the scent of flowers: 683; the smell of Albertine's cheeks: 949, 996; 11 377. Coarse, stale, mouldy smell of the barracks at Doncières: 11 72; "peculiar odour" of the soap in the Grand Hotel, Balbec: 791–2; M compares his desires for different girls to the perfumes of antiquity: 869; smell of rhino-gomenol exuded by Mme Verdurin on musical evenings: 111 242; smells evoked by a spring morning: 418; "cool smell" of a forest: 900.

SNOBBERY. Legrandin's tirades against snobbery — "the unforgivable sin": 1 73; his own snobbery: 138–41 (cf. 111 6, 683). Princes "know themselves to be princes, and are not snobs": 561. Bloch taxes M with snobbery: 795, 799 (cf. 11 1140). Snobbish distinctions among the lower classes more surprising because more obscure: 904. Offensive snobbishness of the Prince de Foix and his friends: 11 418. "Evangelical snobbery" of the Princesse de Parme: 433. Bréauté's hatred of snobs derives from his own snobbishness: 523 (cf. 468). Craven snobbishness of Mme de Saint-Euverte: 727. Artistic snobbery (Mme de Cambremer-Legrandin) and its effect on reputations: 839–46 (cf. 986–7). "Congenital and morbid" snobbery (of Mme de Cambremer) which renders its victim immune to other vices: 955. "Snobbery is a grave disease, but it is localised and so does not utterly corrupt the soul": III 6. Gilberte's snobbery, which has "something of Swann's intelligent curiosity": 597–600. Element of sincerity in snobbery: 601. The snobbery of the gutter: 859. How snobbery changes in form: 1003.

SOLITUDE. M's exhilaration in the solitude of autumn walks: I 169–70. M can be truly happy only when alone: 790. Reasons for Elstir's life of solitude; the practice of solitude engenders a love for it: 886–7. "An artist, if he is to be absolutely true to the life of the spirit, must be alone": 923. The "solitary work of artistic creation": 968. "Each of us is indeed alone": II 328. Ideas are like goddesses who appear only to the solitary mortal: 413. "Exhilarating virtues of solitude": III 17. M's fears that marriage will deprive him of "the joys of solitude": 19–20. "The fortifying thrill of solitude": 201. Impression of solitude in Venice: 667. Solitude can be preserved in the midst of social life: 957–8; but M proposes to return to a solitary life to write his book: 1034–6.

SPEECH. *See* Language.

STOCK EXCHANGE. M's stocks and shares; Norpois's advice on his portfolio: I 489–90 (cf. III 654). Peculiar credulity of the Stock Exchange — sensational war-time rumours: III 762.

SUN. Afternoon sun behind closed shutters at Combray: I 89. Rays of the setting sun in Aunt Léonie's room: 145. Sunlight on a balcony: 430–31 (cf. II 318); on the snow in the Champs-Elysées: 433; in M's classroom: 439. Sunlight in the train to Balbec: 701; sunrise from the train: 704–5. Morning sun on the roof of the Grand Hotel annex: 720; on the sea: 723–4; in M's and his grandmother's rooms: 724, 757, 1017–18. Balbec sunsets: 860–63. Exaltation of sunlight at Doncières: II 79. Desolating sunrise on M's last day at Balbec, symbolising "the bloody sacrifice I was about to have to make of all joy, every morning, until the end of my life": 1166–8. Play of sunlight on bathroom windows: III 2–3. Sunset and painful memories: 488–9.

TEARS. M's childhood tears; sobs that still echo in the silence of evening; "a manumission of tears": I 40–42. "Quite half the human race in tears": II 386. Lowering of temperatures caused by a certain kind of tears: 409. Effect of tears on Françoise: 805 (cf. III 490). Upper-class people pretend not to notice tears whereas simple people are distressed by them: 986. Our own (suppressed) tears in other people's eyes are infuriating: III 103. "People are not always very tolerant of the tears which they themselves have provoked": 316.

TELEPHONE. Mme Cottard's wonder at the novelty of the telephone: I 653. M considers it improper that the telephone should play pander between Saint-Loup and his mistress: II 124. M's abortive conversation with his grandmother; magic of the telephone; the "Vigilant Virgins"; gabblings of the "vociferous stump": 133–9. "Purposeless smiles" of people on the telephone: 596 (cf. III 95). Françoise's resistance to the telephone: 756–7 (cf. III 96, 152). M's call from Albertine; the "top-like whirr" of the telephone: 756–60. Familiarity of a "supernatural instrument before whose miracles we used to stand amazed": III 24. M invokes the "implacable deities" (telephone call to Andrée); genre scene for a modern painter: "At the Telephone": 94–7. "A flying squadron of sounds" (M's conversation with the telephonist speaking for Françoise): 152. Mme Verdurin's war-time telephoning: 754–5.

THEATRE. M's platonic love for the theatre as a child; his classification of actors: I 79–80. Swann advises him to go and see Berma in *Phèdre*: 105; he does so at last: 473–86; expectations before seeing Berma; preconceptions about the art of acting: 475–80; first impressions on entering a theatre: 481–3; disappointment with Berma: 483–6; retrospective reappraisal, influenced by (1) Norpois's opinion: 492–3; (2) an enthusiastic newspaper review: 517–18; (3) Bergotte's views: 603–5; (4) Swann's views: 610–11. Waning of M's enthusiasm for the art of acting: II 32, 40–42. Second experience of Berma; a gala night at the Opéra: 32–55; M recognises and appreciates Berma's dramatic genius, and realises why he had failed to do so before; reflections on the art of acting; interpretative genius transcends mediocre material: 43–9. Rachel on theatre: 170–71. Reflections on actors: 175–6. A case of theatrical bitchiness: 176–7.

Backstage at the theatre: 179–85. The language of the theatrical profession: III 1055. Unpleasant aspects of theatrical life (Berma and Rachel): 1067–8.

TIME. Distortion of time during sleep: I 5–9 (cf. 878–80; II 1013–16; III 116–17). Time the fourth dimension of Combray Church: 66. Imaginary Time of the armchair traveller: 426. M's realisation that he is not situated somewhere outside Time but subject to its laws: 520. Time is elastic, the passions we feel expand it, those we inspire contract it: 659. Life is careless of chronology, "interpolating so many anachronisms into the sequence of our days": 691. Time accurately measured by the body during sleep: 879. For M, far from Mme de Guermantes, the arithmetical divisions of time assume "a dolorous and poetic aspect": II 120. Lengthening of time in solitude: 362–3, or while waiting for a rendezvous: 397. Reappearance of Albertine "like an enchantress offering me a mirror that reflected time": 364. Phenomena of memory make Time appear to consist of a series of different parallel lines: 784. We take account of minutes, the Romans scarcely of hours: 853. "We can sometimes find a person again, but we cannot abolish time": 913. Sleep has its own time, different from waking time — or perhaps is outside time: 1013–16 (cf. III 116–18). Albertine "a mighty goddess of Time": III 393. "As there is a geometry in space, so there is a psychology in time": 568 (cf. 1087). Time brings forgetfulness, which in turn alters our notion of time; "there are optical errors in time as there are in space": 606. Man an "ageless creature" who floats between the walls of time "as in a pool the surface-level of which is constantly changing": 627. Recapturing Lost Time; extra-temporal sensations; "a fragment of time in the pure state"; "a minute freed from the order of time" recreates "the man freed from the order of time": 904–6; a work of art "the sole means of rediscovering Lost Time": 935 (cf. 971, 974); dreams, in spite of "the extraordinary effects which they achieve with Time", cannot enable us to rediscover it: 950. Guests at the Guermantes *matinée* "puppets which exteriorised Time"; M. d'Argencourt a revelation of Time made visible; "the distorting perspective of Time": 964–6; recreative power of Time; "Time, the artist": 977–8, 983; variations in the *tempo* of Time: 986–7; "balancing mechanism of Time": 991–2; "the chemistry of Time . . . at work upon society": 1000–16, 1042–3. The young Mme de Saint-Euverte a symbol of Time's continuity: 1079. Time, "colourless and inapprehensible", materialised in Mlle de Saint-Loup: 1087–8. Time a spur to M: 1088–92; fundamental importance of Time in his book; he will describe men as "occupying a place . . . prolonged past measure . . . in the dimension of Time": 1103–7.

TRAINS. *See* Railways.

TREES. Trees in the Bois de Boulogne (Allée des Acacias): 1 452; autumn in the Bois: 456–9; 11 404. The three trees of Hudimesnil: 1 770–73 (cf. 111∫899). Trees on the roads round Balbec seem to M to be silently warning him to get down to work: 11 1045–6. Row of sunlit trees by a railway line: 111 886, 900.

(*See* Apple-trees; Flowers; Hawthorns.)

TRUTH. The search for Truth the "vague but permanent" object of the young M's thoughts: 1 91. 'The truth which one puts into one's words is not irresistibly self-evident": 659. Fortuitous stumblings on the truth give some support to the theory of presentiment: 920. "Truth has no need to be uttered to be made apparent": 11 62–3. Elusiveness of truth in politics: 248–9. Truth in the context of diplomacy: 268–9. Under the stress of exceptional emotion, people do sometimes say what they think: 525. Truth a current which flows from what people say rather than the actual thing they say: 1133. The truth comes to us, unexpectedly, from without: 1151. Truth, even if logically necessary, not always foreseeable as a whole: 111 1. "The truth is so variable for each of us . . . ": 12. A single small fact may be enough to reveal the truth about a whole category of analogous facts: 524. "How difficult it is to know the truth in this world": 634. "Truth and life are very difficult to fathom": 637. Truths which the intellect apprehends directly less profound and necessary than those received through intuition: 912, 914, 934–5. Truth for the writer: 924–5. Truth unknown to three people out of four: 1077.

VICE. "Perhaps it is only in really vicious lives that the problem of morality can arise in all its disquieting strength"; vice can arise from hypersensitiveness as much as from the lack of it; vice in a writer not incompatible with morality in his books (Bergotte): 1 601–2. "The variety of our defects is no less remarkable than the similarity of our virtues": 796–7. The bad habit of denouncing our own defects in others: 798. "Every vice, like every profession, requires and develops a special knowledge which we are never loath to display": 799. Sexual inversion "improperly" called a vice: II 640. People with the same vice recognise each other instinctively: 662. Nothing so isolates us as an inner vice: III 208. There is no one we appreciate more than a person who places his virtues at the service of our vices: 214. Nothing is more limited than vice: 856. Internal and external signs of vice: 866. The greatest vice of all — lack of will-power: 866.

(*See* Inversion; Sadism.)

VIRTUE. "The impassive, unsympathetic, sublime face of true goodness": I 89. Our virtues are not free and floating qualities but closely linked to the actions in conjunction with which we exercise them: 466. "The frequency of the virtues that are identical in us all is not more wonderful than the multiplicity of the defects that are peculiar to each one of us": 796. It is not common sense, but kindness, that is "the commonest thing in the world": 796. Other people more capable of kind acts than we suppose: III 331–2. "Kindness, a simple process of maturation": 1016.

WAR. Françoise and the gardener at Combray discuss the possibility of war: I 95–6. Discussions at Doncières on the art of war; Saint-Loup's theories: II 108–17 (cf. III 782–3, 1029–31). Françoise's reaction to the Russo-Japanese war: 342. Saint-Loup on the possibility of a Franco-German war; his predictions as to the cosmic nature of a future war: 428. M's interest in the Boer War: 630. Preparations for war provoke war: III 368–9. The 1914–18 war: 743–85 *passim*; war-time Paris: 743–55; profound changes brought about by the war in inverse ratio to the quality of the minds it touched: 748; the misery of the soldier: 756; patriotism, courage and cowardice, heroism of the *poilu*; the ethos of the soldier (Saint-Loup): 760–69, 775–6; the butler "puts the wind up" Françoise; "a good blood-letting is useful now and again": 770; relation of 1914–18 war to previous wars: 782–4; the war considered as a struggle between two human bodies: 795–6; "scum of universal fatuousness" which the war left in its wake: 884. Saint-Loup's theories about war vindicated:

1029–31. "War is something that is lived like a love or a hatred and could be told like a novel": 1031.

WEATHER. M's father's meterological preoccupations: I 11, 99 (inherited by M: III 72–3). Sonorous atmosphere of hot weather: 89. Atmospheric variations provoke changes of key in M's sensibility: 419–20. Importance of weather for M's hopes of meeting Gilberte in the Champs-Elysées: 429–30. Cold weather at Doncières: II 96–7. Profound and unpredictable psychological effect of atmosphere: 144. "A change in the weather is sufficient to create the world and ourselves anew": 358. Evocation of a spring day: 808–9. Hot weather at Balbec and its effect on M's love affairs: 866 (cf. 1026–7). Changes in the weather fill M with joy since they herald changes in his own life: 1008. M in bed reads the weather from the quality of street sounds: III 1. The "barometric mannikin": 4. Moments of inspiration and elation due to the weather: 17–18. Various kinds of weather and their interest for the idle man: 76–9. A spring day in winter: III. Fine spring weather reawakens M's desire for women and travel: 411, 417–19. Atmospheric changes provoke other changes in the inner man, awaken forgotten selves: 500.

MORE ABOUT PENGUINS, PELICANS AND PUFFINS

For further information about books available from Penguins please write to Dept EP, Penguin Books Ltd, Harmondsworth, Middlesex UB7 0DA.

In the U.S.A.: For a complete list of books available from Penguins in the United States write to Dept DG, Penguin Books, 299 Murray Hill Parkway, East Rutherford, New Jersey 07073.

In Canada: For a complete list of books available from Penguins in Canada write to Penguin Books Canada Ltd, 2801 John Street, Markham, Ontario L3R 1B4.

In Australia: For a complete list of books available from Penguins in Australia write to the Marketing Department, Penguin Books Australia Ltd, P.O. Box 257, Ringwood, Victoria 3134.

In New Zealand: For a complete list of books available from Penguins in New Zealand write to the Marketing Department, Penguin Books (N.Z.) Ltd, Private Bag, Takapuna, Auckland 9.

In India: For a complete list of books available from Penguins in India write to Penguin Overseas Ltd, 706 Eros Apartments, 56 Nehru Place, New Delhi 110019.

CLASSICS IN TRANSLATION
IN PENGUINS

☐ *The Treasure of the City of Ladies*
Christine de Pisan £2.95

This practical survival handbook for women (whether royal courtiers or prostitutes) paints a vivid picture of their lives and preoccupations in France, c. 1405. First English translation.

☐ *Berlin Alexanderplatz* **Alfred Döblin** £4.95

The picaresque tale of an ex-murderer's progress through underworld Berlin. 'One of the great experimental fictions . . . the German equivalent of *Ulysses* and Dos Passos' *U.S.A.*' – *Time Out*

☐ *Metamorphoses* **Ovid** £2.50

The whole of Western literature has found inspiration in Ovid's poem, a golden treasury of myths and legends that are linked by the theme of transformation.

☐ *Darkness at Noon* **Arthur Koestler** £1.95

'Koestler approaches the problem of ends and means, of love and truth and social organization, through the thoughts of an Old Bolshevik, Rubashov, as he awaits death in a G.P.U. prison' – *New Statesman*

☐ *War and Peace* **Leo Tolstoy** £4.95

'A complete picture of human life;' wrote one critic, 'a complete picture of the Russia of that day; a complete picture of everything in which people place their happiness and greatness, their grief and humiliation.'

☐ *The Divine Comedy: 1 Hell* **Dante** £2.25

A new translation by Mark Musa, in which the poet is conducted by the spirit of Virgil down through the twenty-four closely described circles of hell.

CLASSICS IN TRANSLATION
IN PENGUINS

☐ *Remembrance of Things Past* **Marcel Proust**
☐ Volume One: *Swann's Way, Within a Budding Grove*   £7.50
☐ Volume Two: *The Guermantes Way, Cities of the Plain*   £7.50
☐ Volume Three: *The Captive, The Fugitive, Time Regained* £7.50

Terence Kilmartin's acclaimed revised version of C. K. Scott Moncrieff's original translation, published in paperback for the first time.

☐ *The Canterbury Tales* **Geoffrey Chaucer**   £2.50

'Every age is a Canterbury Pilgrimage . . . nor can a child be born who is not one of these characters of Chaucer' – William Blake

☐ *Gargantua & Pantagruel* **Rabelais**   £3.95

The fantastic adventures of two giants through which Rabelais (1495–1553) caricatured his life and times in a masterpiece of exuberance and glorious exaggeration.

☐ *The Brothers Karamazov* **Fyodor Dostoevsky**   £3.95

A detective story on many levels, profoundly involving the question of the existence of God, Dostoevsky's great drama of parricide and fraternal jealousy triumphantly fulfilled his aim: 'to find the man in man . . . [to] depict all the depths of the human soul.'

☐ *Fables of Aesop*   £1.95

This translation recovers all the old magic of fables in which, too often, the fox steps forward as the cynical hero and a lamb is an ass to lie down with a lion.

☐ *The Three Theban Plays* **Sophocles**   £2.95

A new translation, by Robert Fagles, of *Antigone, Oedipus the King* and *Oedipus at Colonus*, plays all based on the legend of the royal house of Thebes.

CLASSICS IN TRANSLATION
IN PENGUINS

☐ *The Magic Mountain* **Thomas Mann** £3.95

Set in a sanatorium high in the Swiss Alps, this is modern German literature's most spectacular exploration of love and death, and the relationships between them.

☐ *The Good Soldier Švejk* **Jaroslav Hašek** £4.95

The first complete English translation, with illustrations by Josef Lada. 'Hašek was a humorist of the highest calibre . . . A later age will perhaps put him on a level with Cervantes and Rabelais' – Max Brod

These books should be available at all good bookshops or newsagents, but if you live in the UK or the Republic of Ireland and have difficulty in getting to a bookshop, they can be ordered by post. Please indicate the titles required and fill in the form below.

NAME_____ BLOCK CAPITALS

ADDRESS_____

_____

Enclose a cheque or postal order payable to The Penguin Bookshop to cover the total price of books ordered, plus 50p for postage. Readers in the Republic of Ireland should send £1R equivalent to the sterling prices, plus 67p for postage. Send to: The Penguin Bookshop, 54/56 Bridlesmith Gate, Nottingham, NG1 2GP.

You can also order by phoning (0602) 599295, and quoting your Barclaycard or Access number.

Every effort is made to ensure the accuracy of the price and availability of books at the time of going to press, but it is sometimes necessary to increase prices and in these circumstances retail prices may be shown on the covers of books which may differ from the prices shown in this list or elsewhere. This list is not an offer to supply any book.

This order service is only available to residents in the UK and the Republic of Ireland.

● ● ●